The Mur

Vincent van Gogh

By Nick van der Leek

Published by Shakedown, Irvine, California, 92618 USA.

www.shakedowntitle.com

Edited by R. Franssen

Cover design: Nick van der Leek

First edition published in May 2018

"Fire, intensity, sunshine."— Albert Aurier's description of Van Gogh's expressionism in Le Moderniste Illustré, 1889

"When one blind man leads another, don't they both fall into a ditch?" — Vincent van Gogh in a cryptic reference to Dr. Paul Gachet, May 24th, 1890, Auvers

Important Note to the Reader:

The #SHAKEDOWN books are unique. Throughout this book, the author has provided hyperlinks to relevant resources including documents, photographs and videos to enhance your interactivity with the story.

TABLE OF CONTENTS

Introduction

In June 1889, about a year before his death, Vincent van Gogh produced the sublimely haunting *Starry Night* while he was in an asylum. *Starry Night* was his view through the window of a madhouse at Saint-Rémy-de-Provence, a madhouse he'd booked *himself* into.

Is the whirly enchantment of Vincent's *Starry Night* in yellow and blue evidence of madness, or brilliance?

In lieu of that question, we must ask another:

How precisely did the world's most beloved artist die?

Did madness play a role in Vincent's death? Almost certainly it did. The question is *how* did it? This is the key to unlocking the greatest mystery bedevilling the world's most beloved, most valuable and most misunderstood "mad" artist.

For the first time these questions are interrogated in meticulous detail using the scalpel of true crime analysis. These cuts and incisions to the conventional, mainstream view, take the narrative of Vincent van Gogh forward for the first time in almost 130 years.

BACKWARDS

"The uglier, older, meaner, iller, poorer I get, the more I wish to avenge myself by doing brilliant colour, well arranged, resplendent." — Vincent Van Gogh to his sister Willemien, September 1888

Suicide or Murder?

"What characterises his works as a whole is its excess....of strength, of nervousness, its violence of expression...in the vehement passion of his drawing and colour, even to the smallest details of his technique, a powerful figure is revealed...masculine, daring, very often brutal...yet sometimes ingeniously delicate." — Albert Aurier's description of Van Gogh's expressionism in Le Moderniste Illustré, 1889

1890 – Summer – Northern France

Officially, Vincent van Gogh committed suicide using a 7mm Lefaucheux à broche revolver on July 27th, 1890. Unofficially, someone – someone besides Vincent – shot the ginger haired Dutchman in the stomach from a low angle. This contradiction between accepted versions and conspiracies raises a perfectly simple, if superficially informal question:

Did Vincent van Gogh commit suicide or was he murdered?

In this narrative I will show what has not been done before: firstly why Vincent didn't commit suicide, and secondly, that he was murdered. I will show who murdered him, how, where and why. Further than this, I will show why another recent theory of an accidental killing is wrong.

Before commencing with our interrogation, let's refresh ourselves on the current perspective on the Vincent van Gogh narrative. What is the popular narrative surrounding the world's most famous artist?

The Official Version

The Van Gogh museum, the Van Gogh family, and most of the art world it seems, subscribes to the version of the brilliant, tortured artist who tragically took himself out of this world, and out of his own story, just as he reached his prime.

He was tortured by the failure to sell his works, he was tortured by mental illness, he was tortured by being a nobody, he was tortured by poverty, whatever it was, *he was a tortured artist* – that much was obvious.

In broad strokes, Vincent famously cut off his ear in December 1888, admitted himself to an insane asylum for a year from May 1889 to May 1890, and committed suicide two months later. Given that timeline, and the context of simmering mental illness, suicide makes sense, it even seems *logical*, doesn't it?

In true crime things are never that simple or that easy, but who's to say a *crime* happened here? In true crime, typically the giveaway that there is criminal intent from a particular person is in prolonged, habitual mendacity. It is in a person living a fundamentally double life. It is a person living a lie, who is suddenly confronted by an arresting truth, often embodied in a person, or crisis.

Simple Questions, Difficult Answers

Concordantly, when a version of events about someone is a little off, and that someone is later found dead, it becomes necessary to ask more difficult questions. If things get real complicated real quick from this point of inquiry onward, there may be something there.

So, for example, *what do we know about the revolver? Who did it belong to? How did Vincent get hold of it? Where did he get it? And what do we know about Vincent slicing off his ear?*

We'll deal with the former questions, but suffice it to say the answers are problematic. As for the latter, what happened to his ear, well, that's an enduring mystery too, because there were no witnesses. The meaty fragment was folded into a piece of paper and conveyed to a prostitute at a brothel, who passed out when she opened it.

Did Vincent slice off his whole ear, or just a piece of it? We know there was an attempt to reconcile the amputated ear fragment with its owner, until the hospital doctor realized the morsel was too deteriorated and mushy to be viable. Predictably, there's no consensus on how much of his ear Vincent cut off.

Seeing Vincent through Ourselves

Those who argue for the whole ear are trying to make the case for the *very* tortured artist; those who maintain it was a small piece of the earlobe, argue for historic verisimilitude, and rational perspective. This discrepancy ought to provide fair warning as to the trustworthiness and inclination to exaggeration of the popular narrative surrounding Vincent's life – and death.

Like art, murder can be subjective, especially 120-odd years later. It's because Vincent was the quintessential struggling artist [he only ever sold one painting* in his career], this reversal of fortune from almost total failure in his life, to the world's most valuable painter, is tragically inspiring.

If Vincent couldn't sell his paintings while he was alive, today his ten most expensive paintings are worth over $1 billion in cumulative value. That's an average of $100 million price tag *per* painting. In fact, Vincent's art is in such great demand these days, they're the favorite choice of art thieves. In this narrative we will deal with one particular heist of Van Gogh's art in the modern era, and examine the motives [and aspersions] the underworld cast on the art world.

More than one "Reasonable Answer"

Just as the art dealing in the underworld reveals baskets full of snakes, and bags filled with cats, scratch the surface of Vincent van Gogh's story even a little, and suicide is not the only reasonable answer. It turns out that some sources, including a pair of Pulitzer prizewinning authors, believe Vincent never shot himself, rather that "others" shot him.

That's a rather large range of uncertainty, isn't it? Don't we owe it to ourselves to know for sure who this most admired artist was, and why – and how, and where – he died? As for the "others" implicated, don't we owe it to ourselves to at least identify these potential suspects? Was it a group who preyed on the artist, or a selection of probable suspects?

Some may say there's very little one can find out 120 years later. That may be true if one is too lazy to try. With the modern technological tools at our disposal, what's hard isn't getting to the information that's out there, it's knowing how to filter and interrogate it. How to separate the wheat from the chaff, as it were.

Incredibly, there's no certainty on exactly when Vincent shot himself, or where he was, how he got hold of the gun, and most curious of all, the Lefaucheux à broche revolver was never recovered. Think about that. Someone commits suicide but the weapon disappears…

What was Vincent's Motive – that he was mad?

Prior to this narrative, I profiled eight mass shooters, most of whom committed suicide after they'd committed mass murder. Curiously, society has been slack at ascribing a motive to these shooters, even when the shooters themselves have gone to great pains to provide detailed and expressive manifestos. Yet despite these massacres garnering enormous attention internationally, the authorities, the media and the public have somehow managed to not know the motives of the monsters [or their madness] spawned in their midst. It bothers me when the whole world is watching, and yet somehow the truth seemingly eludes everyone.

So when I watched *Loving Vincent*, the first fully oil painted animation feature film, I was both moved by the art and troubled by the lack of certainty, *the controversy*, around Vincent van Gogh's death. Surely these were matters of forensic fact? Surely the newspaper reports at the time were factually accurate? I was appalled that the same entropy in dealing with motive with mass shooters – something one imagines matters a great deal to damaged communities – had reared its ugly head over the last several decades, in failing to deal with what actually happened to this world famous Dutch artist.

If that is happening, we also need to ask why? Why can't societies examine their own members, why don't they *thoroughly* interrogate their most famous and infamous members?

Red Flags and Clanging Alarm Bells

As I watched *Loving Vincent,* and as I saw the fictional investigation into his death gain momentum, more and more alarm bells started to go off. Are those in the art world not familiar with the rippling psychological patterns of true crime? Or the tried and tested webs of behaviour spinning into the twinkling motives of true crime? Or the moon polishing the whispering cedars of true crime? The same familiar flourishes in art appear in consistent psychological formations in true crime. What happens when we mix the two?

Are true crime aficionados *au fait* with the links between art and corruption? Even if we accept Vincent's death at 37 as suicide, one must still look for a motive, and when no suicide note exists, one must look *especially* hard.

Having probed the psychological chain links between mass shooters and mental illness in *Slaughter*, it makes sense to take these scintillating intuitions into an entirely new area while they are still fresh. What better arena to test this clairvoyance than the world's most famous "mad" artist? Can any new knowledge be scraped from the centuries old canvas? Did his madness really drive him to reach for a revolver, in order to bring his own paint-spattered life to a bloody end?

The suicide version clearly makes for a good story, but is it true?

If Vincent did commit suicide, why would the master of expressionism fail to express himself on his own death? Why would a man whose art, beloved for its effusiveness, remain mum on this most primary of primary motives; why not reveal his motives for putting out his own yellow flame? Why would someone who wrote so many letters – 830 that we know of, at a rate of almost a letter a day – fail to write a suicide note on the day of his death? Why would anyone who wanted to escape his painful existence, shoot himself in the stomach, only to endure an agonising 29 hour exit?

**The Red Vineyard* was the only painting Vincent van Gogh sold while he was alive. He sold it to Ann Boch in 1890 for 400 francs [about S1000], a few months before his death.

The Shooting

"I often think that the night is more alive and more richly colored than the day." —Vincent Van Gogh

Let's get the obvious stuff out of the way.

In order to get ourselves onto the right track, it's important to lay the cards of the various versions of the shooting on the table, examine them one by one, while being careful not to become confused or overwhelmed by them. This is easier said than done; the mixed metaphors in the various versions are by their very nature sticky and compelling, so our forays will require cautious concentration, especially in this psychologically meaty area of the shooting.

The same way a magician must keep track of the card when executing a trick, or a weaver must keep an eye on a thread, or a painter may keep his primary colors separate on the palette, if not in the execution itself, we must place each version on a separate canvas of the mind.

What we want to do is look at each card as dispassionately as we can, and then consider the cards on their own merits. How do they stack up relative to one another? How do they appear in isolation? Are any cards that should be on the table, not on the table? If so, what's missing, and why? Most important, does the card fit in with the hand Vincent was dealt all his life?

This last question is an important one, because it raises the prospect of our familiarity with Van Gogh's life. How do we put ourselves in the artist's shoes?

Once we've gone through this process, we must brush away the cards and look at the final letters written at the time of Vincent's death. Once again, we must allow the letters – valuable because they are first-hand accounts from the protagonists themselves – to guide us, rather than read too much or too little from them. This means we must let the Van Gogh's speak for themselves as far as possible, and not try to intrude with our own interpretations. God knows there is enough expressive material [paintings, sketches and a stream of private correspondence] to allow for their self-expression to stand on its own.

With the various versions, including the letters, added to our archive, we can evaluate the various narratives as well as the modern narratives, and see how they hold up.

This narrative wouldn't be of any worth if it didn't add to what is already there, and so, by the end of this chapter, and again in the final chapter, I will provide what I believe is the more likely scenario. The likeliest scenario is that which integrates the maximum of accurate information in a way that resonates not only with reality, but Vincent's emotional and psychological reality, whatever that is.

Worth playing for?

5 Versions

#1: The Mainstream Version

Auvers, 17 miles [27.2 km] north of the center of Paris. On July 27th, 1890, a Sunday, Vincent left the Ravoux Inn on the northern outskirts of the town [across the Oise River] after breakfast. By dusk, Vincent hadn't returned and the Ravoux family who ran the Inn where Vincent had been staying for two-and-a-half months, became concerned. At around 21:00, Vincent stepped out of the night, clutching his stomach. Adeline Louise Touillet, the Innkeeper's wife, asked Vincent what was wrong. Vincent groaned: "No, but I have [a problem]…" Vincent lurched up the wooden stairs to room 5 in the second storey attic.

Arthur Gustave Ravoux, the Innkeeper, hearing Vincent groaning in agony as he made his way upstairs, followed Vincent into his tiny room [75 square feet, or 7 squares meters]. When Arthur asked his lodger what was wrong, Vincent pulled up his shirt to reveal a small pea-sized wound near his heart. Vincent curled up in his bed like a foetus, drawing his knees to his chin. Then Vincent volunteered: "I tried to kill myself." According to the Innkeeper and his daughter, Vincent said he'd gone to a wheat field where he'd been painting, shot himself and then passed out. The coolness of the evening revived him several hours later. When he came to, Vincent cast about in search of the revolver but couldn't find it in the dark. So he returned to the inn.

#2: Slight Variations on the Mainstream Version

In another version of the same story, this time told by the Innkeeper's daughter, the mother disappears from the scene, and it is only the Innkeeper who "thinks he can hear groans", and so heads upstairs to find out what's the matter with Vincent. When the Innkeeper sees the wound, he asks Vincent "What have you done" and Vincent replies: "I have tried to kill myself."

#3 The Bernadette Murphy Version

In July 2016, Bernadette Murphy, a British expat living in the South of France published *Van Gogh's Ear: The True Story.*

According to Murphy's research, Vincent didn't leave after breakfast, but after lunch, which was unusual because Vincent typically left at five in the morning and returned at nine each night, like clockwork.

Vincent was paying three-and-a-half francs a month for half board, in other words for bed, breakfast and dinner. Murphy's version is otherwise much the same as the mainstream version, except for the Innkeeper explaining "Oh no!" in sympathy, when seeing the bullet wound on Vincent's chest. Moreover, Murphy discounts the "Village-Rumor" version [see #4 below], implicating René Sécretan, noting that Sécretan [sixteen-years-old at the time] "never questioned his suicide." Murphy notes that the Van Gogh Museum "refuted" the "Village-Rumor" version in an official press release in 2013.

In sum, Murphy's position is that she supports the "suicide" version.

So far so good. Three out of three versions that are all mostly consistent with one another. If we stopped here, we might feel confident that we have the basic story. But we're here not to accept the stories at face value, but to interrogate them, test them, and if necessary, develop a brand new true-crime flavored palette of events.

As soon as we scratch the surface from this point onwards, things get exceedingly difficult, and not a little troubling.

#4 The Naifeh-Smith-Village-Rumor Version

In 2011, Steven Naifeh and Gregory White Smith presented a different theory; that Vincent had been killed by a group of teenagers – accidentally.

This theory, as Murphy points out, is hardly new. The whole village was awash with the rumor from the get go. Trouble is, as Naifeh and Smith point out, so was the suicide yarn.

I will deal with the suicide rumor mill in the next chapter. For now we just want to get a handle on the five versions.

Naifeh and Smith claim their reconstruction is based on an analysis of "all the evidence", including "circumstantial" evidence. Promising as this sounds, the authors then piggyback on John Rewald, a scholar they described as having "unparalleled integrity" and "thoroughness", and what's more, became "an ultimate authority" etc. After setting up their reconstruction quite nicely, their "reconstruction" seems to amount to a single sentence, rather than any cogent analysis.

The authors say Rewald had heard a story about "young boys [that had] shot Vincent accidentally." This gang were reluctant, according to the authors, to own up to events for fear of being accused of murder. Vincent, for reasons unknown, decided to protect the teenagers and "be a martyr." In other words, despite saying he'd killed himself, he hadn't.

I might as well be explicit right here and say that none of these versions have a ring of truth about them, except for the bit at the end about Vincent protecting someone.

#5 The He-Who-Should-Not-Be-Named Version

In *Loving Vincent*, the filmmakers tease their audience with two suggestions. Firstly that there was an argument between Vincent's doctor [Gachet], and secondly, that there appeared to be symptoms of a romance between Vincent and the good doctor's 21-year-old daughter, Marguerite. From these suggestions, a myriad of inferences can be drawn, not so?

The relationship between the doctor and his patient, it turns out, went far beyond the ordinary. Gachet was an aspiring artist himself, in fact he made several portraits of Vincent on his deathbed, and after Vincent's death, Gachet spent years copying Vincent's art, in an effort to achieve some sort of artistic par [it goes without saying, Gachet did not succeed in this enterprise].

When Vincent was dying, Gachet was one of three doctors who attended to him. Gachet's diagnosis suggested hopelessness, and thus the treatment Vincent got from him was limited and abrupt. In fact, Gachet appeared to others on the scene to be angry, a frankly inappropriate and patently unsympathetic reaction to Vincent's malaise, given that Gachet was a doctor and what little we know about the circumstances.

Widening the Viewfinder on the "Circumstances"

Vincent and Gachet appeared to have established a close friendship in the space of two months. Vincent had painted the doctor's garden, his portrait [it eventually sold in 1990, 100 years after the artist's death, for over $80 million], and the doctor had given his permission for his young daughter [described as "the shyest person in the world"] to sit for the artist [twice] as well.

Furthermore, Vincent and his brother, had lunched on occasion with the Gachets. So why this antithesis to Vincent's hearty reception that summer? From whence this coldness on his deathbed?

When Vincent begged that a doctor "open his belly" to remove the bullet, Gachet [with a military background] refused, declaring that he knew any procedure was futile. It couldn't have been that serious if Vincent was able to hike from the area where he was shot, climb two flights of stairs, and then smoke a pipe while waiting an entire day and night to die…

It looks a little like Gachet didn't want to try, and as explanation – or excuse – afterwards, claimed Vincent had said: "If you save me I'll have to do it all over again."

So why bother, right?

In that anecdote is the good doctor's justification for not trying to save Vincent. See how the suicide narrative isn't simply a story, but in a way necessary for the doctor to save face? How would the doctor look if Vincent *did* want to live and…we have an *inkling* that he did, don't we?

In *Loving Vincent,* Marguerite is confronted over the fact that she was taking flowers – daily – to Vincent's grave. What lay behind this gesture? Were they lovers? *Loving Vincent* notes too, that Dr. Gachet took many of Vincent's paintings as "payment" for his medical services, such as they were.

Although the version in *Loving Vincent* alerts us to certain possibilities, few are fleshed out in fact or sufficiently detailed circumstantial evidence, and like Naifeh-Smith, after setting up the scenario, the film quickly demolishes their argument by animating the apparently good doctor's admission that *from a certain point of view*, he *had* caused Vincent's death.

How pray tell?

During an argument in which Vincent accused the doctor of being a fraud, a man living a lie while he lived and struggled for the truth. Stung by this, the doctor lashed out at Vincent. Gachet told Vincent that his younger brother had advanced syphilis and would be dead in a few months. How is that for truth?

Knowing this, Vincent was distraught and alarmed. If he didn't want to be a burden to the fragile health of this brother, he couldn't bear the thought of losing his lifeline, his lifetime benefactor either…So there's this sense once again that Vincent is being a martyr, that he has good reason to be, only this time his martyrdom is for his brother, rather than a group of teenagers boys.

Again, although it's true that Theo had syphilis [Vincent did too for that matter], what matters most here isn't the *version* of the argument, but the narrative consistency that there *was* an argument between Gachet and Vincent within days of his death. That's not nearly enough to accuse the doctor of murder, of course, but it's a start.

We also have the psychological substance reinforced here, that Vincent, by committing suicide, was *protecting* someone else. I don't think Gachet's version washes, but for reasons I will make explicit in the final chapter, Vincent *was* protecting someone.

If it seems these aspersions feel flimsy, loose or even silly at this point, that's because we're simply at the stage of identifying them. We have yet to tie them together, and I will do so *en route* to the final chapter, and in the final chapter itself.

Before we get there, we have to understand better who the card players are, and then lean over their shoulders to see what hands they appear to be dealt. What anxieties were they carrying with them? Which demons haunted their steps, and Vincent's above all?

We begin to clear away the cobwebs via the crucial correspondence floating to and from Vincent in the last days of his life. As we move on, bear in mind that the Gachet theory as an unusual suspect isn't a lone voice crying out in the wilderness. Far from it; the theory has been fielded via a cornucopia of alternative sources, cited here by vangoghdeath.com:

Antonin Artaud shouted it [that Gachet killed Vincent] in his 1948 book Van Gogh le Suicidé de la Société. The 1991 French film, Van Gogh, clumsily hints at it. Several of the Fauve artists, perhaps even Matisse, suspected Gachet's glaring eccentricity might include a penchant for euthanasia…

Isn't it time for "shouts" and "clumsy hints" on this particular theory to be remedied by *actual* analysis?

3 Letters*

None can speak as eloquently for Vincent, than Vincent himself, and the same applies to the other characters in this spiel: his brother Theo, Vincent's fellow lodger Anton Hirschigg, Adeline Ravoux [the Innkeeper's daughter], and Gachet.

With that in mind, let's turn to the correspondence as it circulated – the words on paper animating like crows over a wheat field – at or relating to the time of Vincent's death.

1. Vincent's Last Letter

In Vincent's last letter, dated July 24th 1890 [three days before the shooting], he begins by thanking Theo for enclosing a 50 franc note. Bear in mind Vincent's daily rent is three francs 50. Theo has essentially provided Vincent with his accommodation and meals paid for, for the following two weeks. If Vincent is concerned he may be a burden to his brother [who has recently married, and even more recently became a dad to a son called Vincent] there's no mention of whether Theo can afford the stipend. There's just a polite acknowledgement and an expression of gratitude.

Instead of pronouncing his intention not to be a burden to Theo, Vincent seems to be doing the opposite. In the third paragraph he tells Theo he's "convinced" that the "peace of your household can be preserved…" but adds that he's just as certain it may be "threatened by storms". Reading between the lines however, Vincent seems to be saying there's just as much reason to see the cup as half full as half empty.

"I am as much convinced that it [the peace of Theo's household] can be preserved as I am that it is threatened by storms…"

It's not clear what Vincent means when he says "I would rather not forget the little French I know", but it sounds as if he's saying he means to stay where he is. He doesn't want to return to Holland [perhaps where family could look after him]. Whatever he means, he seems to have the future in mind; he wants to hold onto what he has…

A few lines further, Vincent becomes even more self-indulgent:

"As far as I am concerned, I am giving my canvases my undivided attention. I am trying to do as well as some painters I have greatly loved and admired."

He sounds motivated and activated, not depressed or a burden. We know that in June and July, the last two months of his life, Vincent's output soared to roughly one canvas a day. This suggests that in spite of his failure to find a buyer, Vincent was determined to anchor himself in a work ethic, and also to reassure his younger brother that whatever fate may have in store, his work ethic couldn't faulted [nor the "ethics" of the work itself, as it turned out].

Further down in the letter Vincent alludes to an "association". It was Vincent's intention to start-up a southern school of artists in Arles, in the far-south of France, that was before he went to the asylum. Here in Auvers, half an hour by train from Paris, Vincent was giving the idea fresh impetus. Paris was where all the great artists lurked, but Gachet seemed to have started something in Auvers: Cezanne, Daubigny, Pissaro, Corot – they were all here. Why not bring them together…? It may be that Vincent was writing about his "association" with his brother in terms of artist and art dealer, but the point remains, he's engaged, he's thinking about collaboration and his future prospects.

So once again, this idea of being part of something, not gloomily apart from it, doesn't feel suicidal at all, does it?

Vincent uses expressions such as "I've noted with pleasure", "good luck in business" and "remember me to Jo [Theo's wife]." None of it has a trace of despair about it.

Besides all this, Vincent asks Theo in the same letter to provide another artist, Anton Hirschigg, who was lodging next door to Vincent at the Ravoux Inn, with painting supplies. It's possible just as Vincent was tutoring Gachet in his craft, he was also giving Hirschigg painting lessons. Now if Vincent thought he was being a burden, why would he order supplies for his lodger, and a significant order for himself, which he conscientiously emphasised to Theo had been cut down to "the absolute minimum."

Vincent sounds demanding, alert, full of ideas – in other words, his good old self. In the same letter Vincent provides a lovely sketch of Daubigny's garden. He also provides a sketch of thatch roofs and two canvasses depicting "vast stretches of wheat after the rain." Does he sound like a madman, or a man on a mission?

2. Theo's Last Letter

In the entire archive of their correspondence, 663 letters from Vincent to Theo have survived. Only 39 letters from Theo to Vincent have survived. As such, it's difficult to be certain about Theo's last letter.

Although excerpts of the letter provided here aren't Theo's final communications, they nevertheless occurred within two months of Vincent's death.

My dear Vincent,

Last week I was very busy with that Raffaëlli exhibition, we stayed open until 10 o'clock in the evening. Without that I would already have replied to your last letter. I hope that the area continues to please you and that your boarding-house is good.

This response suggests that even after the birth of his firstborn son, Theo maintained dutiful and regular contact with his older sibling. Conscientiously, Theo provides advice on good value, budget accommodation in Auvers. He mentions it costing 50 francs if one stays somewhere for a long time. He adds:

I must come one time, and I'm very receptive to your proposal that I should come with Jo and the little one, for I feel quite emptied, and the countryside would do me good...If I can have around 3 weeks' holiday, we'd first go to you and then to Holland. That would be at the beginning of August, probably.

Theo adds that Vincent's correspondence regarding doctor Gachet interests him "a great deal", and expresses the hope that Vincent will become good friends with the doctor.

I'd very much like to have a friend who was a doctor, for at every turn one would like to know, especially for the little one, where illnesses come from... We'll be happy to have good news from you. If you were here the little one would smile nicely at you. How detached from all other preoccupations is the smile of a child. Good handshake, and warm regards from Jo and the little one.

Theo

There's not a trace of anxiety about Vincent's mental health in this letter, dated June 6th. Here's no mention of burdens of health concerns. So, despite the cynical version we get from Gachet, it's obvious the bond between the brothers, whatever the complications, was as strong as ever in the summer of 1890.

3. Hirschigg's letter

21 years after his fellow lodger's sudden death, Hirschigg wrote a revealing missive to Albert Plasschaert. This letter sketched an entirely different version of events to those spun by the InnKeeper, his daughter or Gachet himself.

[Vincent] lay in his attic room under a tin roof. It was terribly hot. It was August [July 27th in fact]. He stayed there alone for some days. Perhaps only a few [30 hours]. Perhaps many. It seemed to me like a lot. At night he cried out, cried out loud. His bed stood just beside the partition of the other attic room where I slept: Isn't there anyone willing to open me up! I don't think there was anyone with him in the middle of the night and it was so hot. I don't think I ever saw any other doctor like his friend the retired army doctor: It's your own fault, what did you have to go kill yourself for? He didn't have any instruments this doctor. He lay there until he died.

*There is a fourth letter to deal with, written at the time of Vincent's death to Theo, that will be dealt with in The Third Van Gogh chapter.

Why None of the Versions of Vincent's Death Wash: A True Crime Analysis

"I think that we must in no way count on Dr Gachet. In the first place he's iller than I am..."
— Vincent van Gogh, May 24th, 1890, Auvers

In order to begin to understand – intuitively – not why the mainstream belief that Vincent committed suicide is incorrect, but how that may be, I have to play a mind trick on you. To simply state these things is to pluck a peach from the air. In order to convince you, I must plant a seed in your mind, and allow it to germinate. Only then can you taste the fruits of its significance.

Of course you may say you do not wish to be tricked, but then I will say, I am only using historical fact to change your consciousness. You may say, how do I know these are facts and not part of the trick, well, facts – like tricks – are easy to trace and confirm once you've been alerted to the *possibilities* of evidence and deception.

It's a difference headspace, true crime is, to art, and it's important that we enter that headspace, while simultaneously putting the pot with creative juices on the stove, and turning up the heat. We need to fire up our own imaginations if we are to penetrate the steaming stew of the world's greatest artist.

Now, in order to hypnotise you, I have to pretend not to be focussing on Vincent's story whatsoever, while I distract you with another. Once I've achieved that, I will swoop in through the back door and your mind will spin around as if on a swivel.

Worth playing for?

The Perspective of Émile Henri Bernard

Émile Henri Bernard, a French Post-Impressionist painter, was a contemporary of Vincent's, albeit fifteen years younger. He was a friend to Paul Gauguin, even though he was twenty years younger than the post-Impressionist.

Between the three of them, they developed interesting artistic experiments with color, including Cloisonnism, Synthetism and Symbolism. Cloisonnism is a pretentious artistic term for painting in a cartoonish style, using outlines.

Consider the use of outlines in *The Night Café*, a painting Vincent produced in September 1888 while Gauguin was collaborating with him in Arles. Look at the heavy outlines of the pool table in the center of the room, the bottles at the rear and the doorway. At the time Vincent said he wanted "to express the idea that the café is a place where one can ruin oneself, go mad, or commit a crime". The contrast in color and the heaviness of the lines are thus symbols of regimented or overly thick mental programming that might get one into trouble. The idea of conveying madness visually, in a highly simplified view of reality, provides some insight into how much the artist must overthink the conventional view of the world. This overthinking is necessary in order to see the world in a new way, which is after all, the central purpose of the artist.

Now, in Gauguin's *Yellow Christ*, notice how the Christ figure is outlined, along with the bonnets of the women, and the road snaking through middle distance. The Christ figure is yellow against a yellow world. Yellow on yellow. What feeling does this *yellowness* give us about the saviour figure? Is it a sense of saturation, a sense of oppressiveness, or a sense of vitality?

Look closer and you can see Gauguin has mischievously transported Christ from Golgotha into his present, his space, he's brought the Lord directly into his France. He shows a man in the distance clambering over a farm's boundary wall. In the foreground, three women are slouched over, each caught up in individual prayer. This is Gauguin's commentary of an overly naive and trusting religious faith. The cartoon color is a kind of satire. The message of the painting is thus psychological allegory.

Bernard's *Breton Women in a Meadow*, painted in August 1888, features the same flat, heavy tones, with minimal texture, and an emphasis of color and shape. The thick outlines are there too. In November 1888, just two months after Bernard's execution, Vincent had a go at *Breton Women in a Meadow*.

While Bernard's version is green and black, Vincent, perhaps influenced by the shades of winter [it was November after all], provides brown tones for the background instead of green, and turns the dresses from black to brown. Vincent preserves a few aspects of Bernard's concept in his copy – the girl with the blonde hair, the dogs, and the group in general. All he's really doing is playing with color. How do colors placed alongside one another, within a particular concept, make one feel. What does it say? What can it say? How can colors play tricks on the mind?

What matters is that we acknowledge that Vincent's psychology was being actively formed and altered, in a sense, by other artists. We know it was happening because the entire art world at the time was in flux. New *genres* and *oeuvres* were being born, which is to say, new ways of looking at the world were being born, and dying. New psychologies were budding and springing up like flowers and crows between fields of wheat. Hardly surprising that the father of modern expressionism came along at the same time as the father of modern psychology – Sigmund Freud was born in 1856, just three years after Vincent.

Now, when Gauguin visited Vincent in the south of France, they went out to paint the same scene. While Vincent painted what was in front of him, including industrial chimneys belching smoke behind a pleasant avenue of trees, Gauguin seemed to transcend where he was, and paint *somewhere else*. If Gauguin worked at measured pace, Vincent sped through his executions, producing three paintings of the world around him, by the time Gauguin had completed his one [from Gauguin's eidetic memory].

What was clear: there was something very different about the way both artists saw the world. Vincent saw the world all right, whereas Gauguin's world was in his mind, somewhere else, somewhere beyond the here and now…somewhere…in…or from…memory.

What does this say about madness? Madness is also a concept of the world, one that is too much to conceive, or else one is too much and the world too little...

When Gauguin was in Arles, Vincent immediately seized upon this psychology, this idea of painting not what was there but what wasn't, after all, Gauguin was the more senior artist, more self-possessed and perhaps most important, more successful.

If Gauguin's magic could rub off, maybe Vincent could finally break through the minds of the masses and make that all important first sale. So Vincent also tried to paint from memory, and as he did, he began to change reality. Suns turned into enormous yellow balloons. His fine tapestry of fiery reality sparking through fields, trees and skies, subdued, replaced by organic Gauguinesque tones of thick green and luxurious brown. In psychological terms, this is an extraordinary important milestone – we see Vincent so insecure in his own view of the world, he takes on Gauguin's psychology wholesale. He gorges on it, but can't seem to swallow it. After begging Gauguin to visit him for months, after just eight weeks together, Gauguin had had enough of Vincent. The guy was very intense, appreciate of Gauguin's art, while having a tendency to lean in and criticise him while he was painting.

Van Gogh wanted Gauguin's friendship, acceptance and seal of approval. He wanted to be treated as his equal. Instead, he found Gauguin conceited and domineering. The artists were soon at loggerheads, and then the quarrels escalated even further. If they didn't see eye to eye in general, when it came to art, they were poles apart.

If Vincent overwhelmed Gauguin with his words, he soon began to fear Gauguin would abandon him, while Gauguin, besides being put off in a general sense, secretly felt something he didn't wish to acknowledge about Vincent's dedication and work ethic – envy.

Inadequacy is the poison of every artist. In the next chapter we'll deal with this aspect of the story in more detail.

That's Cloisonnism. Now Synthetism.

Synthetism is almost a dismantling of the sculpted one-dimensionality of Cloisonnism. Imagine seeing an artwork through distorted glass, such as those used in bathrooms, or through turbid water, and you have the sense of the fluid symbolism of shapes and colors that suggests things broadly, without going into any grainy description of them.

It's a wonky version of trees and clouds and roads, rather than the road itself. It's how the clouds and trees *feel* on a warm autumn day, as opposed to an exact duplicate of what they look like.

All of this may seem old hat to us sitting on his side of history, but in 1888 it was revolutionary. The Impressionists were hell-bent on softening the world into a flowery mist, but some artists were sickened by the marshmallow sentimentality of Monet and all the rest. They wanted something more vivid, visceral or sensual. Something stronger than this cold, diluted tea that had the art world in raptures, but after thirty years, was in dire need of something fresh and new. Bernard, Gauguin and Vincent were determined to be part of that renewal, but only Gauguin was really getting anywhere, and even his work went through the flush of time, unappreciated until after his death.

If we translate these artistic concepts into the paraphernalia of true crime, they're really two different ways of seeing reality. The psychology is either of generously explicating reality into a simpler form, almost over focusing it, or depriving the viewer entirely of any semblance of focus, but providing a gist of the scene. In one sense it's a reductive technique, but in another sense – also depending on the resources of the artist – it can be very expressive. Color must make up for a reality stripped of its imminent features. Thus, in a sense, Cloisonnism and Synthetism are two poles straddling a third artistic psychology – Symbolism.

Don't be disheartened if these concepts are Greek to you. What matters is that this trio of artists – Bernard, Gauguin and yes, Vincent – kicked them around a little between themselves. It also matters that these psychologies – this way of looking at and interpreting the world – changed over time, and an artist allowed himself to be influenced by another artist's psychology [his view of the world], as he developed his *oeuvre*.

This is perhaps most explicit in the portraits artists painted of their fellow artists. When Bernard painted Gauguin, was he painting Gauguin or his view of Gauguin [in other words, imposing himself on the portrait, more than allowing the subject to speak, and thus painting himself.] When Gauguin painted Vincent and showed his portrait to him, Vincent was silent. Gauguin, he thought, had painted a madman. In reality, and artists are all about shifting reality to their own benefit, Gauguin had painted himself. This is a self-portrait of Gauguin. This is Gauguin's version of Vincent. And here's Vincent's version of Gauguin.

To fully appreciate the range of an artist's psychology, and thus his reality, consider the many portraits of Vincent by Vincent. The dour Dutchman with a thick beard and pipe in Paris, in 1886, couldn't further from the blinding ginger figure glaring back at him while he was at the asylum in St Rémy, in 1889.

What we see in this transformation, besides a change in hairstyle and overall grooming, is primarily a change in psychological color. The one image is dark, the other [including the background] is not just light, but radiant. Even the subject radiates.

In sum, then, expressionism's typical trait is to find an idiosyncratic voice in which to express the world [or oneself]. The idea isn't to color within the lines but not to. The distortions aren't meant to weaken reality, but strengthen it. A scene is meant to convey more than what it is, it's meant to evoke and emphasise a mood – in Vincent's case aloneness, or joy.

In his own words, Vincent said he wished his art to show to the world a person with a lot of feeling, and then to console the viewer with those feelings, to soothe the troubled soul with color as music warms the lonely ear. Expressionism at its core, is the desire to express emotional experience not physical reality. Vincent at his core, has the desire to express his emotions, less so his physical reality.

Which brings us back to Bernard. If Gauguin became a successful artist, and despite all appearances, Vincent achieved virtually unparalleled success posthumously, Bernard – despite his forward thinking – fared less well. Bernard's best work was achieved at a young age, between 1886 and 1897 [just as Vincent approached his zenith].

Bernard also achieved some renown as a writer. He wrote poems, art criticism and art history. His first-hand reports on the goings-on behind the scenes at this crucial time in the evolution of modern art are of some value.

It is through Bernard's writing that we get a strange new perspective on Vincent [and on Bernard himself]. Bernard had a lot of praise for Gauguin, not so much for Vincent, but then, Gauguin was the successful artist, Vincent and Bernard weren't. Not then, anyway. In Paris, at the Académie Julian, the artists displayed their work side-by-side in a restaurant, prompting Vincent to refer to the group in 1886 as the School of Petit-Boulevard.

In 1887 Bernard headed to Pont-Aven on France's far west coast, on foot. In Pont-Aven Bernard encountered Gauguin and the two rapidly struck up a strong friendship. Bernard shared his ideas and concepts with Gauguin, and the more senior artist was receptive to them. Bernard told Gauguin he wished to develop a style of art "of the most extreme simplicity and that would be accessible to all…"

Gauguin liked Bernard's eloquence. He could express himself in words just as well as with a paintbrush. Then came the offer from Theo – to sponsor Gauguin, board and lodging, in return for one canvas each month, and a trip to Arles where Vincent had prepared a room for him…

Despite Bernard's praise of Gauguin, he was gutted to discover Gauguin didn't [or perhaps wouldn't] reciprocate. In Gauguin's letters, published after his death, he didn't mention Bernard's influence on him, nothing about Bernard's ideas on pictorial symbolism and whatnot. In 2002, when the Art Institute of Chicago and the Van Gogh Museum held a joint exhibition on Vincent and Gauguin, Bernard's contribution to both artists was finally placed in perspective. And yet that's not the perspective we are interested in.

It's this:

On July 30th, 1890, Bernard visited Auvers to attend Vincent's funeral. He found a coffin festooned with sunflowers, some provided by Dr. Gachet himself. Then, two days later,

Bernard wrote a letter to Albert Aurier, an art critic. Bernard's letter contained the first version of the shooting incident, and yes, the first suggestion of suicide.

On Sunday evening [Vincent] went into the Auvers countryside, placed his easel against a haystack and went behind the château to shoot himself with a revolver.

What's wrong with Bernard's story? Let's look at those versions again.

#1/2 The Mainstream Version

On July 27th, 1890, a Sunday, Vincent left the Ravoux Inn on the northern outskirts of the town [across the Oise River] after breakfast...

On Sunday evening [Vincent] went into the Auvers countryside...

So did he go out at night or in the morning? And if he went out at night, why the hell would he take his easel along?

He placed his easel against a haystack and went behind the château...

This sounds like Bernard knew where Vincent went that day, or that someone who knew where Vincent went, told him.

According to the Innkeeper and his daughter, Vincent said he'd gone to a wheat field where he'd been painting, shot himself and then passed out. The coolness of the evening revived him several hours later.

None of that makes sense given Bernard's version. The Innkeeper's version has Vincent out in a wheat field, seemingly away from civilization or human structures. He has his art paraphernalia with him, and he shoots himself where he's painting, presumably in broad daylight, and during the heat of the day. In Bernard's version, there can be no "cool of the night" to revive him, if he's gone out at night to begin with.

We also have a sense from Bernard's version about the purposefulness of the suicide. Who knows why he took his easel with him, perhaps so as not to raise suspicion. Whatever the reason, he puts the easel down, then walks somewhere else – behind a building – in order to kill himself. This suggests that far from a spontaneous impulse, Vincent's been planning to do this, knows where he wants to do this. The only problem with the "purposeful" plan is Vincent shooting himself in the stomach. What's purposeful about that?

#3 The Bernadette Murphy Version

Bernadette Murphy's version doesn't have Vincent heading out at his usual time [the early morning], instead he heads out after lunch. This is closer to Bernard's version, but in effect we have *three* scenarios. Vincent heading out in the morning. Vincent heading out at lunch. Vincent heading out in the evening. On such a simple question as when he went out, there's no consensus. Why?

One possible [and I think probable] reason for this bizarre uncertainty is that a consistent story where Vincent heads out early begs the question *where was he*, and *didn't anyone see him* if he was out all day, or all afternoon?

Since his easel and the revolver disappears, it's virtually certain that *someone* knew where Vincent was that day, and whoever it was, found it necessary to remove the evidence lest it implicate them. In other words, where the gun was, and where the easel was, that's where Vincent was shot, and that's where we'll find Vincent's murderer too.

Thus a story of Vincent heading out in the anonymous wheat fields, far from any homesteads, suits the suicide version. And yet we have Bernard saying that's not what happened.

He leaves home but what he does that day no one quite knows. Why would that be? Why is there consensus on when he returns but not on when he leaves? He arrives home at approximately the usual time he normally arrived, except this time he's injured, and he has no canvas.

What all the versions are clear on, is *when Vincent arrived back* – at night. This may not seem significant but it is. The fact of his arrival back home is of little consequence to the murderer. The fact of his arrival or departure from the original crime scene presents a problem for the murderer, which is why there is so much uncertainty around that side of the story. There's a lack of clarity about where and when *on purpose*.

#4 The Naifeh-Smith-Village-Rumor Version

In Naifeh-Smith's account, they do great work on neutralising the suicide narrative. Unfortunately, after taking that away they do a slapdash job of replacing that debunked narrative with a cogent counter narrative.

According to Naifeh-Smith, in his letters to his wife Jo from Vincent's bedside, Theo makes no mention of Vincent attempting suicide. Since Vincent had spoken about suicide often, and just spent a year in the madhouse, one can hardly explain this reticence on the basis of a family taboo. Indeed, we have evidence – through Vincent's letters – that he brought up suicide of his own volition, such as this instance, to Theo, on April 30th, 1889 [shortly before he booked himself into the asylum in early May]:

"...If I were without your friendship, they [it's not clear if Vincent refers here to hospitals, doctors or other artists] would drive me remorselessly to suicide, and coward that I am, I should end by committing it. At this point, I hope, we are permitted to protest against society and to defend ourselves. You can be fairly sure that the Marseilles artist who committed suicide in no way did it under the influence of absinthe..."

Those same letters achieve in a more general sense, a tone opposed to suicide. Vincent refers to it as "terrible" and "wicked" such as in this instance in a long 3500+ word letter dated May 14th, 1882:

"Ought I to have despaired then, jumped into the water or something? God forbid—I should have if I had been a wicked man."

At the time Vincent was 29 years old, and clearly terrified his 26-year-old brother was about to stop supporting him, because of Vincent's temerity to contradict him. One senses that in his desperation, Vincent intended to drown his younger brother in a deluge of written angst, and it worked, because eight years later, Theo was still paying the piper on behalf of his older brother. What this reveals is the obvious psychology from Vincent himself – that the thought of his brother no longer supporting him was terrifying. It stirred up terrors and anxieties, and yes, thoughts of suicide. But we must take these admissions and drop them into the contextual pool as it was in late July 1890. Theo, instead of writing his brother off, was more considerate of his needs than ever, hence arranging doctor Gachet to tend to him, in Auvers, advising him on accommodation and so on.

There's also this, written from the asylum in early September, 1889:

"...I am trying to recover, like someone who has meant to commit suicide, but then makes for the bank because he finds the water too cold."

Note how Vincent frames his psychology of suicide as someone who wishes to drown himself. If this seems more like the cup being half full of suicide for Vincent, than half empty, it's not. Vincent is communicating that although miserable, troubled, unhappy and terribly lonely, and despite the idea of ending his life coming up from time to time in his thoughts, his heart's not quite in it. The *water too cold* is a metaphor for Vincent saying he's not ready to die, he's not comfortable with death, and probably, he is afraid of the whole sad business.

The real value of Naifeh-Smith's research is the manner in which it pertains to Bernard. The authors described Bernard as the "first commentator" to raise the spectre of suicide, even though Bernard wasn't a witness of any sort. He only arrived on the scene *post mortem*.

It turns out, not surprisingly, that Bernard had been informed of events chiefly by Vincent's landlord, Gustave Ravoux. According to Naifeh-Smith, Bernard's version was only "fleshed out" in the 1950s, as the centenary approached of Vincent's birth in 1953. During the decade following, interest in Vincent swelled, until it became a celebration of his tragic life that continues to the present day. As biographers and historians pored through the archives, they invariably came upon Bernard's canonical texts, which referred them in turn to the last surviving key witness, the Innkeeper's daughter Adeline Ravoux.

Adeline in turn claimed her father as her source, and so it wasn't that surprising that the Ravoux version and Bernard's were consistent, more or less.

Adeline's Cloisonnism

In 1956 Adeline maintains that Vincent went toward the wheat field where he had painted before [ostensibly to paint]. She said this wheat field was situated behind the château of

Auvers. Adeline helpfully adds that this château was over half a kilometer from "our house" [meaning the Ravoux Inn presumably.]

According to Google Maps, Adeline's right – it's 500 meters away, about one minute by car, but approximately 14 minutes on foot, so, quite a hike. Adeline describes the route to the château as a "steep slope" as one moves away from the Inn, as well as big trees shading the route [or concealing an injured person from line of sight, as he made his way].

Adeline describes the precise area where Vincent shot himself:

"…in the deep path that lies along the wall of the château…"

Adeline reinforces the impression of Vincent fainting after shooting himself, and being revived later, by the coolness of the night. She doesn't say how long he lay there, in fact in her 1956 account she provides no time scale whatsoever, except that she's certain he was shot in the afternoon and he came to at night. She's also very specific about what she didn't know.

"We do not know how far away he stood from the château…"

We?

Then the very specific detail of Vincent crawling "on all fours", searching for the gun "to finish himself off." To attempt suicide again. Vincent can't find the gun, gives up on his suicide attempt [the water is too cold], and stumbles back to the Inn, and asks for a doctor.

Adeline is also clear that Vincent couldn't find the gun, and no one found it the next day, or any time since.

What we get from Bernard and Adeline and the Innkeeper, is a little like three artists trying to find the best way to express themselves about the same *hypothetical* reality. Two of them broadly agree [Adeline and the Innkeeper], but Bernard sees the same thing through the reality of his reality – expressionism. And as an artist, art critic and art commentator, Bernard has a vested interest.

Of course 66 years after Bernard's version of events has become lore, Adeline is in a sense just like Vincent, copying *Breton Women in a Meadow* from Bernard's version, but providing some of her own colors. In a weird sense, she's being influenced by a copy of a copy of a copy. The first copy is her father's, then Bernard's, then hers, and what ultimate reaches the world is a mishmash of stories run through the mill of a thousand journalists, each adding their own nuances to the original. What remains of the original? Is it salvageable more than 128 years later?

In December 2016 I investigated a famous American cold case about a six year old girl who'd been discovered dead in the family basement. Officially, for twenty years, no one could say what had happened to the child. A three page ransom note was in the house, referring to kidnapping, but the kidnappers had forgotten to take the child. After twenty years, could this difficult case be solved? With some effort, yes. And so, I have the confidence that with enough biographical information, enough original statements by the people involved [which we get through the letters], yes, the *original narrative* is salvageable as long as we're prepared to sit with the material, listen to it, and reflect it as it is, not as we see it.

Thus, instead of Bernard's *Breton Women in a Meadow*, we're in pursuit of the true meaning of Bernard's *Suicidal madman behind the Château*. It makes for an adequate picture, but for true crime purposes it just won't do. We need a better artist than Bernard to decipher the reality here.

What is the reality that's missing in Adeline's version of Bernard's version of the Innkeeper's version? The haystack and the easel. How on earth *can* there be a haystack anywhere near the château?

"We do not know how far away he stood from the château..."

Returning to Google Maps, it turns out Dr. Gachet's house is also behind the château. Drawing a line, the château is due west of the Inn, and Gachet's house is on the same line, due west of the château.

The total distance from the Ravoux Inn to Dr. Gachet's house is just 2.1 kilometers, a fifteen minute walk. From the château to Dr. Gachet is 1.5 kilometers, a thirteen minute walk. The whole walk, end to end, from Dr. Gachet to the Inn takes 27 minutes, and goes right by the château.

Adeline's Synthetism

Out of the muddle and murk of amnesia, Adeline, through a series of interviews during the 50's and 60's, suddenly recalls important and strategic information. After providing a version just short of 4000 words in 1956, a few years later Adeline reveals that the revolver Vincent shot himself with was her father's. If this is true, there's very little regret, guilt or unease expressed by the Innkeeper himself, or by Adeline. One would imagine if it was something of theirs that Vincent used to kill himself, they'd feel very awful indeed, and yet there's the admission – at the denouement of Adeline's life – but without the appropriate emotion.

It doesn't ring true.

Neither does this latest revelation from Adeline: Vincent, in the moments before his death, confided in Gustave [but not his own brother Theo] exactly what happened when he shot himself. In this way Adeline is able to synthesise a new narrative seemingly out of the ether, resurrected from the grave, more than 70 years later.

As Adeline was the only living source at a time when Vincent's legacy had become world famous, she soon came to be regarded as a definitive source, and the more details she was able to give, the more the journalists came pouring back for more.

Naifeh-Smith accuse Adeline of "fitting her account to the [narrative] requirements of the moment". The sudden disclosure after 70 years about the ownership of the revolver, something the authors rightly emphasise was never brought up by the Innkeeper himself, is a kind of narrative expressionism, isn't it?

We've said that expressionism is about finding a unique voice in which to color purposefully not within the lines, but over them.

The distortions aren't meant to weaken reality, but strengthen it.

Unfortunately, while it makes for great PR, and while it brings Vincent's death to life [ironic as that sounds], it's a disaster when it comes to true crime. Distortions in a version, in the legal sense, can *never* strengthen reality, only undermine it, and the storyteller.

And do you see, the same trick all these card players have pulled on the world for over 128 years, I have pulled on you. I do not have to prove Vincent was murdered, as much as I must show why the suicide story is just a badly executed copy of another badly executed copy.

Understanding the Message Hidden in the Noise

What we can say about distortions, is that wherever we find distortions in a criminal case, red flags automatically flicker into being. Distortions, just like the absence of evidence, is evidence of a sort. The distortion is really pushing you away from something. So it's important that there are distortions, because that means, by hook or by crook, something is being hidden. Where there are distortions, we must not look at the distortions, but try to find our way to whatever the distortions are trying to draw us away from.

After countering Adeline's version of events, Naifeh-Smith, unfortunately, do no better. They throw out the pieces they don't agree with, but say that Adeline's story that the revolver was her father's is a match to René Secrétan's story. But isn't it just the same thing all over again, one storyteller borrowing or recycling from another?

Now, we ought not to be too harsh on Naifeh-Smith. In true crime one cannot throw the baby out with the bathwater, just because the bathwater has become cloudy with dirt and soap. People may lie, embellish, forget, remember incorrectly or simply err in some way. No matter how cloudy the water, it's never of no use.

The trick is knowing what and where to filter in and out, and in order to do that, we need to find the authentic thread running through the whole case.

We find this thread by deciphering the most difficult code of all: the identity of the perpetrator and the victim, and the motive that arises out of their relationship.

Before we do, there's a final cup of Adeline's bathwater to scoop out of the tub and examine closely in order to test the fifth version – and the version of this narrative.

#5 The Gachet-Did-It Theory

After seeing [Vincent's] injury in the region of the heart, Father descended rapidly from the bedroom...and asked Hirschigg to [find] a physician... [But the local] physician was absent. Father [then sent Hirschigg] to Dr. Gachet who resided in the upper part of the town, but did not practice in Auvers. What was Dr. Gachet's connection with Van Gogh? Father ignored him completely, the physician had never come to the house, and the scene in which my father assisted did not to make him suppose any existed, in fact on the contrary.

Imagine that, Vincent's best buddy, his personal doctor and contact in Auvers, comes to attend to him, and Gustave Ravoux assumes he's a complete stranger. Moreover, Gachet *allows* the Innkeeper to be misled by this impression.

After [Gachet's] visit, Father told us: "Dr. Gachet has examined Mr. Vincent and has dressed his wound with bandages that he had himself brought" (someone had warned him that it concerned a casualty).

How did Gachet know to bring bandages? The idea that a mysterious someone had told him, and not Hirschigg, who'd summoned him, is peculiar, isn't it? From Adeline's version of events it doesn't sound like Hirschigg saw Vincent before summoning the doctor, but perhaps the Innkeeper told him what sort of wounds he'd suffered, and to relay these to the doctor. Adeline's account simply doesn't provide this detail.

Gachet judged the case hopeless and left immediately. I am absolutely certain that he did not return: neither that evening, nor the following day. Father told us again: "During the examination and when he was bandaging the wound, Dr. Gachet did not say a word to Monsieur Vincent."

Curiouser and curiouser.

In the 1991 French film *Van Gogh*, which examines the last 67 days of Vincent's life, the entry of Gachet into Vincent's room [at 2 hours 26 minutes] is dramatized with Vincent lashing out at the doctor when he sees him. The artist twice attempts to punch the doctor in the face.

Other accounts go further than describing Gachet as merely tight-lipped; *Gachet seems angry about something*, but won't say what it is. Oddly, Vincent doesn't say much either in the last 30 hours of his life. He's not incommunicado by any stretch, but neither is he particularly forthcoming. For once he's less than expressive. Is this entirely due to his ailment, or is there something else eating at him?

When the police arrived, they interrogated Vincent, who seemed then as if he might survive. The gendarmes sharply asked Vincent whether he had tried to commit suicide, and Vincent replied softly, "Yes, I believe."

When the cops pressed Vincent for more details, Vincent was reluctant to answer, and Ravoux intervened. If it was Ravoux's gun, perhaps he had a reason to. Whatever it was, in the end, history right then was denied many answers, and upon that hinge, many questionable answers were sketched into giddy possibility.

Most peculiar of all, was this response from Vincent in defense of the allegation of a suicide attempt:

"My body is mine and I am free to do what I want with it. Do not accuse anybody, it is I that wished to commit suicide."

My body, not my life. I am free to do with my body, what I want, not my life. Do not accuse anybody, but don't ask me any questions either. *This* is Vincent's last painting; once again it's a blurring of reality, a distortion, an attempt not to strengthen emotion, conviction or understanding, but frustrate it. It's an effort to sublimate expression.

Vincent had a secret. Gachet had a secret.

He was protecting someone. He was protecting someone.

What was the secret? What was the secret?

We find the answers to these simple questions by doing the most difficult thing. We must learn as best we can who Vincent really was, and so, from here, we must stagger with him slowly, backwards through time to his very beginning.

The Mysterious Ear

"I can still him see with his cut off ear and his wild eyes, in which was resting something crazy and which I didn't dare look into…" — Anton Hirschigg, excerpt from his letter to Abraham Bredius in 1934

[Warning: Image links in "The Ear in Death" paragraphs may upset sensitive readers]

1888 – Winter – Southern France

The mystery of Vincent's death is mirrored around another mystery – the mystery surrounding his ear. More particularly, mystery surrounds the *size* of the left ear he sawed off his head on the night of December 23rd, 1888 in the south of France.

When it comes to the ear, size does matter, because if he cut off the whole ear, this sets a precedent for self-harm and madness. The bigger the piece of ear removed, the larger the madness, and the better the case for suicide, at least, that's the argument we must soldier through if we are to speak with any authority about Vincent's death being a homicide.

Now, in order to find our way back to the original surface layer – the original canvas that was Vincent as he really was, and Vincent's reality not anyone else's version of it, we must initiate a process of removing the muck and grime from the image that exists today. We must strip it away until we're left with the bare white bones. This unravelling of the murk, to the paint underneath, scraping our way to the original crisp canvas, is like painting in reverse. That is what we must do to unlearn what we have learned.

1. The Ear in movies, documentaries and books

In October 1992, the *New York Times* published a review of French filmmaker [and artist] Maurice Pialat's movie, *Van Gogh.*

[After the screening] at the Cannes International Film Festival in 1991, some members of the audience emerged feeling vaguely cheated and disoriented. "What happened to his ear?" one woman asked her friend. She might have more properly wondered, "What didn't happen to his ear?" All sensational reports to the contrary, Vincent van Gogh did not cut his ear entirely off. He took some nasty swipes at it.

Jacques Dutronc, the actor playing Pialat's version of Vincent in the last three months of his life, has a good head of brown hair on his head, stubble on his face sans freckles, and yes, *both ears intact.* Besides the oddly intact pinnae, Dutronc seems miscast, simply because his version of Vincent is less a man on the cusp, but a man returned from the brink; rather than deeply troubled, this version of Vincent in the last summer of life is resolute, serious and sobered up.

Once again, turds floating in the bathwater shouldn't prompt us to throw the cinematic baby out with it, tempting as that may be. I happen to agree completely with Pialat's version of Vincent's psychology, even if the appearances are [to my mind] far off].

When Adeline Ravoux published her first-hand account of Vincent in 1956, describing herself accurately if somewhat pompously then, as "without doubt the last surviving person who personally knew Vincent Van Gogh in Auvers", she was strident on the fact that the "Vincent of Auvers" was decent and respectable. He wasn't dirty. He didn't drink. As Adeline put it:

He never drank alcohol. I insist on this point. The day of his suicide, he was not in the least intoxicated, as some claim...

If Dutronc doesn't quite look the part of tortured artist, it may be that the sober aspect at least is accurate. In November 2013, the *Guardian* provided a rather different view, in their review of the "classic DVD" version of the same French film.

At the centre of Van Gogh is a tough, uningratiating portrait by the handsome Jacques Dutronc (who won a César for his performance)....

Was Vincent handsome? Would any man missing an ear, or a fraction of it, be handsome, whether he was handsome to begin with or not? Looking at Vincent's self-portraits, he seems to me to be quite an ugly fellow. Don't judge me for saying that – his art is beautiful, that doesn't mean he has to be.

In his last self-portraits, those in Arles and the asylum at Saint-Rémy, Vincent is especially horrible looking. Since there are no self-portraits from those last three months in Auvers, it's not clear whether [even in *his* reflection of himself], he'd become easier on the eye.

Thus, once again we must rely on the Innkeeper's daughter for a portrait of the artist crafted in semantics, rather than oil paint. Given that Vincent painted the teenager's portrait twice, giving one completed canvas to her afterwards, it seems only right that she returned the favor.

Adeline describes Vincent as having a good build but a neglected appearance, a guy who liked to wear hats, and an agreeable smile, at least in her company. But nowhere in her descriptors is the word handsome [or for that matter, not handsome] mentioned, and at thirteen, she was at an age where she ought to have remembered, either way.

Adeline evaluates the portrait of herself, politely describing the execution of the world's greatest artist of her own portrait as *disappointing*, adding she was "poorly satisfied" that he'd even captured her resemblance. Of course the girl, and the 76-year-old woman recalling Vincent's work, is absolutely right, so her description of the painter is likely trustworthy as well. Her failure to judge Vincent as either ugly or nondescript, seems to be a generous omission on her part. One thing is certain, Vincent wasn't good looking.

Returning to the *Guardian's* review, the assessment seems preoccupied with appearances, yet fails to remark on the issue of the ear.

Pialat's visually striking picture concentrates entirely on the painter's final three months at Auvers-sur-Oise, being cared for by the kindly art collector Dr Gachet (Gérard Séty).

It's difficult to agree with the reviewer's assessment that Gachet was kindly. Perhaps to begin with. By the end of the film both characters appear on the verge of tearing at one another's throats.

Much of what happens [in Van Gogh] is invented by Pialat, including an affair between Van Gogh and his host's daughter (Alexandra London) that casts a new light on the painter's character. Where this well-acted film excels is in the realistic set pieces: a party in a Parisian brothel; an idyllic dance beside the Oise; and a jolly alfresco lunch...

Once again, it's hard to see eye to eye with this view of the French film Vincent. Although there are no collars with lipstick, sticky condoms or abandoned pantyhose of Marguerite in the Van Gogh museum, it's easy to imagine that there was an affair. If there was, between the 37-year-old loser with a screw loose [and perhaps only one ear], and Gachet's precious and unsullied 21-year-old daughter, it would have scandalised the doctor and the town.

Vincent's love life is a vital aspect central to his identity not only as an artist, but as a man, but now is too early to drill down into those messy details. Near the end of this section, in the *Vincent's Muse* chapter, we will deal with this critical area of his story in-depth, and attempt to reconcile Vincent's tempestuous relations with the opposite sex with a deeper sense of his psychology.

The *Guardian's* reviewer does raise an interesting point in his references to the "realistic" set pieces in *Van Gogh*. Far from being a loner and an outcast, this version of Vincent depicts a self-possessed man-about-town, a lover, not a loner or a letch, a man on a mission, not a madman. This Vincent seems socialised, even charming. So how could be suicidal?

The *New York Times* reviewer keys into the same vibe of a functional Vincent in Auvers, as opposed to the dysfunctional man of Arles and Saint-Rémy.

Forget all of the hysterical melodrama of Lust for Life. This Van Gogh is an almost serene consideration of the remarkably productive final two months in the artist's life, ending on the day of his death, July 29, 1890, two days after he suffered a self-inflicted gunshot wound.

In the 35 years since Kirk Douglas' tortured depiction in *Lust for Life[1956*]*, Vincent was recast from mad to handsome, from a man missing one ear, to a man for all seasons. Ironically, though Douglas was nominated for an Academy Award for his performance as Vincent, Anthony Quinn's Gauguin was the more compelling, and won the Oscar for best supporting role.

In Simon Schama's excellent *Power of Art* series, in the June 2007 episode dedicated to Vincent, he describes the package delivered to the brothel containing "a large piece of ear." Just how large was it?

2. The Ear as a Symptom of Madness

The reason that audience in Cannes felt "cheated" and "disoriented" by Pialat playing loose and fast with the facts surrounding the artist, is precisely because the amputated ear, more even than the suicide itself, is symbolic of madness.

By giving Vincent back his ear, as Christ did when he restored the ear of Malchus during his arrest, something is minimised. The madness, the suffering, in a word – the psychology. Dipping once more into the 1992 *New York Times* review:

[Dutronc's Vincent] is a man who works very hard, and who no longer has the time or the constitution for out-of-control debauchery. He is plagued by headaches and by fears of the return of the bouts of madness that earlier sent him into the asylum. Yet he is not a madman.

Once again, I agree with Pialat's interpretation. Vincent in Auvers seemed to be mostly well, as well as can be for someone on his second month outside a madhouse he'd booked himself into and out of.

If Vincent in Auvers wasn't mad, however, it doesn't mean he never was, and by the same token, if he once cut off his ear, that doesn't automatically invoke suicide. While the cutting of the ear and suicide go together like two peas in a pod, and while it may seem simple and satisfying enough at a quick glance, Vincent is too important, and the circumstances of his death too obscure, to leave it at that.

Vincent's madness, however persistent, pervasive or paralysing a role it was in his life or death, is nevertheless a slippery concept. Modern psychologist can't be sure whether Vincent was an epileptic, whether he had bipolar disorder, schizophrenia, Xanthopsia or hypochondria, or some crazy combination of these. Some even suppose his suicide was brought on by a bad case of sunstroke.

Far more interesting than these messy medical diagnoses, is the way society has tried to portray Vincent. In virtually every portrayal I've seen, I see the words, circumstances and sometimes aspects of the psychological reality depicted, but the actors never seem quite fit for the role. The transition from whoever Vincent was when he wasn't "mad", also doesn't ring true in any of these performances. We get glimpses, but we don't get a real handle on what's really driving [and torturing] Vincent.

If Dutronc was too handsome, Kirk Douglas was too histrionic. If Benedict Cumberbatch was brilliant, but altogether too charming and likable in *Painted with Words* [2010], Andy Serkis was too dark, and perhaps too British to pass for the fair-skinned Dutchman in Schama's seminal seventh episode in the *Power of Art* series.

My choice for the right looking actor, with the right temperament, would probably be Anton Yeltsin. Alas, Yeltsin is no longer with us, he died in an unfortunate accident at his home at the age of 27.

3. The Ear in Death

Given the Innkeeper's daughter's description of Gachet, which I'll repeat in a moment, it beggars belief that he returned to Vincent's deathbed and spent more time with the corpse – sketching it, and not very well – than he did attending to his former patient when he needed him most.

One can clearly see from Gachet's sketch of Vincent *post mortem*, that though he was a practised artist, he wasn't particularly good. I say this because Gachet's sketch is our best forensic evidence regarding Vincent's ear. Gachet's sketch is so bad, it's difficult to tell whether he's drawn an ear or not.

When Bernadette Murphy, author of *Van Gogh's Ear*, reviewed Gachet's sketch she saw what she judged to be a mostly intact ear. I didn't, however. I saw what I believed one would see if all that remained were the folds embedded beneath the exterior of the jaw and skull, and the mutilated scar tissue.

An updated sketch also by Gachet is even worse, since it appears to depict the tip of a small, cat-sized ear. Since the nose, eyes and lips appear to be approximately the right proportions, the ear is altogether too small to be the original ear, unmutilated. To test this, measure your own ear in terms of the size of your nose, and you'll see why the updated sketch appears to depict an ear, but I believe poorly depicts the ear cavity instead.

In order to test my subjectivity on this issue, I invited an artist to evaluate both drawings. She immediately saw what Murphy saw, the remnants of an ear. When I explained what I was seeing, hoping to transform what she was seeing, she obstinately refused to unsee the ear that she was seeing.

One way around this impasse, is to imagine what someone without an ear would like, and compare that to Gachet's frustratingly bad renderings. As it happens, there is a well-known congenital deformity in humans called *Anotia* ["no ear"], in which babies come into the world sans external ears. This is what it looks like. And here's Gachet's drawing once again.

Now, if you have the stomach for it, here's a real life version of a man who had his ears cut off by an attacker. Doesn't that resemble this?

Gachet's sketch makes it impossible not to wonder: 1) Did Vincent cut off his ear? and 2) If he did, how much did he cut off? If you think about it, the fact that the only real autopsy evidence more than 128 years after Vincent's death does more to raise uncertainty than to quell it, shows to what extent Gachet is at best a lousy witness in this case.

But I want to take the point further. Adeline Ravoux's description of Gachet's movements to and from the Inn at the time of Vincent's fatal injury suggests the doctor spent very little time tending to the slowly dying artist.

She wrote of the doctor:

Gachet judged the case hopeless and left immediately. I am absolutely certain that he did not return...[and] Dr. Gachet did not say a word to Monsieur Vincent.

We know Gachet did return, after his patient had expired. Perhaps that's what Adeline meant – the doctor didn't return to treat or care for his patient. What's clear in his "not saying a word" is this sense of Gachet as an asshole. He doesn't have time for Vincent while the 37-year-old fights for his life, but once he's dead, he has all the time in the world to sit next to him, flip open a sketch pad, and scribble the now helpless, and eternally silent figure. Then he does another sketch as well, perhaps hoping to ride the coattails of the publicity surrounding the incident, and insodoing, find his way onto the art train through some sort of hybrid tradecraft – the doctor as coroner-artist.

I hope it is clear now from Gachet's behaviour at the scene of the crime, that he's far from a kind man, in fact, he seems quite cruel and heartless towards Vincent. Might that not make him, at the very least, a candidate for his murder?

If we are willing to at least countenance this possibility, then we should usher in the probability that comes with it. If the man tried to murder Vincent and failed, and if he then visited him under the guise of treatment, could his quick entry and exit not have involved a second murder attempt? Did Gachet attempt to poison his patient, who after all, was well enough after sustaining the injury to walk a mile, climb the steps to his room and talk before his condition worsened?

It may be then, that if the doctor did murder Vincent, he more than anyone else, needed proof of the missing ear to wield as proof of madness, and also, proof of a suicidal tendency. And so, Gachet himself went about getting that proof. Makes sense, doesn't it?

And with that in mind, don't these words, written on May 24th, 1890, in the first days after Vincent's arrival in Auvers, have a haunting ring of authenticity:

"...he's iller than I am... Now when one blind man leads another blind man, do they not both fall into the ditch?"

Isn't that exactly what happened?

4. The Ear at the Inn

I know what you're thinking, and you're right. Surely if Vincent was missing one ear, especially an entire ear, everyone in the village would know about it, and so it wouldn't be necessary for Gachet to record or provide evidence of it.

The thing is, and we get valuable confirmation of this through Adeline Ravoux as well, that Vincent wore hats much of the time when he was outdoors, and that, perhaps in combination with a certain hairstyle, might allow him to mislead casual acquaintances from noticing the missing left ear. The Innkeeper's daughter observed the following about his appearance:

Of his dress, I remember only a blue drill jacket...which he wore constantly. [Vincent] did not wear either collar or tie. For headgear, he wore a felt hat with large flaps [which would have concealed his ears], and when the sun shone a straw hat like those worn by gardeners or fishermen. Overall his appearance was neglected [suggesting long, unkempt hair and stubble, or a beard, perhaps].

What does she say about the ear though? Not very much admittedly, but not nothing:

He was a man of good build, one shoulder slightly leaning on the side of his wounded ear, a very penetrating glance, gentle and calm, but not a very communicative character. When one spoke to him, he always replied with an agreeable smile.

It's a very incidental description isn't it? And wounded is very vague. Wounded says nothing about the scale of the injury, or the status of it. Has the wound healed? Is the ear difficult to look at without wincing? Is it concealed or if one makes the effort, can one steal a glimpse of it?

During early research I glimpsed the possibility that the author of *Van Gogh's Ear* had missed the most obvious and clearest answer to her questions from the start. Wasn't the mystery surrounding Vincent's ear solved simply by looking at his own self-portraits, specifically those date after December 1888 [and there are many], and those showing the left ear. It quickly becomes apparent that the left ear is entirely intact in every instance, until one sees the portrait as the artist painted it. In order to see himself, he had to use a mirror-reflection, so the right side in the image is actually the left side of his face. To make it more confusing, Vincent's left ear is on the right side of his face from the perspective of someone else, in other words, *his* left. See how easily reality can play tricks even when you're looking right at it.

Before we deal with the most critical information regarding the ear [arising out of the circumstances Vincent was in when he cut it off, in other words, within the correct psychological context of time, place and people], there's one final nugget to take from the Innkeeper's description. The Vincent she describes is friendly if quiet, someone who smiles when spoken too, but in terms of his constitution, he has a good appetite. He remember, if he committed suicide, he shot himself in his stomach, presumably because that's where he felt the most discomfort, or even pain. And yet by Adeline's account, there was nothing wrong with Vincent's health, or indeed his appetite, which is approximately the same thing.

I do not remember…Vincent having any food preference [but] he never refused a dish. He was not a difficult boarder.

If Gauguin [who we deal with imminently], and Theo and Vincent's parents found Vincent hard to live with, evidently by the summer of 1890 he'd found his way to being not unpleasant to live with. But it's hard to know how much of Adeline's story to believe, given what she writes next:

Vincent did not visit anybody in the village, to the best of my knowledge.

Adeline's clearly wrong about that. Vincent was visiting Gachet often. The best of her knowledge is not enough to rely on, which means we must source Vincent's identity elsewhere. Hence, we need Gauguin's impression.

5. The Ear in Arles

One of the few areas of psychological consistency between the Vincent of Arles, and the Vincent of Auvers, is his loneliness. He appeared friendless for the most part whether in the north or the south, though one has the impression the Yellow House was a more maddening domicile than the warmer, more convivial company of the Ravoux family.

In the former he ate his dinner alone, or in the company of whores, in the latter, he was near several families, not only the Ravouxs but the Gachets, and also Theo's family, just down the track in Paris.

It may seem sacrilegious to only deal with three aspects of Vincent's ear in Arles [the handover to Rachel, her reaction, and who cut the ear off], given that Murphy wrote a book about the sorry affair, which spawned a documentary, and the Van Gogh museum took the trouble to rewrite its annuls in respect to Murphy's ear narrative.

I will deal with the merits [and flaws] of Murphy's work in due course, and especially in the final moments of this narrative. While Murphy has made a big deal of the fact that Rachel may have had another name, and may not have been a prostitute but a cleaner working in a brothel, I find such ruminations of cursory value. In my view, what matters is that Vincent was in a relationship with one woman in particular, in Arles. Whether her name was Rachel or Gaby, whether she was a prostitute or a cleaner, is less relevant to me than the fact that he handed her his severed ear.

In *Power of Art*, Simon Schama begins by wondering why Vincent would kill himself in the context of having sold his first piece, having gotten his first review and of finding his stride as an artist ["painting like a demon"] which culminated in the execution of the incredible *Wheat field with Crows*.

I'm afraid I'm not convinced by Schama's answer to the question. It's the conventional answer, it's the lowest psychological fruit on the tree – that five years after their father's death, after five years of taking and demanding handouts, Vincent suddenly couldn't bear the thought of himself as a burden. Wasn't he less of a burden out of the asylum than in it? Wasn't he less of a burden as a motivated artist, heading out each day, indefatigable, optimistic, recharged? Wasn't he more of a burden dead, by suicide, than alive, on the road to recovery?

We find all the psychological fruit we need in Arles. We see that Vincent is capable of self-harm, all right, and in keeping with his intensity, and his vivid expressionism, he saws off not a little piece of ear, but as much of it as he can. Unwrapped, it must be identifiable as a severed ear, not some morsel that one might throw into a pot of stew if hungry.

We have several psychological curtains to draw. There's the girl somewhere off stage or on. There's the man, somewhere off stage or on, but clearly on his way off it. There's also the winter setting in, and clock ticking its way to Christmas. Finally, there's the Vincent leading up to Gauguin's arrival, with his great expectations and dreams running feverishly through his head and across his canvasses.

We must examine these ingredients as genuine precursors to a genuine breakdown, and then test the psychology against the ingredients as they were in Auvers. Although we can already intuit a disconnect between the madness surrounding the ear and the Vincent floating with the crows around the sun-drenched wheat fields of Auvers, that's not enough to disprove suicide.

We need to pluck the low hanging psychological fruit in Arles and eat it as though we were Vincent. We must cut off our own ears and fathom why we'd want to give it anyone, let alone someone in particular.

Briefly now, let's interrogate our three questions within the psychological maze that was Vincent's reality that winter in Arles.

1. **Why did Vincent give his ear to someone?**

The primary reason for Gauguin joining Vincent in Arles to begin with, was to address the problem of Vincent's credibility. He wasn't selling any of his art, Gauguin was, and with Gauguin's seal of approval, Vincent could be on his way. Of course there was more to it than that, but primarily, Gauguin's entry presented the promise of validation, even fraternity, but by the time he'd left, the opposite had happened. Vincent had felt invalidated, and – it's easy to miss – abandoned. It's difficult to imagine loneliness as a terrifying, debilitating and maddening condition when you're not in that situation yourself, or worse, unable to extricate yourself from it. It's less difficult to imagine Vincent pinning more than just his artistic hopes on Gauguin, but hoping the man would be a companion, a friend, a support, like he was to Emile Bernard. In this sense, Vincent was hoping Gauguin would bring him back into society, as an equal, as someone simply worthy of attention, and even love.

In the next chapter we'll pursue this more deeply. The answer to the question has a lot to do with the timing of Gauguin's exit. Even Theo's support of Vincent had cooled while Gauguin was there [which we'll also interrogate]. The cutting off of the ear, and giving it to the only other person in Arles he cared about, was a desperate gesture intended to secure not only her attention, but in a warped sense, communicate his commitment. By giving her his ear, he was in effect saying, “Pay attention, I’m giving you my attention and it’s worth something!”

But the gesture was understandably overwhelming. Vincent was an overwhelming person. His loneliness meant when someone showed him the least bit of kindness, he could overload them with his busy mental landscapes. The poor girl passing out is symbolic of this psychological short-circuiting that went on whenever Vincent let loose his torrents of built-up, held-back, crushed-inward expressing of himself. This overzealous intensity wasn’t an aberration, it had been there all along.

Vincent had written to Theo in July 1882:

Whether in figures or in landscapes, I would like to express not something sentimentally melancholic but deep sorrow. In short, I want to reach the point where people say of my work, that man feels deeply and that man feels subtly.

If Vincent wanted to express deep sorrow in 1882, in 1888, 1889 and 1890 he wished to express something else deeply. It wasn’t sorrow. So what was it?

What am I in the eyes of most people? A nonentity or an oddity or a disagreeable person — someone who has and will have no position in society, in short a little lower than the lowest.

In 1882 Vincent saw himself, and accepted himself, as a nobody, but almost seven years later, he felt he was a somebody, or close to becoming a somebody, even if nobody else did. Hence the excruciating humiliation that was Gauguin’s spirit uprooting Vincent’s psychological anchors, such as they were.

In the same letter written in 1882, Vincent answers the question. If he wasn’t to express sorrow in his art, he would express soothing love, that warm thing he was pursuing day and night himself…

This is my ambition, which is based less on resentment than on love in spite of everything, based more on a feeling of serenity than on passion. Even though I’m often in a mess, inside me there’s still a calm, pure harmony and music.

When Vincent described the filthiest corner of the poorest house containing drawings and paintings, he’s talking about himself. His saying he adds value to an uncaring world, whether people see it or not. Of course, the longer people don’t see one’s value, the harder it is to convince oneself of one’s intrinsic value. And thus, Vincent wants a love, want to love, in order to redeem himself. More than just a love for his craft. He wants the world to love him back…

I want them to say ‘he feels deeply, he feels tenderly’

But the world can only say that once they love Vincent, as they do now.

2. Is her reaction credible?

When Vincent hands over his ear, the recipient faints. On this, Simon Schama says rhetorically, "You would, wouldn't you?" But would you? Would you *really lose consciousness* if you saw an ear? The recipient lived or worked in a whorehouse; one would imagine a strong constitution, perhaps not for amputated ears, but certainly for the sterner stuff in life.

I'm also not terribly convinced that if Vincent nearly bled to death that night, as has been widely reported, that he'd be in any state to hand-deliver his ear without passing out himself. It's an oddly similar scenario to him shooting himself, and then having to hike about while bleeding, before returning to his bed while the neighborhood goes berserk overnight.

Now it's certainly possible, given the history of corsets as it stood in 1888, that the recipient of the ear *did* pass out. It's easy to imagine a particular dress-code, even for female cleaners, in a whorehouse, calculated to warm the blood of male visitors. When one resuscitates [pun intended] the mechanism of the corset on the body, as it was well-known at the time, the possibility that the recipient of the ear passed out shifts, in my view at least, from possible to probable.

Consider this for context, from todayifoundout.com:

...well-bred ladies [as well as not-so-well-bred ladies] in the 1800s struggled to maintain consciousness when faced with even the slightest emotional or physical shock. Over the years there have been several theories as to why this seemed to happen, from the women's garb to simply conforming to societal expectations...

The corset was a crushing cage displacing the ribs, squashing the lungs, and flattening the stomach, as well as crushing other organs. Besides making it hard to breathe, a woman might not be capable of eating much, or having eaten, digesting anything.

In addition to making it hard to breathe, hearts struggled to pump and, guts struggled to digest what little food they could get down. As one Victorian lady is reported, "I had only eaten two bites of my biscuit there was no room beneath my corset for a third."

This was the strange, cruel world Vincent was walking through, and trying to soften. Vincent wanted to enter the world, whereas Gauguin wished to flee from it. Strange as it was, Vincent was still a stranger to it, and a stranger in it, even if he didn't wish to be. Lending his ear – to anyone – wasn't going to change that.

But there is a third, extremely disquieting possibility to disentangle.

3. Did Vincent cut off his own ear, or did Gauguin?

In order to answer this question to satisfaction, we must plumb the true identity and circumstances of Gauguin, just as we've done, and must continue to do, with Gachet. There is no doubt the events in Arles surrounding the ear and those in Auvers are linked in some way.

Is it Vincent's madness boomeranging back, as the mainstream believe, or was Vincent, in his compromised state, the victim of the capricious behaviour of some other party? Are there two murderers to deal with, as opposed to a single madman?

On July 30th 1890, Gauguin's pal Émile Bernard arrived in Auvers to attend Vincent's funeral. Bernard wasn't Vincent's friend per se, but since he was in the area, and it was something to write about, perhaps he was there doing his duty, like an art journalist. Gauguin, significantly, wasn't there.

I have already mentioned Bernard writing to Albert Aurier, the art critic, informing him of Vincent's death two days later. Bernard did exactly the same thing two years earlier, sensationalising the incident in Arles, based on Gauguin's apparently traumatised accounting of the incident.

In true crime red flags are raised whenever a version changes over time. It seems when it comes to artists, reality is like a painting: *there is no reality*. If the mainstream believe the licentiousness of artists entitles them to play the same manipulative games with fact as they do with color, light, perspective and artistic suggestion, they're mistaken. When lives are at stake, and Vincent's was, then sober reality – as much as the artist [as witness] can muster – is the only sketch required. No embellishments, no fancy flourishes – just cold truth.

As you are about to see, Gauguin's handle on truth is more than a little tricksy. And since Gauguin wasn't known for his honesty, but rather, was well-known for his arrogance, we're left in a quandary by the very man who should be the best witness in this critical ear dicing business.

The déjà vu is unpleasant, isn't it. Because here we are again, in a different place, but with oddly similar circumstances. Like Gachet, Gauguin in the worst witness, as if he is frustrating the pursuit of justice, instead of painting a reliable, trustworthy and beneficial version of reality.

In the end, what's more important to our criminal investigation isn't the size of the ear, but the circumstances surrounding its amputation. What prompted this self-harm? And now we want certainty on what we initially thought to be the most certain question of all: who cut off Vincent's ear?

*The Irving Stone novel, on which the 1956 film Lust for Life was based, was published in 1935.

Gauguin – Best Supporting Actor?

"The murderer fled."— The last line of an article appearing in L'Intransigeant, the local newspaper in Arles, on December 23rd, 1888.

After Vincent's death, Gauguin wrote to Bernard:

However sad one is at this death, I do not really lament it, because I foresaw it and I knew the suffering of that poor boy, battling his madness. Dying now is great good luck for him, it means the end of his suffering, and if he ever returns in another life he will reap the rewards of his good behaviour in this world...He took with him the consolation that he was not forsaken by his brother and was understood by some artists.

Everything Gauguin's written here is wrong. No, that's stating it too mildly. It's bullshit.

In the context of suicide, this is an incomprehensible response. Gauguin's essentially saying, don't be sad about Vincent's death, I saw it coming all along so I'm not surprised, and not sorry either, in fact I'm relieved, and you should also be.

Calling Vincent's early death "good luck" reveals just what a jerk Gauguin could be, even – perhaps especially – in the most extenuating of circumstances. We know from his own history separate from Vincent that he outlived three of his own children, and if he abandoned Vincent, he did the same to his own wife and children.

As for Vincent *reaping the rewards* of good behaviour in another life, what's that all about? What, in the context of the popular narrative – suicide, madness, lopping off his own ear, and being so disagreeable Gauguin packed up and ran off, never to see Vincent again – has anything to do with *good behaviour*? It beggars belief.

The last sentence is also a crock of shit. Vincent didn't have the consolation of friendships, instead, the closest to a friend he had in Auvers – Gachet – seemed to abandon him when he needed him the most. If he means he had the consolation of his blood brother Theo, then that doesn't hold up either. Surely the popular reason for Vincent killing himself was because he felt could no longer rely on Theo, or that he could no longer be a burden to him. If Vincent was understood by some artists, that *some* didn't include Gauguin himself, for all his arrogant talk of what he "foresaw" in the "poor boy".

True to the true crime pattern, the absence of grief, even worse, the stated absence of it ["I do not really lament Vincent's death"] is a serious problem. It doesn't necessarily confirm culpability, but it certainly rolls out the red carpet to the probability of it. What is Gauguin culpable of? Besides being the originator of the persistent mad narrative [and he mentions it here as well, reiterating the poor boy "battling his madness" to the very end], besides his unsympathetic response to Vincent's death, besides skipping town the morning after Vincent's "breakdown", I want to contend here that it was Gauguin who confronted, and removed Vincent's ear.

I understand it feels like another pestering blasphemy that the Van Gogh Museum would deal with with a flyswatter, if they deal with it at all. At this point, though I'm certain about Gachet's cold-bloodedness, I simply wish to sit with the idea of Gauguin's, and see where it leads. As we go further backwards, perhaps the story that's buried will reveal itself. If it reinforces Gauguin as a piece of work, and so far it looks like it does, then we are left with a peculiar circumstance indeed: that almost the entirety of Vincent's legacy is myth, and the madness aspect means it is more myth than reality. It also means there is more than one murderer to contend with, and perhaps a degree of collusion – up to the present – that is well-nigh incomprehensible to comprehend. And yet we must. If Vincent was battling his madness, we must battle our way through this writhing snake pit of shifting reality.

Excising the Madness and the Madhouses – for a moment…

Going backwards in time, from the dead man lying in the bed of room 5 of the Ravoux Inn in July 1890, all the way back to the last time Vincent and Gauguin saw each other in the blood-soaked interior of the Yellow House in Arles in December 1888, is it the same Vincent throughout?

Clearly in the year-and-a-half separating the one incident from the other, Vincent suddenly went completely mad, and arguably has remained mad ever since. The man with him at the starting line of this unravelling [but not the end], was one Paul Gauguin.

In my brushes with Vincent, I don't see someone tumbling down the rabbit hole of madness. Instead, I see someone labouring across a vast and dazzling field, perhaps getting lost or disoriented on his way from time to time. By and large, I see him getting to where he was going towards, on the sun-drenched horizon, and despite his disorientation, he makes steady, even impressive progress.

Gauguin asks us to see another version of Vincent. This whole time, Vincent hasn't been a struggling artist, he's been battling his own madness. There's a fine line between the two, and it's especially fine when the artist himself accepts the narrative that's floating about – not of a world gone mad, but of his world gone mad. Artist's, let's face it, are particularly susceptible to distortions like these, and if a community gets it into their head, who is an artist – especially a nobody artist – to defy society's diagnosis?

One thing that hasn't changed since Vincent's day – a nobody can't accuse a somebody of committing a crime.

If Gauguin cut off Vincent's ear, how would he get away with it?

Like Gachet, as I've said, *Gauguin was a piece of work.* But whatever aspersions we cast over Gauguin, we have an enormous hurdle to overcome hence the question mark attenuating the chapter title. If Gauguin sliced off his rivals ear [for by the end, that's what they'd become], how is it that Vincent maintained a kind of solidarity with him, if not the other way round?

To understand these dynamics, we have to understand who Gauguin was, we have to get to know Vincent better than we already do, we have to plumb the dynamics of the men as they were together, and apart from one another. And we have to reinterpret the broader social fabric in both men were moving through, and hoping to establish themselves, in the late 19th century.

In this step back, I've skipped completely the two internments in two separate madhouses, these accommodations that held Vincent together, which contrived to produce arguably the world's best art, in order to draw the thread as clearly as possible between the Vincent before his madness, and the Vincent after. Is such an idea even sensible given what we know about Vincent?

It's through Gauguin that the lens of madness comes into position to begin with. What is left to do now is to examine that lens, not by looking through it at the madness itself [which we will get to in due course], but the *lens itself* and Gauguin's role in it, if any.

On July 7th, 1890, Gauguin wrote to Vincent's brother.

"I have had 2 quite calm letters from Vincent, which I enjoyed."

We seem to get a different impression of Gauguin, and Gauguin's version of Vincent in his correspondence with Theo, the art dealing younger sibling. Despite the incident in Arles, the pair – Vincent and Gauguin – stayed in touch, albeit at a distance. We will deal with the meat and potatoes of that section of correspondence separately, but it suffices to note that though the correspondence continued, the tone after the incident changed dramatically.

I have purposefully not attempted to deal at length with Gauguin doing something and how he would get away with it, because I want to get more comfortable with the notion that Gauguin was the sort of character capable of this sort of behaviour in the first place.

Had he assaulted anyone before?

Was he known for violence, deception and malice towards anyone else?

We need to make our way a little further before we can revisit these possibilities with confidence, but even so, we need to keep the question uppermost in our minds.

If he did it, how could he get away with it, and if he did it, why he did he do it?

The Execution of Prado in Paris

We begin the slow process of interrogating these simple, but far from easy questions by trawling through the apposite history. As we bait our psychological hooks and push our way through currents of apposite time, penetrating protected coves and inlets of apposite space, we get a few bites. Like this one.

Are you sure you want to hear this?

Four days after skedaddling from Arles [in such a hurry he left behind his fencing gear] Gauguin was in Paris, attending the execution at dawn of...well...nobody quite knew *who* he really was, where he was from, or even his real name.

At about 02:30, almost five hours before dawn on December 28th, 1888, Gauguin pushed his way through a thick throng of Parisians. It was cold and dark, but the smell of blood and taste of metal was in the air, just as it had been in Arles. Gauguin was only in Paris to begin with because he was on a two-day layover to somewhere else – Brittany. He was going back the way he'd come, but if he was going to the trouble to attend an execution, would he make the effort to visit Vincent's younger brother in Paris [Theo had his art, after all]?

The scene for the execution scheduled for shortly after seven was a courtyard somewhere within the labyrinth of the monstrous Prison de la Roquette, a colossal fortress in the shape of a pentagon. Six towers bulged out of each of the six corners of the structure, while more buildings radiated inward, like thick spokes, towards a central, domed hub, and the largest tower of all.

The prison was situated just 1.4 kilometers [18 minutes' walk] in a northerly direction from Gare de Lyon, the station for southbound trains. From the prison to Saint Lazarre station, where Gauguin would take a train west to Brittany, was a 6 kilometer [90 minute] hike due west. From the Eiffel Tower* the site of the prison [today's square de la Roquette] is 90 minutes on foot due east.

Capital punishment in France initially occurred in large public spaces, such as the Place de la Concorde. Nearing the end of the 19th century, although executions maintained a regular pace, they were moved to local prisons, perhaps for security purposes. There offenders were dispatched, sometimes by firing squad, or as Gauguin intended to see for himself, by guillotine. The first execution by guillotine occurred in 1791, almost 100 years prior to the one Gauguin wished to attend. The last execution by guillotine in France occurred as recently as 1977.

Getting into the golden circle, where one had an unobstructed view of the criminal's head rolling into a basket placed on the ground, was the trick. On December 28th, the size of the crowd presented both a problem and an opportunity. There was nowhere near enough capacity for everyone, and in any event, only the well-connected got a ticket. Gauguin may have been further along the road as an artist in comparison to Vincent, especially now, but for purposes such as these, he was still a nobody. He wasn't going to let that stop him, however.

In Gauguin's autobiography, he recalls his scepticism regarding the guilt of the convict, an infamous fellow called "Prado" by Parisian and international press. Gauguin, in his own account, makes no bones about his own bloodlust. Like the bloodthirsty crowd, he's swept up in the same feverish excitement. As the horizon begins to illuminate, and clock towers chime seven bells, and the crowd grows restless. Guards shove Gauguin, in his words "brutally" backward.

"I wanted to see, and when I want something, I'm stubborn," he wrote afterward.

At about 06:00, Prado is roused and prepared for slaughter. Unexpectedly, the wily Spaniard makes a statement to his captors, declaring that he wishes his body to be buried after decapitation. There is no such protocol in place; typically convict corpses were sent to the Paris Medical School where they were sliced and diced in the name of scientific study. In the case of infamous criminals, with no oversight, the temptation to seize souvenirs of flesh by the mob *post mortem* [skin for book bindings, a skull for punch bowl] was all too real.

While Prado attempts to arrange limits for the potential desecration of his body, a crowd of about 600 waits impatiently in the cold courtyard. Because of the size of the crowd, security is stretched. At the first sight of the prisoners, the crowd cranes their necks. Sadistic jeers directed at the doomed men are met with a cacophony of excited cheering. When the crowd are settled and guards distracted, the mischievous Gauguin finds an opening to slip through and bolts. Because the execution is underway, the guards can do little to stop him. Gauguin forces his way to the very front, despite being pushed back "three times" by some in the throng.

The meaty curiosity of Gauguin, gaping near the front, is rewarded with an uncommonly grotesque and gratuitous scene. The Spaniard, known as the "gentlemanly burglar", thought to be the son of a South American president by some, has an unfortunate exit from this world, to put it mildly. The guillotine slips from its rail and smashes into the side of Prado's face. Prado, who's maintained an impressive stoicism until then, screams and struggles, and tries to stand. Guards rush to subdue him, while the guillotine is raised a second time.

When the shining, bloodied blade falls the second time, Gauguin, in the commotion, appears to miss what one author distastefully called "the money shot." When Prado's severed head is lifted from the basket, and held aloft, Gauguin stretches and strains among heaving shoulders, and misses the moment.

Such was the impression made by Prado's execution, Gauguin rushed to create a severed head [which he described as a self-portrait] made of glazed stone in the shape of jug. The head was missing both ears, and lavishly decorated in greasy veneers of blood red. By casting this severed head as a jug, there was the disturbed suggestion of drinking a dead man's thoughts, at his own expense. In short, a sadistic execution of a sadistic execution.

Gauguin's Sick Psychology

One writer, Bradley Collins, is adamant that Gauguin would have "strongly associated" the execution in Paris, with Vincent's ear cutting. In Collins' interpretation:

"If Gauguin had been terrified by the sight of the near-dead Vincent curled up in his bloody sheets, he may have had the counterphobic desire to reassure himself of his courage

by taking an unflinching look at Prado's execution...to glory in his own innocence and another's guilt."

It's an outlandish theory in my view. Was Gauguin "terrified" by the sight of Vincent? If he was, if he'd been traumatised in any way, the last thing he'd want to endure would be another spectacle dripping with blood. And yet, that's what he did want.

Since Gauguin didn't believe Prado was guilty, if he was glorying in anything, it wasn't in innocence, he was revelling in the suffering and condemnation of another up close. If he thought Prado was innocent, then this slaughter was all the more barbaric. Gauguin's not there to oppose it, or to protest it, but to experience this dog-eat-dog barbarism first-hand. Gauguin, it's clear, is a sadist.

Collins also seems to miss the fact that Gauguin himself writes about his excitement [which might be another word for enjoyment] at the visceral entertainment in the prison grounds that December day. Given this image of Gauguin desperate to see the gore up-close, we have a sense of bloody satisfaction from him, in the sense of a man's transformation into a salivating wolf in his relations to another man.

Ironically, to take the man-as-wolf allegory further, when Gauguin described finding Vincent curled up in his blood-soaked bed, he compared the wounded artist to a lifeless "dog's leg". There's plenty of dehumanising cruelty in that assessment – the psychology isn't sympathetic in the least, instead it debases Vincent into something beyond an animal; he's reduced the vulnerable artist to nothing more than an animal's limb. But the real animal is Gauguin*, and Vincent's like a dead-weight he feels he's been forced to carry, isn't that roughly the sum of it?

Was this really the best person, the most sensitive person, to have as housemate? I submit not, that Gauguin, in his attraction to the primitive savagery of the world, was a callous and insensitive person, and if Vincent was kind and tender, this was someone who not only could, but *would* walk all over him.

Prado's Gift

The execution of Prado is a gift, for it in it, we're provided with an extensive psychological window into the mind-set clouding Paris, France, and the wider world. Bear in mind, the world was moving inexorably to two world wars in 1890, the first barely 20 years away. If Prado was fascinating France, Jack the Ripper held Britain in his terrifying embrace at precisely the same time. It's difficult to look back at the world, trying to imagine things coming into existence, like chocolate, the Eiffel Tower and Vincent's expressionism, from the perspective of them already in existence. Moreover, it's difficult to imagine things going out of existence, like corsets, rural France and Vincent himself, without relying entirely on perspectives handed down and recycled.

To repeat what I have said, to see the world as Vincent knew it, as Vincent lived it, and not as some shallow inauthentic post-truth, we must unlearn what we have learned while we are learning and painting a new, authentic picture together.

So, for example, the attitude to artists as thought leaders then was of far greater significance than it is today. That was a world without confidence in reality, a society that was clearly cautious about flashy expressionism, and unclear about science and psychology. Artists like Gauguin shaped some of the early attitudes to new things, even if posthumously, just as Vincent did. Gauguin called the Eiffel Tower "a triumph of iron, not only with regard to machines but also with regard to architecture…"

Curiously, through the *entire archive* of correspondence between Vincent and Theo, the word "Eiffel Tower" isn't mentioned once, even though Theo was living in Paris while it was under construction. The closest reference is to the imminent exhibition of Dutch artists at the World Fair, in a letter to Theo dated February 1st, 1890. Instead of references to architecture, which crops up a few times in their correspondence, Vincent writes about reputation and sunflowers.

It was also a world where visiting a brothel, for a bachelor, was commonplace, and not necessarily a sign of moral decrepitude.

There is much more to learn about the social fabric in the historical context of the time. Thanks to world famous, very high profile court cases and executions, such as Prado's [reported here in a Philadelphia newspaper], and the role of these highly charged newspaper stories in raising the profile of rising crime and its relationship to a rise in immigrants burning through France at the time, they had a *direct impact* on Vincent [a Dutch immigrant living in France].

In fact, so compelling and powerful was this true crime case [Prado's trial ran over nine days in November 1889], society itself felt itself challenged by it. Vincent and Gauguin discussed, and disagreed about the Prado case [he was accused of stealing from, and murdering high-class Paris prostitutes].

One can imagine, for two regulars to houses of ill repute, news of a mysterious, but evidently wealthy assassin, dealing in death to the ladies of the night [seemingly with the consent of his own wife and mistress] was clearly relevant to their own pursuits. One has to wonder whether, given the coverage Prado and Jack the Ripper were getting for their handiwork, whether both struggling artists may have seen crime [or even the appearance of it] as a shortcut to fame, of a sort.

In *The Sudden Onset on Insanity* chapter I examine these ideas within the canvas of Vincent and Gauguin in the Yellow House before the ear cutting incident.

Now, however, we must interrogate Gauguin's account of what happened to Vincent before taking in the savagery first-hand at the Prison de la Roquette. Does Gauguin's account add up? If not, why not?

*When Gauguin attended the execution of Prado in Paris on December 28th, 1888 the Eiffel Tower was still under construction. Three months later, on March 31st 1889, the world's tallest man-made structure at the time was complete, and inaugurated to great and colorful fanfare. The wrought iron lattice tower was meant to serve simply as a prominent entrance to the 1889 World Fair, which kicked off on May 5th. It was meant to be demolished after the fair packed up in October the same year, something that seemed inevitable given the protests of about three-hundred of Paris' leading artists who were opposed to structure. The artists of the day felt there needed to be a functional relationship between engineering and architecture. By 1918, less than thirty years after it had been erected, the Eiffel Tower was widely seen [by the French and internationally] as a quintessential symbol of France. It remained the tallest structure in the world for 41 years until the Chrysler Building in New York superseded it. The French Tower reclaimed the titled when new antennae were fitted. In 2004 the Millau Viaduct overtook the Eiffel Tower as the tallest structure in France. Even so, the Eiffel Tower remains one of the world's most recognisable man-made structures, and is the most visited paid-monument on Earth, with over 6 million visitors per year, three times as many as to the Van Gogh Museum in Amsterdam.

**Gauguin's biographer, Nancy Mowll Mathews, returns the "dog" insult to Vincent by framing her prose thus: *"By the end of the year [1891], Gauguin was like a cornered dog…[desperately] harrying friends for cash…"*

Gauguin's Dodgy Version of December 23rd, 1888

"And the memories of all we have loved stay and come back to us in the evening of our life. They are not dead but sleep, and it is well to gather a treasure of them." — Vincent van Gogh,

Vincent and Gauguin spent 63 days in one another's company in the Yellow House in Arles. Not much was achieved in these two months, besides Vincent very briefly taking on Gauguin's style of painting *psychological* realities, drawing from the mind rather than the real world, and losing his left ear in the process.

Something did happen somewhere in those 63 days. Something woke Vincent from his sanity.

What was it?

In *Loving Vincent*, as the question arises for the first time around Vincent's sanity, a character in a restaurant attests:

"He wasn't [mad]. Things only got strange when that friend of his – Gauguin – came."

So what precisely did Gauguin bring to the party?

What was it!

Gauguin's version is that Vincent awoke [after behaving badly] and with preternatural calmness, told Gauguin:

"I have a vague memory…[I] offended you last night."

Gauguin [speaking on his own behalf] is gracious and forgiving in his response. As he puts it:

"I gladly forgive you with all my heart, but yesterday's scene could happen again, and if I were struck I might lose control of myself and strangle you. So permit me to write your brother and announce my return."

This is an astonishing statement. There's a clear mismatch here between Gauguin's generous pardon, and the threat of imminent loss of control, and worse. On his own accord, he admits to wanting to kill – to throttle – Vincent. He admits to having motive to affect violence on his tender, if tempestuous friend. Vincent is a guy who writes letters abounding with sensitivities to his brother almost every day. Who stops in a field to take a moment when a crow lands beside his lunch. A man who paints friendly yellow suns and warm, whirling stars. Gauguin reveals himself as totally disingenuous here – of course he doesn't forgive Vincent. His words mean little, with one exception:

…yesterday's scene could happen again, and if I were struck I might lose control of myself…

Think about it, those are the words of a madman. Is Vincent mad, or Gauguin? Then he writes about the fateful events:

"My God, what a day! When evening had arrived and I had quickly eaten my dinner, I felt the need to go out alone and take the air, scented with flowering laurels. I had already almost crossed the Place Victor Hugo, when I heard behind me a familiar short footstep, rapid and irregular."

Gauguin actually provides no details, no context about what happens that day. Probably they argued. Possibly neither felt ready to forgive the other for slights, but perhaps Vincent wanted to be reassured Gauguin wouldn't leave [who knows, perhaps that he should leave] because of whatever they were bickering about. Given what happened that night, and the fact that Vincent ended up at death's door, and the apartment a bloody mess, Gauguin's exit that evening seems too harmless. He doesn't mention Vincent whatsoever. He doesn't say whether he said goodbye to Vincent, or told him where he was going. Seemingly out of nowhere, Gauguin "felt the need" to go out alone. This zen-like centeredness feels a million miles away from the opposite psychological pole, the ragged sense of *if I were struck I might lose control...*

As Gauguin tells it, he leaves the house calmly, in complete control. Then, with his back turned, for no reason at all:

"...Vincent rushed towards me, an open razor in his hand. My look at that moment must have been powerful indeed, for he stopped, and lowering his head, took off running in the direction of the house."

There are more mismatches here. Vincent "rushes" [charges] Gauguin, carrying a weapon. There's no reason given. No words, no context, no rhyme or reason. Vincent confronts Gauguin, not the other way round, for reasons unknown. Gauguin appears to do almost nothing. He doesn't, according to him, confront Vincent. He doesn't even ask Vincent what's going on. Again, just because Gauguin's account doesn't hold water, we shouldn't discard it. It's a psychological painting not of the scene, but of "post truth", reality the way Gauguin wishes us to see it. So, what Gauguin does reveal is the psychological symbolism of him turning his back on Vincent, and [for reasons that are unclear] Vincent pursuing Gauguin. Vincent has a bone to pick with Gauguin. I'm sure he did.

Let's examine the image closer, and more carefully now.

In the scenario given, Vincent rushes Gauguin from behind, armed and dangerous, and all Gauguin does in response is flash him a defiant look. It's enough to make Vincent turn tail, and run off. Gauguin clearly has a high opinion of himself, if he thinks someone with murderous malcontent can be dissuaded by a dirty look. Vincent doesn't simply stop what he's doing, he runs away. The mismatch here lies in the purposeful pursuit and the sudden, inexplicable, urgent flight. Anytime there is a mismatch in a version surrounding a criminal scenario, there's a credibility problem.

Just as Gauguin claimed to not lament Vincent's death, he says he did not "reproach" himself at all for not trying to talk to Vincent, or calm him down. On behalf of the critical he writes:

"Often I have questioned my conscience, but I do not reproach myself at all. Let him who will cast the stone at me."

Shouldn't he feel a little bit bad about what happened? He's Vincent's only friend, and whatever he did or didn't do, had lasting consequences for Vincent. Again he says something that makes no sense. He has a conscience, he tells us, but he doesn't have any problem with what he did [or didn't do]. By saying he accepts people will cast stones at him, he acknowledges that to the outside view, his behaviour isn't beyond reproach.

Despite Vincent appearing in a state, Gauguin simply walks on and checks into a "good" hotel in Arles. He finds a room and goes to bed. In this version he couldn't be more innocent, and Vincent couldn't be more guilty. Vincent is running around, armed and dangerous, saying nothing, and Gauguin is taking in the air, also saying nothing. It's not credible at all.

I want to highlight Gauguin's use of the word "good" here. I will deal in more detail with a potential love triangle between Vincent, Gauguin and "Rachel" [the recipient of the ear] in due course, but for now the *good* is intended to steer us away from the bad. Gauguin's specifically letting us know he didn't leave the Yellow House to spend the night in a brothel.

Well, what if he did? For starters, that would cast Gauguin as a callous villain, a hedonist who not only doesn't care about Vincent, but is so good at not reproaching himself, so good at being unaffected by matters of conscience, he can revel in a brothel while Vincent suffers. I believe Gauguin did go to a brothel that night, the same one Vincent went to while seriously injured, to *deliver a message*. As a result of that message, Gauguin left the brothel and booked himself into a proper hotel.

In Gauguin's version, he adds that he was agitated that night, and couldn't fall asleep until about three in the morning. As a result he woke up late.

Now, why is Gauguin agitated when he's alone, but unruffled when Vincent rushes him with a razor. Why is there no reproach right then, but when he's alone, then he's agitated? The agitation and the going to bed late is psychological padding for the fact that Gauguin's night wasn't incident free, and he slept late not because he went to bed early, but because of unrevealed goings-on that night, of all, nights, that kept him occupied.

As for Gauguin's version of the ear slicing incident, this is how he puts it:

"[Vincent] returned to the [Yellow House] and, immediately, cut off his ear close to the head. [Vincent] must have taken some time in stopping the hemorrhage, for the next day there were many wet towels scattered about on the floor tiles of the two rooms downstairs."

In other words, immediately after stalking Gauguin for no reason, and despite Gauguin being completely innocent, saying nothing nasty to the Dutch artist, and making no aggressive move except shooting him a look, Vincent scuttles back and lops off his ear. The only way that ridiculous story gains any traction is if we accept Vincent was mad, and what he did and why he did it made no sense. In true crime, there's a tendency to write off inexplicable behaviour as monstrous or mad, but what it really reveals is laziness. Just because we can't see a reason for extreme behaviour doesn't mean there isn't one. Typically, the motive is hidden, and a habit of hiding things, or misleading, or misdirecting, or habitual mendacity in everyday life [living a lie] in the context of crime, tends to reinforce a pattern that often feels like criminal intent.

The Other Gauguin

In a general sense, Vincent is an artist trying to enter the world. That's the message of his art. It's inside the world. His journey as an artist involves repeated, exhaustive forays into real landscapes, rain or shine, during the heat of the day or the cool of the night, whether calm or blustery, to get his fix on reality first-hand. Vincent pained 800 paintings in 8 years, that's an average of 100 per year, or roughly one every three to four days. Factoring in his year in the loony bin, that's an incredible output, mad or not. Gauguin on the other hand is fleeing the world. He has an idea of the world as a more visceral thing, a thing of the mind that is somehow more real than the real world. In Gauguin's idyllic childhood, and short-lived success as a stock broker, we can understand the more cerebral pace in executing his art, and in his trips to Tahiti, Panama and the Caribbean, we have sense of a childish* and spoiled man intent on escaping civilization.

In Gauguin's praise of the Eiffel Tower, a truly man-made, modern symbol, we have yet another mismatch, from a man who seems to have no compunction against saying what sounds popular, and yet this clearly seems at odds with who he was. Gauguin's hunger, above all, was for the primal.

Taking this psychology into Gauguin's pencil-sketch of the scene, what can we say about what happens when any man runs *into* the world? He gets hurt. What happens when you flee constantly *from* the real world? In this conceited attempt to escape pain and seek pleasure, you invariably hurt others.

Which of the two was running repeatedly into the real world, and who got hurt?

Who was running repeatedly away [and imminently to Paris, and then Tahiti], who had hurt others, including his own family?

If this seems like cerebral psychology, we have evidence – besides the fact that Gauguin was a pugilist [an old European term for a boxer], a party animal**, a pedophile*** and hedonist**** – of Gauguin being involved in a brawl, while drunk, in Brittany in 1894. This was no simple scuffle; Gauguin shattered his ankle so badly during the altercation, the fracture never healed.

In 1897 Gauguin attempted suicide by walking up a hill and swallowing arsenic. That tends to be the way you'd expect an artist to kill themselves, through poison. In 1903, the year of his death at 54 years of age, Gauguin spent time in prison, as a result of political activism against the local Tahitian police. This idea of Gauguin as a violent troublemaker capable of hypersensitivity and brutal indifference is thus a pattern, and one founded in a psychology of escape interrupted by a traffic jam of unpleasant confrontations.

One may argue Vincent was doing the same, but even if we accept it, Gauguin was clearly far more extreme in both his escape attempts, and his confrontations. Gauguin's biographer*****happens to be critical of the artist too, calling Gauguin a "twisted and bitter man, having alienated everyone both at home and in Tahiti" at the time of his death.

Compared to Gauguin, Vincent feels like a more impressionable and modest fellow, in almost every respect, besides his art, doesn't he? The Dutchman signing into the sanatorium at Saint-Rémy is hardly the kind of thing we'd associate with either escape or confrontation. Cowards confront others, masters confront themselves.

In fact it seems like a very sane thing for a man who thinks he is mad to do. Can we imagine Gauguin voluntarily signing up for a stint in the madhouse? I can't, and yet Gauguin – his life from beginning to end – reads more like a legacy of a guy off his rocker, than Vincent does. The difference between them: Vincent's story is stronger and more cohesive, just as his art is. If there is uncertainty about Vincent, it's couched in tragedy, not debauchery, misleading public relations and mendacity, which is the case with Gauguin.

Vincent's letters to his brother are another strong signal of someone who wished to be in a decent relationship with his family, unlike Gauguin who wished to escape his responsibilities to his family, and the real world.

I hope by now the possibility of Gauguin having at least the *propensity* to lash out at Vincent is now manifestly clear. This isn't a guy who is afraid to fight, or afraid of blood, or to damage those closest to him.

"What have you done, sir, to your comrade?"

Even in Gauguin's version of events, suspicion from the cops in Arles, immediately fell on him. It made sense, they boarded together, and the crime happened in the home they shared. In other words, it was a little like the murder of Meredith Kercher in Perugia, with Gauguin playing the role of Amanda Knox, in other words, as the prime suspect who lived with the victim, but couldn't remember where he was, or who he was with, or whether he was awake or asleep at the time of the incident.

In addition, instead of Gauguin finding Vincent – as you'd expect in a situation where he lived with the guy – just as in the Knox case, the cops find him before he does, so that when he arrives he's bewildered.

According to Gauguin Vincent's blood was all over the house. Besides staining two rooms, it had splattered the staircase leading up to "their" bedroom. In fact there were two separate bedrooms, but Gauguin's vague description seems to fuse them into one, raising the spectre of blood in Gauguin's room. Why would there be blood in his room if he wasn't there? Vincent would have no need, let alone the wherewithal, to go into his room either…

Since the razor [the likely implement used to sever the ear, and implied by Gauguin] was found in the kitchen, one would expect most of the blood there. Gauguin doesn't mention the kitchen*****, but the kitchen [in a scenario of two men sharing space], feels like a likely space for an altercation.

Describing the aftermath of the ear cutting, Gauguin's painting skills go up a notch:

When [Vincent] was in good enough condition to go out, his head covered up by a Basque beret pulled all the way down, he went straight to a house where, for want of a fellow-countrywoman, one can find a chance acquaintance, and gave the "sentry" his ear, carefully washed and enclosed in an envelope.

It's interesting that in both self-portraits Vincent did after the incident, he paints himself wearing a blue beret. Some versions of this story say the ear was wrapped in newspaper. The newspaper sounds right, given that Vincent supposedly thrust a piece of newspaper into Gauguin's hand earlier that evening, underlining the words in an article "and the murderer took flight." This seems to be a very non-confrontational way of saying, "Please leave" or "If you don't leave I'll cut of my ear [and then I might cut you]."

On the other hand, since Vincent was a machine when it came to writing letters, he likely had a stack of envelopes at the ready, and so, what safer place to protect and convey a message than an envelope. It was simply an ear inside an envelope, this time, instead of a neatly scribbled page.

At about 23:30, Vincent delivered his package to "Rachel" at rue Bout d'Arles, instructing the poor girl to take care of it. This differs from Gauguin's account, which has Vincent tell an anonymous "sentry" to remember him. These differences are less subtle than they seem. Cutting off one's ear, taking the care to wrap it, going to the trouble to deliver it – only to deliver it to some unknown doorkeeper at a brothel smacks of a drunken lack of reason. Asking someone you don't know, or who doesn't know you, someone whose job is gatekeeper, essentially, to remember you, also has a fatalistic tinge to it. It's as if Vincent [in Gauguin's version] is desperately suicidal. He wants someone, anyone to notice him. It feels like it may be true, except there's a mismatch between the preparations around his ear and giving it to someone who wouldn't care one way or the other how it was wrapped.

I believe both Vincent and Gauguin knew the girl in question. Knew is the wrong word. I think both artists were *familiar* with her, and she was no sentry. I think she was special, and since Vincent had lived in Arles longer than Gauguin, he probably knew the girl better. Gauguin may have tried to have had his way with her, or tried to come between them.

Ordinarily, two guys interested in the same girl may not necessarily lead to a deleterious outcome. But there's reason to believe Vincent was more agitated than usual on December 23rd. One theory is that Vincent received a letter from Theo announcing his engagement to Gauguin, and this traumatised Vincent. I have a better theory that builds onto this one.

Vincent may have communicated his financial concerns, but Gauguin – who was also being sponsored by Theo – may have taken them to heart, and taken matters into his own hands.

Either as a result of the imminent arrival of Christmas, or the news of his brother's engagement, or because of Gauguin's own greedy conceits, or a combination of these factors, Vincent drowned his sorrows more than usual that day. And so did Gauguin. If the money was up, wasn't it all over? What was there to do but drink? Given the infernally cold weather there was little else to do. Under these circumstances, Gauguin was either more irritated than usual by his companion, or Gauguin chose this moment to get his own back on both brothers: he'd steal Vincent's muse and what remained of Theo's purse from him. Maybe he needed money to buy the muse. Was it money or sex? Given what we know, it feels like it was both. Violent deeds such as this as often precipitated by greed and sex.

I'm convinced "Rachel" has a pivotal role in this, either as part of a love triangle, or as a witness to what Vincent feared could be his imminent demise at the hands of Gauguin, who I suspect was also drinking heavily, and also very unhinged. Giving Rachel the ear might have served as an insurance policy, having already been attacked by Gauguin. If Gauguin had attacked Vincent, and if Vincent had escaped, he could easily lead Gauguin to believe that whoever he gave the ear to, *knew* something about the crime.

If Vincent suspected Gauguin meant to spend that night with Rachel, then giving her his ear was sure to put paid to Gauguin's antics, and as we know, wherever he started the night away from home, he ended it sleeping in a "good" hotel.

Thus, if these conjectures are true, then Vincent succeeded in his plan, which was to show Rachel what a jerk Gauguin was, at his expense. Gauguin's response was to show Arles what a madman they had in their midst. Touché!

As someone who briefly went through a phase of self-harm as a teenager [hand, wrists and leg], it's clear that the ear isn't an obvious choice, and if one was in the habit of it, there would be signs of escalating mutilation on the arms, hands and legs.

Off With the Ear, and then to bed?

After handing over the package, Vincent went home, to bed and slept. This part of the story feels like Vincent in Auvers after he was shot. Instead of "I tried to kill myself", this time it's "I cut off my ear."

But in Arles, he closes the shutters, lights and lamp and puts it on a table near the window and goes to sleep. That doesn't make any sense. When Vincent shot himself, he went home and lay on his bed, not to sleep but to recover. In Arles, there is somehow an impression that he did go to bed to sleep, but how could anyone sleep with one side of their head on fire? Remember, you sleep with your head on a pillow, but one side of your head is gushing blood, a pain so excruciating it feels like a candle is burning into the side of it. Sleep would only be possible if Vincent passed out, due to a combination of blood loss, exhaustion and perhaps intoxication.

The closed shutters only make sense if someone was in the house with Vincent, doing something but didn't want to be seen. The idea of a lamp lit through the night, suggests while Vincent was bleeding to death, his would-be-murderer was cleaning up the scene. Well, we know from Gauguin's own version that he only slept from 03:00 that night, and the ear incident took place three hours earlier. Three hours seems like the right amount of time to sneak out of the hotel, cover up evidence [perhaps pack his things too], and sneak back.

In Gauguin's version, he arrives back at the Yellow House the next morning, the last to know what had happened. Despite the commotion in Arles, and despite Gauguin being on his own and agitated, he's completely unaware of what's happened.

I had not the slightest inkling of all this when I appeared on the threshold of our house and the gentleman with the bowler hat said to me point-blank, in a more than severe tone:

"What have you done, sir, to your comrade? Oh yes...you know very well...he is dead."

The police, confronted with such a macabre scene splattered with scarlet, assumed they had a murder on their hands.

At this accusation Gauguin isn't surprised, and crucially, shows zero interest or concern for his friend. He doesn't ask how he is, because he knows exactly how he is. Instead, his concern is – resonantly given the true circumstances – for himself.

"I would not wish anyone such a moment, and it took me a few long minutes to be able to think clearly and repress the beating of my heart."

An innocent person wouldn't care about thinking clearly or how their own heart was beating in guilty trepidation, they'd be caught up in the emergency of trying to save their friend. We don't seem to get a trace of shock, surprise, sympathy or concern from Gauguin. All he's trying to do is think clearly, and he's not enjoying the looks he's getting. He talks about "anger and indignation" as well as "the shame of all those gazes tearing my entire being to pieces" and how this "suffocated" him, causing him to "stutter".

Let Sleeping Dogs Lie

If Gauguin had cut off Vincent's ear, and then arrived back hours later, did he expect to find Vincent dead? From his own version, clearly, he did expect to find Vincent dead. This means, if Gauguin was involved, it was attempted murder.

In the bed, Vincent lay completely enveloped in the sheets, curled up like a dog's rear leg; he appeared lifeless. Gently, very gently, I touched the body, whose warmth surely announced life. For me it was as if I had regained all my powers of thought and energy.

I've written about several true crime cases where the perpetrators, within a scenario of death or murder, describe their feelings of relief. John Ramsey, when he discovers his six-year old daughter dead, describes *relief* rushing over him. Gauguin feeling relief that Vincent is alive only makes sense if Gauguin harmed him in the first place and now, sobered up, has to face the music with the cops at his side. Of course, Vincent being alive presents another problem – what story to tell while Vincent himself is not *compos mentis* to tell it himself?

Gauguin admits whispering to the commissioner of police to do him a favor and waken Vincent "carefully", and immediately tell him Gauguin has gone to Paris. Then, the ingenuous wriggle. *If he sees me, that could kill him [because he's mad]*. And so, for his own sake, for his own safety, Gauguin flees to Paris – Vincent being just another discarded human being littering his cannonball-like trail of destruction.

Naturally, if Vincent awoke only to discover he had [according to everyone] cut off his own ear, and Gauguin had abandoned him, and Vincent's dream of a Southern Colony for Artists was gone with it, then the betrayal and disappointment would be difficult to bear.

When Vincent woke up, Gauguin relates, one of the first things he did was check the box downstairs containing their money. And so, there's your motive.

*According to the *Washington Post* Gauguin was *"...a child all his life. You sense that in his manner, in his bragging and his rages, in his pier-side brawls and show-off clothes, his greatcoats and his wooden shoes, his cowboy hats and hand-carved canes."* Besides all this, Gauguin himself wrote: *"Men of science, forgive these poor artists who have forever remained children..."*

**Gauguin named his tropical home in Tahiti *La Maison du Jouir* – House of Pleasure. The walls of Gauguin's home were decorated with 45 pornographic images purchased in Port Said. Gauguin also produced a statue intended to ridicule the local bishop for his "sexual hypocrisy" [The fact that Bishop Martin had a mistress seems the cause of Gauguin's lampooning him].

***Gauguin's local wife in Tahiti Vaeoho, was 14 years old, and she wasn't the only child Gauguin had sex with.

****Nancy Mowll Mathews is a Czech-American art historian, and author of *Paul Gauguin: An Erotic Life*, published in 2001.

*****In one of Vincent's letters to Theo describing his early impressions of life with Gauguin, the Dutch artist enthused: "I must tell you that he knows how to cook perfectly..." This suggests Gauguin spent a lot of time in the kitchen of the Yellow House. Crime scenes tend to be where the perpetrator either spends the most time, or feels the most comfortable. Whether the razor was more likely to be in the kitchen than somewhere else in the house, is another matter. The idea of Vincent sitting down in the kitchen to a plate of Gauguin's food, while left the table in a huff, only to return, approaching Vincent from behind [while he was eating], and sliced off his ear unexpectedly, is difficult to evade.

Vincent's Sexual Psychology

"Concentrate your strengths against your competitor's relative weaknesses." — Paul Gauguin

1888 – Spring/Summer/Fall – Southern France

In order to more seriously test the probability of Gauguin as Vincent's attacker, we must float through to time, to examine the motives that brought Gauguin to Arles in the first place, and also Vincent's motive, in bringing Gauguin there. What was the purpose for the one, in terms of the other? We can also look at the portraits painted by both immediately after the incident as a mental projection of the events.

On the issue of portraits, Vincent's portrait of Gauguin [painted in December 1888] is exceptional in that the subject is turned away from the painter. *Man in a Red Beret* has his back turned on the artist – while a small art work drifts in the background above Gauguin's left shoulder. Gauguin, meanwhile, is leering elsewhere. The tones of the painting are thick, dark and smudged, symptoms of Vincent's emotional claustrophobia regarding Gauguin. A *Guardian* review intuits "a coldness and enclosed quality" in Gauguin, exposed by Vincent. The review adds presciently:

The big matted hulk of [Gauguin's] back is a wall keeping us out, his swirling red beret giving life to a head that is otherwise blank. The eye is a void, the nose and beard as sharp as daggers. Van Gogh sees Gauguin as a remote figure, someone he is scared to tap on the shoulder and talk to.

Who was helping who, again?

In hindsight, it's easy to imagine Vincent as a pathetic and tortured failure, and Gauguin as the more functional artist. This perception of Gauguin as the superior art force, and human being, was crafted, after all, by none more than Gauguin himself, the son of a journalist who knew the power and potential in telling stories.

Gauguin was a boxer and a fencer; he was physically stronger and more combative [including in temperament] than Vincent, and more creative – in the sense of wiliness, or craftiness – but was Vincent really the more disturbed of the two? Gauguin's disturbia was a kind of depravity, which made Vincent's mental illness seem like mere moodiness, not madness, by comparison.

Vincent arrived in Arles in late February 1888. When he arrived, Gauguin sent Vincent a rare missive from 13 place de la Mairie, a boarding house in Pont-Aven. He complains at some length in this letter about having no money. He refers to funds, pressing debts, having nothing in a month or money five times in the barely 100 words of the note. In other words, he's laying the begging bowl at Vincent's door, and laying it on quite thick.

In a way, it's not even a letter to Vincent but to his brother. Gauguin's asking Vincent [using him] to make contact with the younger brother and art dealer, who, for reasons unknown, is slow to respond to Gauguin. Perhaps Gauguin, knowing Vincent is receiving a regular stipend from his brother, wants in on the same situation, but slyly realizes his chances of getting an allowance are greater if Vincent petitions his brother on his behalf, than if he does, directly.

I wanted to write to your brother but I know you see each other every day and I'm afraid to trouble him, occupied as he is with business from morning till night.

That's a manipulative way of weaselling through the door of the one sibling through the relationship with the other. How *troubling* could it be to receive a letter, let alone a letter as short as this? As for this idea of I know you see each other every day; Gauguin's addressed his letter to Arles. Theo's in Paris. So it comes down to a letter from Vincent on Gauguin's behalf, passing on correspondence effectively, or a letter from Gauguin saying effectively, hey Vincent's brother, can I also have some money?

To rub it in even further, Gauguin paints himself the victim, not only struggling to make ends meet but struck down with fever.

Ironically, Gauguin also pressures Vincent with the idea of Gauguin desperately seeking peace of mind, and needing Vincent's help and encouragement in order to foment the mental calm he craves.

I don't want to put pressure on your brother, but a brief word from you on this subject would set my mind at rest, or at least enable me to hold on. My God, how terrible these money matters are for an artist!

Actually, by using the one brother to get into the good graces of the other, pressure is precisely what Gauguin's after. The idea of Gauguin "holding on" is also designed to exert pressure. He also uses the term "eke things out". We know that Gauguin ultimately succeeded in his schemes – both brothers came around to encourage, sponsor and support him, yet after the invitation was extended for Gauguin to go to Arles [board loadings and materials paid for], Gauguin procrastinated. Gauguin seemed to want money but no strings attached. Going to Arles and living cheek by jowl with Vincent, meant his work ethic would be exposed to his patron, directly or indirectly, on a daily basis. There'd be no hiding behind words, so Gauguin was lukewarm about it.

A final observation on Gauguin's letter of February 29th, 1888: Gauguin makes absolutely zero reference to Vincent in it, other than that Vincent is the addressee, and in the instance where he asks Vincent for "a word for you" to be sent to Theo on Gauguin's behalf.

Now, Gauguin had some reason to complain because he *was* ill throughout 1888 – he'd picked up malaria, dysentery and hepatitis on his trip to Panama and the Caribbean for seven months in 1887. The point is that artistically, financially and mentally, Gauguin – before his arrival in Arles – was in a more pathetic state than Vincent. The only area where Gauguin was more on the ball than Vincent, in 1888, was in his social *nous*. Vincent's weakness was that his passion for art had made him not only lonely, but socially inept and it has to be said, naïve. This made him easy to deceive and manipulate, an easy target for the likes of Gauguin.

Statistical Analysis of the Correspondence

Gauguin's letter in late February was the first of six to Vincent in 1888. For Gauguin that was a lot of letter writing.

In 1887 Gauguin wrote a single letter to Vincent, and in 1889, when Vincent was essentially a prisoner stuck in a madhouse, largely thanks to Gauguin, he sent Vincent just four letters. In 1890, until the summer of Vincent's death, Gauguin wrote five letters. If the archive is reliable, and complete, this means in the two-and-a-half years between December 1887 and July 1890, the artists corresponded 21 times. Of those, Gauguin wrote to Vincent 16 times [76%], and Vincent five letters to Gauguin [24%].

The semantics of Gauguin's letters to Vincent, besides the repeated requests for money, are worth digging into in great detail. I burrow through these in depth in the *Last Letters* chapter. What is interesting to consider for the moment, is the issue of hypochondria.

In 1888 Gauguin was poor and in bad health, but when comparing the two artists, the French artist seems to exaggerate and wallow in his symptoms, quickly losing motivation and focus in his work, whereas Vincent, despite suffering symptoms that are infinitely worse, seems more resilient to them, at least in his writing and in his artistic output. Although there is a sense, occasionally, of Vincent playing the sympathy card with Theo, on whom he was dependent, the timbre of virtually all his correspondence is on Vincent's impressive enterprise. He works hard throughout. Gauguin doesn't. Gauguin's erratic, as the following excerpts from 1888 attest…

...my sickly state and my worries often leave me in a state of prostration, in which I sink into inaction...

...I've neglected [work] a bit owing to illness...

...I'm beginning to recover the full use of my faculties: my illness had weakened me...

...I'm terribly bored and I'm suffering from stomach trouble...

...If you were familiar with my life you would understand that after having struggled so much (in every way) I'm in the process of drawing breath, and at the moment I'm lying dormant...

[I'm] waiting for better times, unless I'm released from this lousy existence, which, aside from work, weighs on me so horribly.

...the collection of boors around here think I'm completely mad and I'm happy about that, because it proves to me that I'm not...

When we consider Vincent stumbling through the night in Arles, despite almost bleeding to death, and hiking back to his room at night in Auvers, despite being shot, we get brief glimpses of a man who can walk off – or walk through – the pain. In Gauguin we see someone who is brittle and *kleinserig*, an Afrikaans word that means babyish, but a more direct translation is *small hurts*.

He moans constantly about things not being the way he wants them, is quick to blame and quick to beg others for help or relief. In this sense, babyish feels more like a man who is infantile, and immature, certainly in his ability to deal with the rigours of life, work and love. In comparison to this, wasn't Vincent a much stronger, more authentic, more internally driven and consistent fellow?

Is it really so difficult to see Gauguin's disturbia in the relentless remoteness of his work? By comparison, Vincent's work is warm, even hot, and warmly sensual at that. But the question is, what more than that?

Sexual Analysis…

One moment Gauguin is overcome by complaints, the next he is gushing enthusiasm, in prose that's meant to butter up and flatter:

I like the way you picture your dream house and its arrangement, and my mouth is watering to see it…Ah well! As far as possible I don't want to think any more about the promised fruit…

On other occasions, it's difficult to tell whether there's sexual allegory or not:

At the top a cascade of foaming water, white pink, and a rainbow on the edge near the frame.

What we do know is of the two artists, Vincent was more infatuated with Gauguin than vice versa. Simon Schama uses this word, but it's difficult to be certain whether this was a kind of captivated admiration, or something to do with a sexual orientation. One may say the absence of undisputable references to homosexuality speaks for itself, but I'm not sure that's necessarily true. Sexual matters, especially in this area, tend to be private, especially for a former preacher, and as the son of a protestant preacher, as Vincent was.

On the other hand, in 1888, prostitution was so popular it was difficult to walk down the street, including in Jack the Ripper's Whitechapel, London, without being accosted by prostitutes. Brothels in the late 19th century were as ubiquitous, and part of the lifestyle, as television is today. Both popular forms of entertainment, only the one could infect you with syphilis while the other made you fat.

In 2002 *Salon* interviewed Nancy Mowll Mathews expressly on the topic of Gauguin's "monstrous" sexuality.

Was there an [openly] gay culture in Paris?...Yeah. I would say it was an open gay culture...and some people...wrote about it and their relationships. Although it's hard to reconstruct...I feel that Gauguin was appealing to that group in writing so openly himself about his attraction to men...

We have to wonder then, if Gauguin was trying to appeal to homosexuals, whether this appeal was the real reason Vincent invited Gauguin to live with him. Was it for the...well, not the promise of sex exactly, but the possibility of it, at least...that Vincent extended the invitation? And what did Theo know? Was Theo trying to enable the whole operation from afar?

The Sal interviewer points out the difficulty of being "a man who loves other men" but has no example of how to go about it. Mathews responds:

I think van Gogh did have access to gay culture. I like to think that that's reflected in the fact that once he moves to Paris, he calls himself impotent. He is no longer interested in women...I think that now that he is in Paris, he has other friends and other ways of looking at things...Would that have been able to make him deal with the Gauguin situation better? I don't know...Now we're really speculating. I do know from his paintings and letters there were several men that van Gogh expressed love for.

The difficulty, of course, when dealing with an expressionist is that they're going to be effusive in general. Vincent loved yellow so much he slurped up tubes of chrome yellow paint. He loved sunflowers. He loved the glare of the sun. When an expressionist is lonely, and Vincent was, it's also easy to misinterpret affection for orientation, affiliation for ardour.

Don't Kick the Chair

In January 2010 the *New Yorker* also hints at simmering signs of homosexuality around the goings on of the Yellow House in Arles.

There was something erotic, ardent, if unrealized, about van Gogh's excitement in Gauguin's presence. [Vincent] was acutely aware of his own sexual inadequacy, especially in comparison with Gauguin's hyperactive sex life: even when they were paying for sex at the brothel, van Gogh admitted ruefully, Gauguin got more value for his franc.

The *New Yorker* article feels authentic and authoritative because it anchors itself in the source material, Vincent's art. Contextualised, we're forced to admit there's smoke, and where there's smoke, isn't there fire?

Van Gogh eventually painted two wonderful symbolic portraits of the artists as their chairs: Gauguin's is robust, lit by a candle, van Gogh's is armless and small. It requires no doctrinaire Freudian to see significant form in the contrast of the erect and flaming candle that sits on Gauguin's chair with the crumpled, flower-shaped handkerchief on van Gogh's.

The erect candle is positioned broadly where the phallus might be, and to make the aspersion even clearer, if Gauguin was seated on the chair, and naked, and aroused, the erection would arise where the candle did. The light winking on the wall also seems to be a flickering, burnishing glow in response to the candle. Since Gauguin's mother was half Peruvian, he had a darker complexion and features, that to the fair-skinned Vincent must have felt exotic. This wild mixture of civilization and the artist taming his animal is reflected in the brown tanned limbs of the chair, which shine with a layer of sweaty varnish. The slightly cursive touches, suggest Vincent's appreciation of the artist's nuance. The green and the brown express Vincent's sense of Gauguin's intoxicating earthiness. The two books are a reminder that they have, at least, an intellectual countryside in common [or so Vincent has been misled to believe]. As an example:

I've just read your interesting letter and I entirely agree with you on the slight importance that accuracy contributes to art. Art is an abstraction; unfortunately we're becoming increasingly misunderstood. I would very much like it if we were to achieve our aims, that is, my coming to Provence. I've always had an itch to interpret bullfights in my own way, as I understand them.

Did Gauguin ever actually paint a bullfight scene? Many did, like Manet, Picasso, and Vincent himself, although the Dutch painter's execution focuses more on the crowd than on the arena. Vincent's *Les Arènes* was painted in December 1888, precisely when Gauguin was around. In April 1888, Vincent wrote to Theo of a toreador crushing one if his balls while leaping a barricade, and again in September of seeing some "very beautiful sights at the bullfights." In 1888 the bullfighting season in Arles ended on October 21st, and Gauguin arrived two days later, on October 23rd. So much for the itch he'd always wanted to scratch.

Gauguin went to Arles but apparently never got round to scratching that itch. The closest he got to depicting a bullfight, arguably, was *Vision after the Sermon*, which features an arena and a bull, but the focal point is a man wrestling with an angel in front of a crowd of devout onlookers. Gauguin painted this in 1888, before he left Pont-Aven for Arles. He also painted a pair of bulls in *Christmas Night*, executed in 1894, in Pont-Aven.

How does Vincent see himself in comparison to Gauguin?

On October 24th, the day after Gauguin's arrival, Vincent wrote to Theo. For all Gauguin's complaints about poor health, Vincent was surprised at how robust and healthy he was. He told Theo:

Gauguin has arrived in good health. He even seems to be in better health than I am.

It's important to know who both of these artists are inside out, but it's not enough. We have to take these separate identities and figure out the dynamic between them. It's clear Gauguin had a huge ego, and a weak work ethic, and Vincent rather the opposite – he felt himself an apprentice at everything, including art, yet he worked like a demon.

In such a scenario it seems almost inevitable that one would trample the emotions of the other. The question is, if Vincent was being trampled, almost like an abused wife, would he add insult to injury [or is it injury to insult] by cutting off his own ear? Personally, I doubt it.

Would any wife with a black eye box her other eye with her own fist to stave off further abuse, or to win the affection of her abuser? Or to convince her abuser not to leave her? Or is it more likely that the abusive partner, intent on leaving, would smash his fist into his victim as he was wont to do all along, and then leave?

Now, Vincent himself describes the dynamic between the two artists as "electric". In fact, in his letter to Theo on December 18th, that word manifests three times. Vincent writes of "excessively electric" discussions, and of emerging from their talks "like an electric battery after its run down." Some might read into that sexual languages, ejaculations and what not. I'm not sure if that's right. It sounds wearying more than anything else. By the end of the letter Vincent describes his lack of motivation in writing to two colleagues as "[not feeling] the necessary electric force."

Electricity, of course, was a fairly new concept in France in 1888. The first gas lamp to illuminate a Paris residence occurred in the winter of 1800, but it took 29 years for street lamps in Paris to get them. In 1876, Los Angeles ordered four arc lamps to illuminate its streets. In May, 1878 gas lamps were replaced with the first electric lights in Paris. London had about 4000 electric arc lights installed by 1881.

So the notion of electricity was fairly new to Arles in 1888, and the experience of streetlights burning out at regular intervals, would have made an impression on the artist.

It feels more like Vincent sees this "electric" energy as an unpleasant kind of current pulsing through the body. When there is too much, the body can be stung, shocked or zapped. When the battery is run down it is like death, and a mechanism – whether light or living body – cannot be revived unless an external charge is re-introduced.

Without current, the machine doesn't work. There is darkness. Now, isn't this allegory aimed more directly at the sharp, unpleasant energy that is generated between people who don't agree, or rub each other the wrong way? There hardly seems to be anything positive, let alone sensual or romantic about this description. It may be, if Vincent was infatuated, but feeling spurned, then this energy fluctuated unpleasantly within. It's difficult to say whether a friendship on edge would differ much to unrequited passion, but if I had to guess, the electric metaphor seems to work better for the sexual dimension. One seldom thinks of sparks flying or electricity where friendship is concerned. In sexual relationships it's a typical way to phrase things.

Vincent's depiction of his own chair really says it all. If Gauguin's chair is brown and exotic, Vincent's is yellow, and quite simple. It lack armrests and is situated modestly besides a box of onions with Vincent's name on it. It's unpretentious. If Gauguin's has an erect candle on its seat, Vincent's has an extinguished pipe lying flat on his. Some tobacco lies in a crumpled bit of paper.

Perhaps the simplest interpretation of the two chairs [painted by Vincent in November 1888] is also the most obvious – neither of them are occupied, as if the artist intuits that both chairs will soon be permanently abandoned, as indeed they were. Vincent got the idea, according to some scholars, from an illustration of a vacant chair in a Charles Dickens book.

Gauguin is often typecast as evil, and that's not wrong, but Vincent is hardly the innocent lamb either. Or perhaps that's unkind. What made Vincent charming on paper made him insufferable in real life. He wouldn't – couldn't – shut up. His loneliness meant that whenever someone shared space, or made the mistake of opening up a dialogue with Vincent, he answered with a deluge from which there was no escape, and no relief. No wonder Vincent writes about a battery being allowed to run completely down. That's what Vincent was doing, and his captive audience, trapped by the weather, had to endure it too. As the weather grew worse and the two were locked for longer intervals indoors, in each other's company, so the relationship unravelled until the fuse blew with a shower of sparks.

Far from a sexual explosion, I wonder whether the cutting off of the ear wasn't a sadistic kind of retribution from Gauguin, who was effectively saying: listening to you is like having your ears melted from your head. *Here, see what it feels like.*

Is the homosexual narrative possible?

Are you sure you want to hear this?

The streets of Arles are purposefully designed to twist and turn, in order to channel, mitigate and frustrate the force of the Mistral; a wind that rises with cold violence each winter in the south of France. It was down these narrow, snaking labyrinths that both artists wandered on the night Vincent lost his ear.

On this night, more than any other, we get a visceral sense of Vincent's sexuality. It's laid bare. He loses an ear, yes, yet it's not enough to dissuade him from getting to the whorehouse. *He must go to the whorehouse!* And where was Gauguin during this slippery nocturnal expedition?

And what was it about the bloody orifice under the ear that spoke visually of another sexual organ?

If we are in the dark to some extent about Vincent's sexuality, we are less in the dark about Gauguin's. But using broad strokes, we see that Vincent heads to almost the furthest corner of France, as far from Theo as he can get, when he summoned Gauguin. Schama describes Vincent preparing the Yellow House for Gauguin "like a groom waiting for his bride". He paints a series of sunflowers in order to decorate Gauguin's room. One man decorating another man's room with flowers – not bullfights, or steam engines, not warriors, or the horses of the Camargue.

With the homosexual narrative, we are left with another theory, plausible for Vincent cutting off his ear, and as I will demonstrate, just as plausible a driving force in his potential suicide.

What if Vincent had become infatuated with René Secrétan, been rebuffed, and then stole René's pistol [as Secrétan claimed later] and shot himself in despair. Having come so far, have we gotten ourselves completely lost in the labyrinth?

INTO THE MURK OF MADNESS

"I shouldn't precisely have chosen madness if there had been any choice, but once such a thing has taken hold of you, you can't very well get out of it." — Vincent van Gogh

Murphy's Lore

"I stand at the edge of the abyss, yet I do not fall in." — Paul Gauguin

1889 – Winter – The Courtyard of the Hospital at Arles

Bernadette Murphy makes a reasonable argument for Vincent heading to Arles not because he was gay, but because he wasn't. He'd had a falling out with his brother, and at the same time, was charmed by a farmer's daughter he'd encountered in a Paris hospital, or *en route* to or from her many treatments.

Enter the Mad Dog

Through Murphy a dog scampers onto the stage [the back stage] of Vincent's story, cast as primary catalyst, or a sort of *deus ex machina*. It's a rabid dog. The neighbor's dog. The dog springs up, and bites an eighteen-year-old Gabrielle Berlatier during a Sunday barbeque on the farm near Arles. The mad hound's jaws fasten on the skin of Gabrielle's lower arm, clenching her flesh through her shawl. The family form a scrum around the foaming hyena, and are able to separate beauty from the beast. But she's bleeding badly.

The Berlatier's, apparently, continue to rally. A local shepherd shoots the dog. Michel Arnaud, the local vet is summoned to check for rabies. Arnaud's assessment is rabies. Next, the farm hands got to work heating up an iron poker, perhaps the sort used to brand bulls fit for the arena at Arles. The molten iron is applied to poor Gabrielle's wound in a sizzle of burning tissue. Gabrielle screams as only young girls can – a piercing shriek. Cauterising the wound would have limited infection, but a vaccination against the incubating virus [typically two weeks] was the only way to be safe.

Gabrielle was bitten on January 8th, 1888. The teenager and her mother arrived by train in Paris, at around 17:40 the next day seeking advanced medical treatment. At about 11:00 on January 10th, a Tuesday, mother and daughter arrived at the Ecole Normale Supérieure, in the rue d'Ulm suburb. This hospital, where Dr. Louis Pasteur was a director of research, was 5.5 kilometers due south of the brother's Van Gogh apartment in Rue Lepic [about 70 minutes walk crossing the river Seine].

If you lived in France and wanted to survive a bite by a rabid dog, then 1888 was just about the right time. Pasteur's world class research was a little like the Eiffel Tower at the time – in medical terms, the foundations had just been laid for a towering achievement.

Pasteur had tested his work on baby rabbits, using at least 50 rabid dogs to fine-tune his vaccine. In the summer of 1885, just two-and-a-half years before Gabrielle knocked on his door, Pasteur was faced with his first genuine case – Joseph Meister*, a nine-year-old boy who'd been mauled by a rabid dog. Pasteur was in a difficult situation. He believed his research could cure little Joseph, but if he failed or miscalculated, he could be sued and ruined. Since he wasn't a licensed doctor, the situation was fraught with risk.

Pasteur backed himself, and injected the little boy over eleven days with thirteen separate doses of rabid rabbit vaccine, basically very dilute doses of virus in the very early stages. Each successive dose had been incubated over a shorter period of time, giving the body's immunity a fighting chance. In other words, the idea was to infect someone *already infected* with rabies [during the early stages] with a much smaller dose, and thus give the body a chance to develop antibodies to ward off the original infection. Brilliant, mad even, but Pasteur's vaccine worked, little Joseph was cured and the doctor went on to become a living legend. That's one version of the story. Another version is that Pasteur treated two other patients, one of whom recovered [but may not have had rabies to begin with], and another who had rabies, and died.

In 1886 Pasteur treated 350 patients, losing only one. And so, it was during this initial *Pasteurization* of Paris, so to speak, that Gabrielle arrived on the scene, bring more microbes for the good doctor to slay. And so he did, over a period of some 20 treatments, starting on the day of her arrival.

For the farm girl, the trauma of the gnashing dog quickly became the adventure of a lifetime. In Paris she saw a larger world. Murphy describes the girl's mother taking her wide-eyed daughter to the theatre, a Jules Verne production involving real horses and mirrors to create the effect on stage of a large army. Gabrielle loved it. If the pair had taken in theatre shows, it's possible they visited the odd art museum as well. The big question is whether Gabrielle from Arles, and Vincent, bumped into each other in Paris.

We know that she attended Jules Verne's *Michel Strogoff* at the Théâtre du Châtelet, which is on the north side of the Seine, roughly halfway between the hospital and the Van Gogh's apartment. After her last inoculation on January 27th, the Berlatier pair boarded a train back to Arles. Vincent followed the same route three weeks later. So did Vincent meet her in Paris, and in stalker-style, did the 35-year-old follow the teenager to Arles, and ultimately hand her his ear?

Squabbling Siblings

Tempting as it is to tie Gabrielle's appearance in Paris to Vincent's in Arles, there are other explanations too. Vincent didn't just leave Paris on a whim, he and Theo had been living together and their relationship by late winter had become rather fraught. Theo's health was also in serious decline at the time, and Vincent would have felt himself a burden to his brother – a not unreasonable realization given he was dependent on his younger sibling, and frequently arguing with him.

The conventional wisdom that Vincent left Paris because he was tired of the hustle and bustle of Paris, and longed for sunshine is only half-true, if that. It reminds me of the conventional wisdom surrounding the exit of the Durrell family to Corfu in 1935, supposedly for the same reason. The reality had more to do with darker, unacknowledged forces, like money troubles, attempts at making a living on foreign shores and terminal afflictions [in the Durrell's case it was chronic alcoholism].

Did Vincent meet Gabrielle in Paris?

I'm not sure whether Murphy believes that Gabrielle and Vincent encountered one another in Paris, but I don't. In any case, she was there chaperoned by her mother, and she was – after all – in a process of medical treatment, not there to paint the town red.

It's possible, given Theo's poor health at the time, that the younger's siblings medical treatment may have brought Vincent at close quarters with the Belatiers. Since the hospital the Belatiers visited was close to the Van Gogh's apartment, it seems natural that they would have sought medical treatment, if they had, somewhere local.

Specifically, Theo was suffering from exhaustion, disfiguring swelling and frozen joints. These are classic symptoms, of course, of secondary stage syphilis, and though neither Van Gogh knew it then, these symptoms would escalate and overcome the younger brother two short years later.

It is not the ambit of this narrative to probe the research methodologies of Pasteur in any depth, even less so as it pertained to syphilis. Nevertheless, it should be noted that a contemporary of Pasteur's, one Joseph Turenne, pursued lifelong research in an effort to find an antidote to syphilis. The research methodology was similar to that of rabies. In 1859 Turenne participated in a controversial experiment where research subjects were purposefully infected with second stage syphilis. They failed.

The main difference between rabies and syphilis is the former is a viral infection, while the latter is bacterial. Currently, in spite of Pasteur's promising research at the time, and despite great leaps in medical science over the past 130 years, no vaccine exists for syphilis.

Doctors and hedonists had no way of knowing that in the 1880's, but it's possible Theo may have sought medical care from the best, most promising expert in the area at the time. And since Theo was afflicted that winter, at the same time Gabrielle Belatier was treated for rabies, it's certainly possible to bring the two together *hypothetically*.

Given Vincent's assessment that Theo's malaise was due to a *shared neurosis*, it's difficult to say for certain whether either Van Gogh's saw Theo's deteriorating condition as more than merely psychosomatic. Since the affliction returned each winter with a vengeance, there was clearly a pattern to it. It was related to Theo's immune system slowly being eaten away by infection. And so, when winter hit, so did the infection.

What is true, is that Vincent's hedonism had imperilled his younger brother, whether he knew it or not, and so from a certain point of view, Vincent's influence *was* a burden [health wise] to Theo, who sometimes frequented brothels on the invitation, instigation and encouragement of his artist brother.

Vincent shouldn't be given *all* the blame for Theo's condition, however. Theo was an art dealer, so Vincent wouldn't be the only artist roping him in – there were a slew of other artists doing the same thing, and this was Paris after all. It's fair to suggest that at some point Theo was whoring it up more than Vincent, especially given the young man's early death.

By all accounts, Theo, despite a pious upbringing, eventually became *completely* caught up in the "bohemian" lifestyle, that was the Paris art scene. Participation was clearly part of the job description.

Worryingly, if the one brother was unattached, the other was in a serious relationship at the time. Through Andries and Johanna Bonger [respectively Theo's future brother-in-law and bride to be at the time] we're provided with an awareness that this kind of behaviour came with a potential health cost.

From Andries:

"[Theo] is ruining his health...[this] extreme lifestyle he is bound to regret later on."

Later, when more seedy anecdotes found their way to Jo in Amsterdam, following her acceptance of Theo's marriage proposal, she worried:

"If I only knew whether I did the right thing [in agreeing to marry Theo]!"

Clearly, we can't dismiss either brother's *complete ignorance* of syphilis either. The fact that Pasteur was around right then, rocking the medical establishment, meant the idea of germs, contagion and disease was already well-formed in the public headspace at the time. In Naifeh-Smith's narrative, *Van Gogh: The Life*, they write:

As for the pleasures of whores and the dangers of syphilis, Vincent...said blithely: "Once you've caught it you'll never catch it again." [Vincent] advised his sister Wil that winter "Enjoy yourself too much rather than too little."

Back to Murphy

Murphy's research contextualises the return of Gabrielle to Arles, and her efforts to relieve the huge medical debts of her treatment on her peasant family. Gabrielle worked as a cleaner, Murphy reckons, servicing houses in a particular prescient of Arles – from number 2 Place Lammartine [Vincent's residence] to the brothels littering backstreets [and one in particular, at rue Bout d'Arles].

Compelling as Murphy's work may be, it's still speculation, and let's face it, the conjecture becomes fraught where Gabrielle changes her name to Rachel. It's problematic. Prostitutes change their names, but why would a cleaner?

In my view it's less important to try to prove that Gabrielle and Vincent had an encounter in Paris, when what's far more likely is them meeting in Arles. If this happened, one can imagine a conversation in which both can recount colourful adventures in Paris. And Gabrielle's brief medical emergency would have captured the attention, and sympathy, I think of Vincent.

Whether Gabrielle cleaned Vincent's Yellow House, or Vincent encountered her at a brothel [cleaning or providing servicing of a different kind] doesn't matter. It's less important where they met, how they met or even whether Gabrielle was Rachel.

What matters is that whoever Vincent gave the severed ear to, mattered to him. The real value in Murphy's version is that she presents a hypothesis that fleshes out how someone – during that particular time and place in history – may have featured in the artist's life. Someone did.

Murphy fleshes out a person with a backstory, and insodoing, fleshes out Vincent's attachment to her. By reimagining a potential context, we suddenly see Vincent's world coming into being, sparking with energy, vitality and most important, authenticity. We have to ask, did Vincent behave like this on other occasions too, and the answer is a resounding yes.

By handing Rachel his ear, by moving through the cold night despite gushing blood to do that, Vincent does what he has done all along. He presents himself once again as a highly charged, highly motivated and highly committed individual. Within that intensity, Murphy observes, there is no room for half measures.

But Murphy's contention that Vincent's Rachel was working as a cleaner at a brothel at 23:30 on a Sunday night in 1888 feels naïve to me; it feels like special pleading, perhaps a sentimental effort to cast Vincent [and Rachel] as redeeming figures, less compromised or unsullied than they really were.

I don't believe the gift of the ear had anything to do with the gallantry in bullfighting [where the bull's ear was cut off and given to women in the crowd]. I don't think there was any religious message in it either. Some have been fast and loose with Vincent's words to her, and associated them with Christ saying, "This is my body, take this in remembrance of me."

What we know is Vincent hastily pulled on a red beret that night, Gauguin's beret, perhaps choosing the beret to camouflage the blood, perhaps dressing in this way to confuse or mislead onlookers on the night a crime was committed. Perhaps he had Gauguin's beret in his hand after the two came to blows, and the beret ended up in Vincent's paws. We don't know whether Vincent was drunk or not, and if or how this may have featured into his faculties. What we do know is Vincent's words.

Take care of this for me.

Are those the words of a madman?

If you ask me, Vincent sought out someone who knew him who was nearby, walking distance from where he was, and he did this to protect his life and his legacy. The modern equivalent might be to turn on one's cell phone during an attack so the police may later be able to tell where you were.

It was an insurance policy having the ear out there, known to someone who not only knew Vincent, but Gauguin too.

Who was chasing who?

In Gauguin's version of events, Vincent pursues him, then he turns around, looks at Vincent, and Vincent runs away. Well, isn't that what happened? Vincent somehow got away from Gauguin during the initial stages of an attempted murder. In Gauguin's version, *Vincent cut off his ear immediately after fleeing Gauguin*, and then immediately after that, couriered his ear in person to Rachel.

On both sides of this version, Vincent is the one doing the running and the fleeing. Vincent's confronting, and cutting off his ear. Gauguin, on his own version, does nothing. The only things that move are Gauguin's eyes. He's standing around harmlessly, or is he?

We know for a fact that Gauguin packed up and left that night. He slept in a hotel. So the idea that Gauguin wasn't activated, moving, lashing out, stretches credibility. Only in a scenario where Vincent is mad [suddenly stricken mad at a time that suits Gauguin very well, wouldn't you say], does Gauguin's entropy make any sense.

Gauguin's Inversion?

Isn't it more probable that Gauguin's version conveniently inverts reality, sticking to certain incidents, but casting the villain as the victim, and the victim as the villain? If Gauguin attacked Vincent, and Vincent went on the run, wouldn't he hand off his ear [something he perhaps wanted back on his head later on] as part of his attempt to escape Gauguin? Think about it. If Vincent expected to pass out soon, he *would* need someone to look after his appendage, wouldn't he? By the same token, rushing into a public venue when someone is chasing you might also be intended to dissuade an attacker from following his prey inside.

And after that?

Vincent had no money for the brothel, so he had to leave. He couldn't sleep there, and was in no state to socialise either. Extended time outside in mid-winter in Arles, in the state he was in, could kill him. It was late, a Sunday night, and he'd lost a lot of blood, so Vincent was forced to return home to his bed.

When he saw a candle had been lit for him, perhaps he saw that as a sign of truce from Gauguin. Perhaps Gauguin wanted to get the little shit back inside before he got them [or more precisely him] into more trouble.

Or was it Gauguin who'd rushed home himself after Vincent darted into the brothel, and hurriedly cleaned up after himself, perhaps stealing from the shared pot of money downstairs, but leaving the candle, then fleeing the scene before Vincent returned to confront, or perhaps accuse him.

If Vincent had died shortly after the delivery of the ear, by delivering the ear he guaranteed that he would be discovered sooner than later, and also that raised the spectre of Gauguin being arrested and detained before he could do more harm, or flee [as he was about to do].

If Gauguin had turned the Yellow House into a gallows for Vincent, then by making this delivery, Vincent was robbing Gauguin of alternative accommodation at his favorite brothel – and in that he succeeded. If Gauguin had stolen money, then by making sure he slept elsewhere, Vincent was settling the financial score somewhat.

Why the need for insurance; why not simply tell the world what Gauguin had done? Because both Vincent and Theo were invested in Gauguin, and if things blew up in a scandal, it could ruin all three of them. Vincent had spent years trying to sell his art. He couldn't have this blowhard squander what little reputation he had, so it was in the name of PR that Gauguin enjoyed the Van Gogh's protection.

The intention behind the ear was to suggest to Gauguin that Vincent had made contact with a witness and given her a vital piece of evidence, and perhaps damning information about Gauguin [that he'd attacked Vincent].

Or it was just as Vincent said:

Take care of this for me.

We know that an attempt was made to reconcile the ear with its owner, but doctor Felix, whose expertise in urology didn't quite translate, judged it too late, and so the ear was discarded. So evidently Rachel, or whoever she was, *didn't* take good care of the ear after all!

Just as with the murder of Meredith Kercher in Perugia in November 2007, where the primes suspect was her house mate Amanda Knox, it's significant that on the night Vincent almost lost his life, instead of his friend being there for him as any real friend would be, there to render aid, there to summon a doctor, instead of being at his home late on a Sunday night, instead of him sleeping in his home on this night of all nights Gauguin sleeps elsewhere. Was that because of what Vincent's done, or because of what Gauguin's done?

To reiterate, those who self-harm typically aim for hands, arms, wrists, ears or legs – never ears.

Also significant are the blades and stabbing weapons Gauguin abandons that night in the Yellow House. But what would it look like to be walking through the streets of Arles with the intent to flee the city, carrying swords, while his friend lay bleeding in their home?

When the police arrive at the Yellow House they think Vincent has been murdered. When Gauguin turns up, even the gendarmes think Gauguin is Vincent's murderer. And so, they seize him. Before Gauguin's lips begin to move, before he spins his tale, Vincent is seen as the true victim. If he had spoken then, would history have turned out very different?

*Joseph Meister, the nine-year-old saved by Pasteur's rabies shots, went on to become a caretaker at the Pasteur Institute. The circumstances of Meister's death in 1940, at 64 years of age, are tragic. Ten days after the German army invaded Paris, Meister committed suicide – incinerating himself in the hospital's gas furnace. Although some versions hold that Meister made a heroic stand, not wanting to allow German forces access to Pasteur's work, his great granddaughter believes Meister killed himself for less noble reasons – out if guilt. Meister had sent his family away, and with German forces occupying Paris, Meister believed he'd sent them to certain death. As it happened, the Meister family returned on the same day – June 24th, 1940 – Meister took his life.

The “Sudden” Onset on Insanity

“No one has ever questioned Gauguin’s own version of the man he was and the life he lived.”— Nancy Arle Mathews

There are those who lay Vincent’s madness, on the night of December 23rd, 1888 in Arles, and July 27th, 1890, in Auvers, entirely at Theo’s door. In both cases, Vincent goes mad because his brother is getting married/having a child, and so may no longer be in a position to support his older brother.

In the next chapter I will fully and finally rubbish this theory. It is not that these theories are completely irrelevant. Every rumor after all needs a grain of truth to gain the traction it needs. Unfortunately, by fixating on these silly, less relevant ideas, history is deprived of the Vincent’s true motives, and thus, the history we hold dear today is hardly accurate, hardly real, hardly reality. It is the ambit of this narrative to straighten out these distortions.

In this chapter I want to challenge the notions of:

a) Vincent going mad *suddenly* on December 23rd, 1888

b) Vincent *staying mad* throughout 1889

c) Vincent *being mad* in the first place

Vincent’s sudden onset of madness on December 23rd becomes less and less inexplicable the more we contextualise the three-way dynamic brewing at the time between and the brothers Van Gogh, and Gauguin. There are other forces at place to deal with besides this three-way dynamic, but we’ll deal with secondary forces secondarily.

A. DID VINCENT GO MAD SUDDENLY, ON DECEMBER 23RD, 1888?

Two Artists and One calling the Other Mad…

If Vincent was so worried about Theo’s engagement plans, he would have brought them up in his letters to Theo. Did he?

In his letter dated December 23rd, 1888* to Theo, the night of the ear incident, Vincent doesn’t so much as mention Theo’s bride-to-be. The entire body of the short missive has to do with Gauguin, and Gauguin’s unhappiness. It’s about Vincent trying to calm Gauguin down, trying to prevent Gauguin from doing anything rash. It’s about Gauguin being out of sorts with the town, and with Vincent. Vincent doesn’t mention being angry at Gauguin, or quarrelling with him, or being desperate for him to stay. He refers to grave difficulties, and Gauguin either definitely leaving or definitely staying where he is.

Curiously, Vincent adds:

“[Gauguin] must have peace. Will he find it anywhere if he does not find it here? I am waiting for him to make a decision with absolute serenity.”

This sounds rather like Gauguin is going mad, or at best, stir crazy. If the two artists were arguing, it sounds like Gauguin was the one instigating the arguments, and Vincent trying to settle him down. That's not to say Vincent was necessarily innocent, coherent or easy to live with. If Vincent was drinking often, and abusing alcohol [by his own admission he left Paris in February for Arles a virtual drunkard] he may have been tiresome to endure, especially when he was drunk. If he was an insomniac, and a drunk one on top of it, well then, even more so.

Gauguin, it is clear, wants to be elsewhere, and wants to find his peace – peace of mind – somewhere else. Vincent's response is that, as an artist, what better place to figure out your shit than in a studio created to that purpose?

Given what happened to Vincent that night, and thereafter, we must ask ourselves whether we believe Vincent when he claims:

I am waiting for him to make a decision with absolute serenity.

From this we have Vincent claiming that he's mentally strong. Well, is he? If Gauguin leaves, he's fine with that? Is he really? Since the letter arrives a day short of Christmas eve, Vincent in his response seems completely unaware of Christmas, of conveying glad tidings to his beneficent sibling, of extending any courtesy to ask Theo how he is. There's zero indication that he cares, or is burdened in any way, by Theo's love life.

Bernadette Murphy and Simon Schama take it a step further. They dispute Vincent's honesty as regards his "absolute serenity", but I have to wonder, what if he meant what he write? If you have had your fill of someone who you and your brother are relying on, then when the arrangement unravels, you may be resigned to accept whatever they do, one way or the other. For example, if someone has undertaken to share rent, and they renege on their side of the deal, but they're hard to live with and are making life difficult, as much as you would like things to work out, there may also be reasons you might want them to do what's right for them, even if that's not good for you. Because what you want at the end of the day is a place where you can work, and be productive, and feel settled and at home.

In other words, this seems to be a polite and respectful [or even sarcastic] way of Vincent saying to his brother, *I don't care what Gauguin decides to do. Whatever he does is fine with me.*

But there's more to it than this. About two weeks prior to the ear incident, on December 11th, something seemed to be simmering vigorously beneath the lid of the Yellow House. Gauguin had written to Theo, asking for money while declaring his intention to bail on the whole partnership. In respectful terms, Gauguin appeared to be saying that the deal is off because he and Vincent are quarrelling too much. This is interesting, because a few days later Gauguin wrote second time, claiming his complaint about arguing, and incompatible temperaments, was just a bad dream. He asks Theo to disregard it. Again, doesn't this feel like Gauguin is the one who is disagreeable and unstable?

On December 22nd, just a day before the ear incident, Gauguin wrote to French artist, Émile Schuffenecker, telling him he'd decided to stay in Arles after all.

"You await me with open arms…but unfortunately I am not coming yet. My situation here is difficult; I owe Van Gogh and Vincent a great deal…despite certain differences of opinion…"

Despite acknowledging how much he owed, Gauguin skedaddled regardless. What matters here is the admission that Gauguin was obligated, didn't want to be, found his situation difficult, and wished to be elsewhere. When it was all over, Gauguin got what he wanted, and Vincent was cast as a madman.

Remember that name – Schuffenecker – because it comes up again in the 1920's, where he's accused of making forgeries of Vincent's work, including a painting Gauguin removed without Vincent's permission, *Sunflowers…*

Gauguin Needed an Escape Clause

I hope from the above it's clear that Gauguin was well aware of his obligations to both Van Goghs, and at the same time, appeared intent to extricate himself from what amounted to contractual obligations. Gauguin wished to cut himself from Vincent. Theo would not have been too chuffed to let Gauguin off the hook, unless he felt Gauguin had really good reasons. By turning the one brother against the other, by turning Vincent's self-deprecating modesty into self-harm, and his intense inner feeling into fiery incompatibility, Gauguin could extricate and exonerate himself from the situation.

More than a century later, we can either take Gauguin's word for it, that Vincent was a pain in the arse and his own worst enemy, or we can intuit Gauguin as a crafty opportunist who'd come into some big money thanks to recent sales, and now wished to escape his duties in the backwoods of Arles [mirrored by similar efforts throughout his life]. He could have achieved this by distorting reality, by deliberately painting in new memories over the original. Thus his fictionalised style of painting extended to fictional storytelling.

I'm certain there's a glimmer of truth in either side of the coin, but what we want to see isn't a glimpse. We want confirmation. Was Vincent mad? Was Gauguin a deceitful wretch?

In order to fully test the authenticity of the Vincent's sudden madness, we need to interrogate the mind-set of the artist before the onset of mental illness, as well as after. Fortunately, because Vincent was as prolific as he was, we have a marvellous record of uninterrupted paintings leading up to the ear incident, and crucially, a record continuing afterward.

There are a few simple techniques we can use to approach this question. Firstly, did the volume of art work change significantly after the ear incident? If it did, this may suggest Vincent did suffer from a suddenly debilitating illness of the mind. On the other hand, if

Vincent was mad to begin with, then his output probably didn't change. If Vincent had suddenly gone mad, what we'd expect to see after the ear incident is a change in tone.

Do the paintings become more vivid, more intense, as a reflection of the fiery malaise within? Or do they become more intense because of Vincent's emotional and existential crisis? There are also Vincent's self-portraits, and the symbolism in them, that may indicate madness, or some other explanation.

Naturally, if Vincent's artwork provides an important before/after archive of his mood, as expressed in colors and tones, his words are an even more valuable archive. What does Vincent say about his madness? What do the doctors say? How does Theo react? The most important version of events, and indeed the most specific and problematic, comes from the witness and prime suspect to these events – Gauguin. It also comes from someone who has much to gain by sinking Vincent's fortunes – he gets to return to Paris, and by painting his rival as the loser, he gets to be the heroic, triumphant artist.

Let's continue our analysis of Vincent's madness by comparing Vincent's artistic output in 1889, to that of 1888.

B. DID VINCENT REMAIN MAD?

Starting with *Landscape with Snow*, Vincent churned out 187 paintings between February 1888 and May 1889. The Arles period is considered to be Vincent's most creative, and included seminal works such as *Starry Night Over the Rhône, The Night Café, Café Terrace at Night* and Vincent's *Sunflowers* series.

From May 1889 to May 1890, Vincent stayed in the madhouse at St. Rémy. There Vincent painted an estimated 150 paintings over one year**, or roughly one every two to three days. While at the asylum Vincent produced arguably his best, most brilliant work, including *Starry Night*, *Road with Cypress and Star* and his *Wheat field with Cypresses* series.

Vincent's output*** in 1888 to May 1889 [over 455 days] averages out to one painting every 2.4 days. His output in the asylum [over approximately 365 days] is exactly the same, one painting every 2.4 days.

January 1889, the month following the ear incident, was one of Vincent's busiest months. He churned out fourteen works in the space of a month, almost one every second day. This was roughly the same pace he'd maintained in December, while Gauguin was around. Does this frenetic pace speak more eloquently of madness, or commitment to his craft?

Reading Between the Lines

It's interesting that for all Gauguin's fear and contempt for his house guest, he left the Yellow House in Arles with two of Vincent's now-famous sunflower paintings. What's more, he took them without Vincent's permission.

More than three weeks later, on January 21st, 1889, Vincent wrote to Gauguin to ask for them back. In the context of Vincent volunteering to "return what belongs to you" [Gauguin had left in such a hurry from Arles he'd left notebooks, artworks and his fencing equipment behind] Vincent seems to be suggesting a swap. I'll give you your stuff if you give me mine.

"...I'll begin by returning what belongs to you, making it plain that it's my intention, after what has happened, to contest categorically your right to the canvas [the Sunflowers] in question..."

Vincent then goes on to say he will paint two more of the missing paintings exactly the same. It's not clear whether Vincent wishes to replace what Gauguin's taken, or give him the exact copies. But there is something sarcastic about Vincent commending Gauguin's "intelligence" for stealing what Vincent considers to be some of his best work. Following this barb, Vincent expresses his hope that they can settle things amicably.

In the tone of this correspondence, we see a focus on things. Who gets what, who took what, when I get my stuff back? It's as if Gauguin is bickering about money all over again, except this time he's appropriated Vincent's art, while demanding the return of his other things.

It's possible that Gauguin's efforts to remove some of Vincent's art is a form of leverage. *If you accuse me of something I will burn or destroy or keep these paintings. If you co-operate, you can have them back.* For a man so terrified of the madman he'd lived with, and so intent to leave, it's strange that he would appropriate the artist's work, and thus insure that they maintain civil to one another.

Another letter from Gauguin that's worth a closer look, is written on January 17th. Gauguin writes to Vincent, telling him not to bother with the studies that I deliberately left in Arles. It's a strange indictment of his own work. He'd gone to Arles to paint, and that was part of why Theo was paying his way, and here he is saying, nah, the work wasn't worth transporting [but Vincent's evidently was].

"On the other hand the sketchbooks contain notes which are useful to me, and I accept your offer to send them to me. As well as the 2 masks and gloves [fencing equipment]..."

Gauguin adds that he regrets "inadvertently" taking something with him, and apologises, which is possibly an oblique reference to the sunflowers. He admits he hasn't been painting at all in two weeks because he's been running errands. He does mention publishing lithographs with Theo's approval to "get myself known." For all his talk in December about moving to Brussels [which Vincent also conveyed to Theo], once again Gauguin has changed his mind, now saying he doesn't know about Brussels, and that it depends on "the money situation."

On January 4th, Vincent sent Gauguin this carefully clipped message:

"I have thought of you a great deal in the hospital, and even in the midst of fever and relative weakness."

One might imagine this is a friendly message. If Gauguin had purposefully sliced off Vincent's ear, then each minute of throbbing recovery, would include a wounded sense of humiliation, and of asking inwardly: why?

When Vincent adds, "Tell me. Was my brother Theo's journey really necessary…" we get a clearer sense of Vincent's pique. He's upset because Gauguin summoned Theo without asking Vincent, and thus unnecessarily worried him, this besides the expense. Now, one might side with Gauguin on this, saying that Gauguin was right to contact Theo in such an emergency. Fact is, Theo arrived on Christmas Day and left the next day, suggesting the entire ear incident was overblown, especially for Vincent.

Vincent goes on to ask Gauguin to "at least reassure him completely…please." Going on to smooth things over, Vincent tells Gauguin to "trust that in fact no evil exists" and that what has happened is "for the best." Whatever did happen, this is a remarkably self-deprecating assessment. Vincent had lost his ear, some of his art works, evidently his friend and an important chance to be validated by a fellow artist. And yet he assures Gauguin not evil exists and that it's for the best. Vincent seems to be a glutton for punishment either way.

Then he adds:

So I want you to give my warm regards to good Schuffenecker – to refrain from saying bad things about our poor little yellow house until more mature reflection on either side – to give my regards to the painters I saw in Paris.

Let's think about what's going on here, within the context of Vincent being mad. Once again, he's trying to soothe things over with Gauguin [Gauguin's not concerned about Vincent's state of mind in his correspondence]. He's also worried about his reputation. He's asking Gauguin not to say "bad things". It's not just about Vincent, Vincent wants the Yellow House to become a regular art studio for artists, and he's right to be worried that this setback could torpedo this scheme. Ironically, in the six months before Vincent's death, Gauguin would float the theory of starting an art studio with the help of the Van Gogh's in Antwerp; a studio that would carry Gauguin's name…

In an unclearly dated letter with no salutation, and with half of it entirely missing, Gauguin writes about sunflowers on a yellow background, and is explicit on where exactly his fencing equipment is in the Yellow House:

"…if you can send me by parcel post my 2 fencing masks and gloves, which I left on the shelf in the little upstairs room…"

Reading Between the Brushstrokes

In Starry Night Over the Rhône, painted on September 28th, 1888, three weeks before Gauguin's arrival, Vincent depicts "two colourful lovers in the foreground", as he described in his letter to Theo.

The painting is undeniably rich, warm and romantic. It's positive, reflecting Vincent's positive feelings prior to Gauguin's arrival. Right then, following a period of abundance, depicting spring orchards and sun-drenched fields, Vincent had every reason to be optimistic.

One would imagine darker and more sombre tones, coming from Saint-Rémy, and yet *Enclosed Wheat Field with Rising Sun* [painted in May 1889] is bright, the lie of the land upward and hopeful. *Green Wheat field*, painted June 1889 is just as fresh and untroubled. *Wheat field behind Saint-Paul* has a lyrical quality to it, the winter sky swept by stormy clouds, the wheat itself blowing in the Mistral.

The major change between Vincent's art in 1888 and 1889 is in his portraiture.1888 contains a cast of vivid characters, including the principal character appropriated for Loving Vincent, Armand Roulin.

In 1889 there are depictions of Doctor Felix Rey, and Augustine Roulin [the postman's wife], but very few characters besides, and only a small handful of self-portraits.

The cheerfully symbolic *First Steps*, painted in January 1890, seemed to suggest Vincent's readiness to take his first steps out of the madhouse, and back into the world. On January 31st 1890, Theo's wife gave birth to Vincent Willem. This suggests an alternate awareness. It's difficult to imagine Vincent not in a sense comparing the arrival of a new born child into the world, with his own effort to enter the world anew, refreshed, reborn in some way. Either way, that kind of mental alacrity doesn't feel like the delirium of madness, does it?

In the final chapters I will deal with Vincent's last paintings, but for now it suffices to note the theme of those paintings: summer and gardens, green and growth, flowers and insects, roots and harvests, rivers and wheat fields, vineyards and thatched cottages. Hardly the subject matter of a madman, let alone a man intent on being done with the world.

The End of Vincent's Tether

Vincent was painting *Madame Roulin* [*La Berceuse* or the *Lullaby*] at the time he and Gauguin had a falling out. He depicted Augustine Roulin holding a rope and using it to rock the cradle, which is out of picture]. Some have pontificated about there being symbolism here, in that Gauguin was also pulling strings from a distance, rocking – essentially – Vincent's cradle from a distance.

The lullaby title also seems to suggest someone hypnotising someone else into a state of unconsciousness, or else, blissful ignorance. I'm not sure how much we should read into this. It's difficult to be entirely dismissive of it, given Vincent's epic 3000+ word letter to Theo on January 17th. In it, he asks Theo rather obliquely, even cryptically, if Gauguin has read *Tartarin of Tarascon,* a book by the French author Alphonse Daudet, published in 1872.

Consider this: Vincent is asking Theo if Gauguin's read a particular book, and shortly after, Vincent writes Gauguin directly and asks him the same thing.

One might see all this as a throwaway comment, until one digs into the plot of the book. It involves an over-imaginative town that gets into its head the notion that Tartarin is about to mount an expedition to the Atlas mountains in Algeria [northern Africa]. This comes about simply because of Tartarin's reaction to seeing an Atlas lion in a travelling menagerie.

Tartarin, a boastful braggart, is so caught up by what the town thinks of him, he decides to mount an expedition "to save face". He purchases an absurd amount of equipment, and *en route* to Algiers, a conman spies all of this equipment, and plots to take advantage of Tartarin. Tartarin finally arrives home, penniless, but to a heroes' welcome. He'd managed to shoot a lion after all [a tame, blind lion]... What the story shows is capacity for almost everyone in the story [barring the unfortunate lion, and conman] to be misled.

"...does [Gauguin] remember Tartarin's illustrious pal [Bompard] from Tarascon who had such an imagination that in one fell swoop he imagined an entire imaginary Switzerland? Does [Gauguin] remember the knot in a rope rediscovered high up in the Alps after the fall? And you, who wish to know how things happened, have you ever read the whole of Tartarin? That would teach you to recognize Gauguin pretty well."

These are pretty strong words from Vincent, but he's not done yet.

"I urge you in all seriousness to look at that passage in Daudet's book again...And then do you remember Bompard...and his happy imagination? This is what we have here, though of another kind, Gauguin has [an]... absolutely complete imagination of the south, with that imagination he's going to work in the north! My word, we may yet see some more funny things!"

This is a very abstract way of saying *don't believe what Gauguin says about me [and about what happened in Arles]*. The full portent of the paragraph becomes clear when one realizes the capacity communities in the south of France had towards embellishment and exaggeration. In the frenchfork blog, this capacity is made manifest:

In France, one commonly known stereotype of people from Marseille, is that they tend to exaggerate. So when someone says something that sounds a tad much, we usually say "il est Marseillais" (he is from Marseilles). The stereotype is usually used for French people from the south of France (du midi) in general.

This is why Vincent tells his brother Gauguin is effectively drawing on "the imagination of the south" and "going to work on the north." It's another way of saying: *Jeepers, he's ruined my reputation here, and if that wasn't bad enough, he's going to be telling stories about me in Paris as well.*

While Vincent doesn't accuse Gauguin of betrayal or cowardice outright, because what he writes is quite cryptic, by comparing Gauguin as a character, to a particularly unreliable, conceited and arrogant character in a particular book, he feels like he's providing a much better description. But Vincent's wrong. Instead of writing a 3000 word letter and not quite getting to the point about what he's saying, or what he's accusing Gauguin of, he beats about the bush. For someone weary or at their wits end with Vincent, it would be easy to glance at the long letter and toss it aside without reading.

Trawling through the torrent Vincent provides another fish for the reader's net:

"...I find it quite odd that [Gauguin's] claiming a painting of sunflowers from me, offering me in exchange I suppose, or as a gift, a few studies that he left here. I'll send back his studies — which will probably have uses for him that they certainly wouldn't have for me."

Do you see the anger and frustration in Vincent's words? Gauguin's taken – stolen – Vincent's work, and pretending it's part of arrangement, a swap of one artist's work for another. And yet Vincent's clearly communicating that he feels his work to be worth more than Gauguin's. Vincent bitterly volunteers to send Gauguin his work as a half-hearted play to get his own work back. And Vincent's still not done:

"If Gauguin were to examine himself properly in Paris or have himself examined by a specialist doctor, my word I don't really know what the result of it would be. Several times over I've seen him do things that you or I wouldn't permit ourselves to do, having consciences that feel things differently – I've heard two or three things said of him in the same vein – but I, who saw him at very, very close quarters, I believed him led by his imagination, by pride perhaps but – quite irresponsible."

It's unfortunate that Vincent can't be more specific about Gauguin's transgressions. When Vincent describes Gauguin "led by his imagination", he seems to be saying Gauguin was a habitual liar. Someone using creative license to explain what he was or wasn't doing. Gauguin deceived Vincent at the Yellow House, just as he deceived him outside of it afterwards.

Even so, one intuits a modicum of generous morality in Vincent that stands in sharp contrast to Gauguin's selfish immorality. But Vincent's suggestion that Gauguin be assessed by a doctor rings hollow now, with Vincent in the state he appears to be in. Gauguin has called him mad, now Vincent says Gauguin is mad. Well, which one is missing his left ear?

Within a few short weeks, the town of Arles felt their imaginations running wild as well. A petition was drawn up in Vincent's absence, with the town's folk growing in their conviction that Vincent was mad. Even his brother had come, and then abandoned him. It wasn't safe to have him around!

Thirty signatures were taken to the mayor, and on this basis, Vincent was removed from his home, taken away and incarcerated, isolated, tethered to a hospital bed. With much of the South now utterly convinced that Vincent was mad, and a danger to society, and the North fast becoming convinced of the same, there was no escape for the Dutch artist, especially at a time when immigrants were being associated with crime.

The only way out seemed to be humble contrition. Accepting that he was mad, and receiving treatment. At least that way, he could continue painting. The correspondence over this period matches this schizophrenic period: Vincent's doctor and the postmaster, Roulin, and Vincent himself, declare him fully recovered from the ear incident by the first week of January. But the good people of Arles decide otherwise, and thus, the sudden onset of insanity.

*There seems to be a strange conflict in records with regard to Vincent's letter to Theo claiming to await Gauguin's decision with "serenity" or "equanimity". Some records, such as the authoritative book *The Letters of Vincent van Gogh* and the exhaustive webexhibits archive of *Van Gogh's Letters*, both have the date of this letter – fatefully - as December 23rd 1888. But others have it on December 11th, 1888. If Vincent describes himself as "serene" on December 23rd, that's a problem for the mad artist version of events. Bernadette Murphy and the Van Gogh Museum appear proponents of the latter date, perhaps not surprisingly.

**While holed up at Saint –Rémy, some might argue that Vincent painted 142 paintings in less than one year. He arrived at the asylum in May, and left for Auvers in late May. However one does the calculation, it still amounts to roughly one painting every 2.4 days.

***It might be more illuminating to compare Vincent's output through his correspondence, rather than his artwork. At a glance, it's clear 1888 was the year Vincent's letters peaked, although since he was living with his brother in January there was no correspondence then, and only a trickle in February, the month he left for Arles. November and December show a slight decline [the months Gauguin was present], but in January 1889 Vincent's letters resumed maximal output. In 1888 Vincent wrote approximately 127 letters, roughly one every two days, words to mirror his efforts on canvas. It's fair to say that in 1889, while Vincent was at Saint-Rémy, his output of letters [just 43 during the year] declined markedly, to an average of roughly one letter a week. However this output was still greater than that of the years 1884-1887 and 1872-1881.

Maddening Money Matters

"[Gauguin] created a life for public consumption as part of his campaign to make his exhibitions - and therefore his future - a success." — Nancy Mowll Mathews

1885 - Peasant Woman Digging

There was one thing, and only one, besides them both being artists, that Vincent and Gauguin had in common. They both had money difficulties. In a way, Vincent had an easier career, given the almost uninterrupted patronage of his brother. For Gauguin it was much tougher, especially since he came from privilege, even worked as stockbroker, and then suddenly had to deal with the effacement of poverty.

Gauguin did sell some of his works, including three pictures in 1888, but overall, he only became popular and successful after his death. I have already mentioned Gauguin was bitter, suffering with advanced syphilis and penniless at the time of his death, so much so he was driven to attempt suicide. The question is, was Vincent similarly twisted and tortured by the rigours of failure and moneylessness?

Although Vincent didn't have it easy, the main difference with Gauguin was that Vincent had been struggling for far longer. He was used to it. He was a self-effacing kind of guy. One might even go so far as to say martyrdom was a default setting for Vincent. Is there any artist who worked as hard, or as long, for his art as this one?

In a December 2014 article published in *Vanity Fair*, the word "martyr" is mentioned four times. These instances are worth close and careful study:

...The chief purveyor of the suicide narrative was Van Gogh's fellow artist Émile Bernard, who wrote the earliest version of artistic self-martyrdom in a letter to a critic whose favor he was currying... Boosted by the gripping tale of his final act of martyrdom, Van Gogh's celebrity took off like a rocket...[Ultimately] Vincent chose to protect them as a final act of martyrdom.

The article ends with a quote from the curator of the Van Gogh Museum no less, saying that what happened to Van Gogh is "self-evident":

"Vincent's suicide has become the grand finale of the story of the martyr for art, it's his crown of thorns."

One could also argue that Vincent chose struggle and hardship [in the same way that he volunteered for treatment at Saint-Rémy], while Gauguin did his best [or is it worst] to avoid these hardships. One artist avoids effacement like the plague, the other is self-effacing to the point of martyrdom. But if this is true, then Vincent was a lot more resilient in life than he's given credit for. Well, resilient people don't kill themselves.

Money forms an important backdrop to the ear incident, the shooting in Auvers and our new theory of resilience. We know how fraught the financial situation was leading up to that fateful Christmas in 1888. We're less clear on how money played into the dynamics eighteen months later, or indeed, for the decades following his death.

Since we are dealing with the world's most valuable artist, with canvases that today are worth tens of millions, it's vital we investigate both ends of this spectrum – how Vincent dealt with having no money, and how and why the world decided he should be worth more than any other artist. Was he really the martyr, in the absolute sense, he's been made out to be?

There seems to me to be the same inversion at work here, where the madder and more troubled the artist, the more valuable his work [as it applies to Vincent van Gogh]. The mirror provided by interminable financial struggle reflects his obsessive commitment and mad frustration. The poorer he was, the greater the struggle, the more valuable, and valiant, his efforts. Conversely, if Vincent was less mad, less of a martyr, and not quite as deprived as he's depicted, then his story is less inspiring and his art "self-evidently" less impressive, and less valuable.

Now let's test the authenticity, and the portent, of the money narrative.

A Peek inside the Purse

More than half of Vincent's correspondence to Theo contains references to the word "money". A handy tool in the webexhibits archive, allows one to track the instances money comes up in their correspondence. It comes up in 372 letters. At a glance one can see that the second-half of the timeline [approximately 1880 – 1890] contains most of these references, far more than the first-half [1872 – 1879].

The period 1880 – 1885 has by far the most references, which is to say, more than at the end of Vincent's life, although there clearly is an uptick to Vincent's demands in the last two months. Did Vincent painting a picture a day, every day for the last 70 days of his life indicate someone who could no longer endure the burden of financial difficulty, or quite the opposite: was he quite practised by then at a certain low-level of meagre existence?

One must bear in mind, that when Vincent asked for money, it wasn't just money for board and lodging, but also for art expenses, canvases, equipment and paint. If Vincent was completely destitute, and if his financial burden was intolerable, why would Theo continue to send him paint supplies? If money was tight, then feeding Vincent's additional and pointless expenses would be profligate in the extreme.

It's important to answer these questions, and in this chapter, I do.

Vincent's money narrative starts early. It follows him like a dark cloud his whole life. By 1888 he's entering the epilogue of his own story, although his story continues without him well after his death in 1890, and the money train continues to rumble on today.

Didn't the money struggle eventually become so much water off the duck's back? And didn't Theo endure it because both brothers were invested in the same market – the one supplying, and the other selling. So Theo's handouts to his brother were less charitable contributions as a kind of strategic investment [and an excellent one as history now shows].

But if we really look at the picture, of one brother giving another brother money, on and on, for years, we have to ponder whether this was a burden to Theo, and if it was, what kind of burden it was. This may seem a silly question, until we personalise it. Have you ever sponsored a sibling for an extended period of time? How did that arrangement begin and end? What caused it to begin and why did it end? Have you ever been on the receiving end, in terms of "charitable donations" from family, especially siblings? Sometimes they're not charitable in the least, but highly-charged, and riddled with emotions, obligations, sympathy, sentiment and guilt.

To fully understand this aspect of the narrative, we must mine the origins of the family, and get a handle on the complete picture of their financial circumstances, their level in society, their lifestyle.

In the *Forwards* section I delve into the money narrative in more detail, asking questions about Vincent's parents [were they wealthy?] and Vincent's attitude to money [how did his early work experiences shape his career as an artist?] deprivation [what did he experience while preaching to the miners in the Borinage?] and affliction [had he been sick/hospitalised previously, and how did he handle that?].

Whether we have the complete financial picture at our disposal or not, there is no better authority on how Vincent endured deprivation than Vincent himself. Without doubt the best evidence in his archive of letters is in the epic 3000 word diatribe written on January 17th, 1888. The reader is advised to spend some time trawling through this letter, absorbing it on your own time, and referring to it frequently, as needed.

Now, if we take this letter and imagine it as a court exhibit, it gushes with insights: there are financial records and calculations, there are extended insights into the dynamic between Gaugin and Vincent, there's the cautious interaction between two brothers that need but are also burdens to each other. Above all we're provided a portrait of the martyr *by the martyr*.

In his January 17th letter Vincent's quite measured in his condemnation of Gauguin, but that's not to say he sucks it up and doesn't complain. Vincent's suffering, not merely from his head wound, but from starvation.

"In short, the result of all this was that by the 8th [of January 1888] I was broke. But a day or two later I borrowed 5 francs. That barely takes us to the 10th. I hoped for a letter from you [Theo] about the 10th, but, this letter did not arrive till today, January 17th, the time between has been a most rigorous fast, the more painful because I cannot recover under such conditions."

He has nothing to eat, and he's annoyed – pissed off – because when he's needed Theo the most, financially and otherwise, Theo's gone AWOL. He hears nothing from his brother for eight days, and is bummed out that after wishing to see his brother for months, his brother has come and gone at great [and as Vincent sees it, unnecessary] expense, and under the worst of circumstances.

On January 9th Vincent had reported to Theo about paying "quite a number of things". Trying to paint a silver lining on his situation, Vincent declares himself "in no sort of a hurry [for money] for several days" but adds, hopefully, "it would be nice if you could send me 50 francs or so within the next few days."

In hindsight it's clear that on January 8th Vincent had no money, and yet, in a bid to reassure his brother, made it his situation seem better than it really was. If one considers the larger narrative, that Vincent went mad on December 23rd, then these two letters don't make any sense. We'd expect him to be more unhinged closer to the incident, and more recovered, calmer, further from it. Instead it's the opposite. Vincent's extremely lucid on his situation, and he's trying his best not to have Theo worry, while hoping that things can simply continue as normal. For someone who's just lost an ear, and much besides, it's obvious how this "damage control" at his own expense plays into Vincent's tendency to martyr himself. If Gauguin had cottoned on to this, we can see how a selfish bastard might take his chance, walk all over a martyr, get away with it and sadistically rub Vincent's nose in it.

Far from being mad, Vincent is painfully aware of their expense account in January 1888, perhaps more so then than ever. While he's even more measured in his opinion of Gauguin and his financial situation at this point [January 9th] than he would be the following week, we can see the walls are already moving in for Vincent – not in terms of madness, but the anxiety that flows from possibly losing his home [which he did].

It's interesting, in this regard, how Gauguin plays into the liquidation of Vincent's finances, at least from Vincent's version of the story. One wonders whether Gauguin intentionally wrecked Vincent's dream, or was simply reckless in leaving so much wreckage behind him.

"I think the mistake in old Gauguin's calculations was that he is rather too much in the habit of ignoring the inevitable expenses of house rent, charwoman, and a lot of worldly things of the kind. Now all those things are weighing more on our shoulders, but once we have accepted them, other artists could stay with me without having those expenses."

Vincent is trying to convince Theo that while Gauguin was a spendthrift, other artists might do better. Despite everything, the colony idea is still viable in his mind. But storm clouds are brewing over Vincent's little Yellow House.

"They have just told me that during my absence [while Vincent was receiving treatment in hospital for his amputated ear] the owner of my house here [the Yellow House] made an

arrangement with a fellow who has a tobacco shop to turn me out and give this tobacconist the house."

Vincent's facing a situation where failure to pay rent may cause him to lose not only his home, but his dream of starting an artist's colony. He may also be aware that regardless of whether he pay rent, the disgrace surrounding him [fanned by Gauguin] may cause him to lose his home anyway. And so he does.

As early as January 9th, Vincent remarks about the disgrace that clouds his return to his home in Arles. It's as if he's returned from the hospital to an alternate reality in which he's the villain of the story, he's the madman. For him it must feel like the world has gone mad.

"This has rather upset me, for I am not much disposed to have myself turned out of this house practically in disgrace when it was I who had it repainted inside and out, and had gas put in, etc. - in fact, who had made habitable a house which had been shut up and uninhabited for a considerable time, and which I took in a very poor condition."

Vincent is referring here to the investments he'd made, in money and personal effort, in kitting out the Yellow House not only for his own habitation, but to make it a suitable sanctuary for Gauguin. If there's any doubt about Vincent's honesty here, we know that Gauguin took the art Vincent had hung, had decorated his room with, as souvenirs, and what's more, Vincent's depictions of the two chairs, supports the idea that the furniture he provided Gauguin was better than the furnishings he chose for himself.

Returning to the letter of January 17th, it's easy to scroll down to Vincent's calculations, to get a sense of what he was going through *financially*, at a glance. When we peek inside the purse we find Vincent starring, like old mother Hubbard, at a bare cupboard. Soon the cupboard would be gone too.

The Threat to Theo

In all this drama it's easy to forget Theo's side of the coin. Johanna's just agreed to marry him after considering the merits of his proposal for a year. Theo doesn't want to spoil his chances by telling his wife-to-be about his earless, wayward, mad older brother. He's scared of losing her, and so, Vincent finds himself abandoned by his friend and his brother, and soon after, the community as well.

It's not a *complete* abandonment – Theo does eventually send Vincent some money, though it's very late considering his needs: specialist hospital care, repayment for the telegram Gauguin sent and a laundry list of expenses, from cleaning up the blood-spattered house, to buying new clothes. Vincent, as always, is careful not to bite the hand that's feeding him.

"It's the 17th today, there are still thirteen days left to get through. Question: how much can I spend per day? Next there must be added the fact that you sent 30 francs to Roulin, out of which he paid the 21.50 for the rent for December..."

When Vincent asks Theo, rhetorically, whether Gauguin "claims to have acted brilliantly in this?" what he's really saying, he's saying quite euphemistically: *This isn't my fault, it's because of Gauguin that we've lost a fortune.* And he's right.

Once again, it's easy to lose sight of the fact that besides Vincent's medical expenses, the costs of Theo going to Arles and back, and probably paying for Gauguin's trip as well, on top of January's rent and everything else, *Gauguin still had to be paid!* Vincent emphasizes this in the same letter:

I can't praise you enough for paying Gauguin in such a way that he couldn't but congratulate himself on the relations he's had with us. Unfortunately, that's another expense, perhaps more sizeable than it should have been, but anyway...

The sum of all of this was that Gauguin emerged from the catastrophe quite well. The Van Goghs, but Vincent in particular, lost everything, even his mind, or so everyone believed. In time Vincent also believed he'd gone mad. Well, wouldn't you if this happened to you, and wouldn't you recover your sanity, given sufficient passage of time and space to separate from this unmitigated disaster?

Money as a Motive for Mutilation?

Now we come to the heart of it. It's easy to look at Vincent's letters, the length and breadth of them, the ramblings, the endless exhortations, as symptoms of a disturbed individual. We may say that the money was precisely why Vincent went nuts. He became so anxious, so sick with worrying about his survive, he carved off his ear in teeth-gritted, snarling frustration.

As fulltime freelancer I know there's a lot of truth to the anxiety, the worry, the sense of disturbance. When you're not in a regular nine to five job, you live by your wits, and yes, you die by them. Isn't that what happened here?

In October 2016 the *Independent* touched on this, in an article about what motivated "the art world's most infamous moments"...

The motivation for such an act of self-mutilation has evaded art historians for more than a century... it was in fact inspired - not by his argument with Gaugin - but by the news that his brother Theo, who supported him closely both financially and emotionally, had become engaged. Though it was previously thought he had only learnt of the impending marriage after his mutilation... Van Gogh actually learnt of it in a letter from Theo delivered on the very same day he cut his ear off; a note which enclosed 100 francs...

This same theory, as I've noted previously, is fielded for why Vincent committed suicide. It has to do with Vincent having an impression that he could be, or would be a burden to his brother, and martyr that he was, decided to do everyone a favour.

The problem with this theory is that the change is happening elsewhere, with other people. Criminals don't change their behaviour because someone else is going through a crisis, they take the law into their hands because they are. In the same way, people don't commit suicide because someone else is going through a crisis.

To be even more logical about this, Vincent after the ear incident is excruciatingly aware of the expense account that's been unleashed. He's doing everything he can to shut it down, and to calm everyone down including Gauguin. Vincent's desperate to keep his show on the road, and that means, the last thing he wants to do is cut of his nose [or ear in this case], to spite his face. But we can't put it past Gauguin.

Why on earth would Vincent injure himself so severely if he knew it was going to require specialist medical care? On the mystery of the size of the sliced off ear, it would make more sense – if it was a case of self-harm – to cut off a smaller piece, and so, not require hospitalisation.

In October 2016 *CNN* suggested Vincent cut off his ear because he was drunk.

We know in hindsight that Vincent cutting his ear off cost the Van Gogh's an arm and a leg as well as the expenses surrounding the treatment of the ear, and we know Vincent was painfully aware of their ongoing expenses, and his role in mitigating them, before, during and after the incident. So it makes no sense that Vincent would purposefully try to aggravate his situation, unless he was mad.

It's far more likely that Gauguin was mad at him, and since Gauguin was being sponsored, he didn't particularly care what the costs were, either to Vincent or Theo. He didn't care who paid the piper as long as someone did. All he cared about was getting himself where he needed to go, and he needed Theo to get his ticket to Paris.

When Theo was summoned by Gauguin, and not because Vincent asked for him, Theo arrived *and left with Gauguin*. Doesn't that sound like a perfectly executed plan if your intention was to get out of Arles, but your patron, who held the purse that could get you out, was somewhere else?

In short, as a freelancer, if you live by your wits you *make sure* you keep your wits about you. That kind of discipline and resilience takes years to achieve, and no one who has endured years of dreams and deprivation is going to throw that away on a whim, especially not during a promising phase of one's personal project.

Even after the ear incident, Vincent kept the faith. In his letter of January 9th he's still a believer, still holding on his goal, still patient that eventually the pendulum of fate *would* turn in his favor.

"I believe that with patience the goal will at last be reached, that the pictures will pay back the money invested in making them."

His faith in himself on January 9th was unshaken, and in his dream of getting an art colony going he was undeterred as ever. Does that sound like someone who could have a breakdown, with so much at stake? Does that sound like someone recovering from a breakdown, or brushing off a betrayal? If Vincent had been tortured so that he cut off his ear, the immediate aftermath would have included self-doubt, and the abandonment of all his hopes. The act itself, which is self-harm, would have been symbolic of his capitulation. So where is the self-doubt, the uncertainty, the insecurity *in himself*? All of his anxiety is directed outwardly, to things and people beyond his control. What does that tell us? Vincent himself was fully self-possessed, firmly in control of himself, disciplined, determined, motivated. Losing an ear wasn't going to disrupt a very internalised sense of mission.

Vincent was disrupted, but that only came much later, when Vincent was completely abandoned, when he'd lost his home and found himself in the asylum, surrounded by people who were actually mad. Any normal person in these circumstances would struggle to hold it together as well. Anyone who'd gained so much only to lose it, would spend sleepless nights trying unravel how they got there, and later, how to get out, and back into the world.

When Vincent came out of all that, he still had the wherewithal he'd had all along – to paint, to make a success, to pull himself up by his bootstraps, but dammit, to get it done and make something of himself. Most people having survived similar circumstances, one would imagine, would quit what they were doing and take up something safe and easy, like sweeping streets, or milking cows for a living. Vincent didn't do any of these things because of how deeply he was anchored to his identity, and his journey, as an artist.

Vincent's Inheritance

The money narrative is incomplete without a look at the events following the death of his father Theodorus on March 26th, 1885. Vincent's father died of a heart attack. A week later Vincent produced one of his seminal works, *The Potato Eaters*.

Vincent had been living with his parents for two years when his father died. During that time he produced about 200 oil paintings, an output averaging one painting every 3.6 days. Vincent had been able to attract interest in an art dealer during this same period, the first quarter of 1885.

Vincent's shenanigans went beyond artistic endeavours. The neighbor's daughter, ten years older than him, fell in love with the artist, but when both families resisted [no doubt Theodorus also disapproved], the poor girl attempted to kill herself by ingesting strychnine. Vincent rushed her to hospital, and she was saved. I deal in more detail with Vincent's love life, including with Margot Begemann [the neighbor's daughter], in the *"Overzealous"* chapter.

I hope the above anecdote demonstrates how long and far Vincent's almost machine-like ability to paint goes back, and even in the four weeks following his father's death, Vincent was able to continue, executing one his most beloved and valuable works, considered by many to be his first masterpiece. There is evidence here of mental fortitude in the face of love, loss, grief and hardship, and Vincent's stamina only developed from there just as his art did.

It's easy to miss the obvious here as well. Didn't Vincent inherit something from his father, and didn't his inheritance make the life of the 32-year-old artist easier, at least for a spell. One might think so, but actually, no. Before we get to why Vincent didn't inherit, let's examine the size of the largesse the late Theodorus had left behind. Was there any inheritance in the first place? Well, actually, there was.

On March 16th, 1889, Theo wrote a letter to his brother. Ironically, just as one brother was being kicked out of his home, and in a sense, removed from society and the life he knew, the other was setting up a new home for himself and his new bride. In the letter Theo writes about "arranging my new apartment" and "rooms so jolly" because they'd been decorated by Vincent's art.

Theo excuses himself for not going down to see his brother, saying if it wasn't so far, he would have made the trip. It was far, 708 kilometers south by train, and about 30 kilometers north east of Arles. But this is a little disingenuous, especially since the doctor [as early as December 29th, 1888] had offered to have Vincent committed in an asylum near Paris, an offer Theo didn't pursue.

"Nevertheless, I will take the liberty to ask you a question and give you some advice. Would you rather have your brother [Vincent] in an asylum close to Paris? Can you afford it? If yes; you should go and find one quickly: his state will certainly allow him to make the journey."*

It's likely an asylum in Paris would be "less affordable" than one further south, in the countryside. But it brings us back to the inheritance. How much was there, after all?

In the archive provided by vangoghletters.org, it's revealed that a few days before Theo's letter to Vincent on March 16th, 1889, the Van Gogh sisters Elisabeth and Willemien had put their share of their inheritance together, to pay for specialist hospital treatment for Vincent, in the event he needed it. The amount wasn't small – 678.23 francs. Using a historical currency converter, it works out to about $3785. Given how Vincent was eeking a living on five franc a day, less when he lived in Auvers, and receiving weekly stipends of about 50 francs from Theo, we can see that this was a fortune for the artist in his day. It could have kept him well-oiled and looked after for six months.

Easy to miss: this was the remainder of the inheritance of the two Van Gogh sisters as it stood in March 1889, four years after they'd received it. More interesting still, Theo notes in a letter dated March 10th :

"...at the moment there's no reason to change [Vincent's] present treatment, which is free. He is well cared for in the municipal hospital [and] it's best to leave him there for the time being to see whether rest and regular care can put him to rights."

It's difficult to know whether Theo truly has Vincent's best interests at heart, or his own. Instead of using the money his sisters have made available, he elects to deposit it with a banker on their behalf, and tells them so. I don't know about you, if you had a close relative in an asylum, a municipal one at that, and he'd cut off his ear months earlier, wouldn't you use resources – especially they were available, and if it didn't mean dipping into your own pocket – to get the best treatment?

Theo continues [this time addressing other family besides the sisters]:

"I appreciate that you would like to contribute if needed, but that probably won't be necessary... As you know, Vincent gave this money to the girls and Cor, influenced by a reproach that he had used more money for his education than the other children."

This revelations changes things, doesn't it? Vincent has not only given up his share of a sizable fortune, but given it to all his siblings [though Theo leaves himself out of it]. We also note a third brother, Cor, who I deal with briefly in the last chapter of this section.

Vincent has given up his share of his own money, apparently out of good conscience. As a result, in some ways at least, he'd been financially vulnerable ever since. And thus, with Vincent in dire straits, the conscience of his family is pricked and they are moved to support him. But Theo says no.

"I don't think that he would take it [his inheritance] back, no matter what the circumstances, if he could judge for himself."

In other words, if Vincent wasn't mad, I don't think he ask for his money/inheritance back.

"It is, however, a reserve in case other means should prove insufficient..."

Why Theo was Indebted...

On March 16th, Theo wrote to his brother about having an exhibition by Claude Monet "at my place". By way of encouragement Theo adds [remember, Vincent hasn't stopped painting]:

"In a little while the public will certainly want paintings by the new school [Vincent's expressionism], for they're certainly exercising the public mind. If you could you would be very kind in giving me or having me given news of you, for apart from the letters from Messrs Rey and Salles I don't know anything about you. I wish you better health and I remain your brother who loves you..."

In March, Vincent has stopped writing, but then, he's also lost his home. We have to trawl all the way back to July 16th, 1885 to find out how and why and when Theo became indebted to his older brother.

Theodorus had left his eldest surviving son an inheritance. A provision was made, but in a classic case of self-sacrifice, of the artist as a martyr, Vincent gives it up. It's not quite as saintly as it seems. The siblings had been bickering about it [see below] for three months, on the basis that if Vincent received any large sum of money, he'd either give it away [as he did during his sojourn at the Borinage], or spend it on whiskey and whores. There seems to be a trade-off here, where Vincent reluctantly but sensibly agrees to go without, in exchange for a stipend, administered by his brother. This makes sense, but it does cast the myth tortured, penniless artist in a less tortured light. Vincent wasn't getting money from Theo out of Theo's good graces, per se, he was to a large extent *entitled* to it.

I know of a woman who currently maintains her ex-husbands finances, as a result of his schizophrenia and alcoholism. The ex-husband, who is also the father of this woman's children, accepts this method of receiving his pension through an allowance. It's a legal arrangement, and also a practical one, given his condition.

The letter making all of this explicit was written one Thursday in July, 1885, from Nuenen, to Vincent's friend Anthon van Rappard. Van Rappard, who mentored Vincent in art, happened to hate *The Potato Eaters.*

"I want you to come right out and take back once and for all, without reservation, what was in your last letters — beginning with the one I sent back to you."

This is how a 32-year-old Vincent corresponds with his mentor – he's bickering, argumentative and intent on settling scores over slights.

Jumping across a few paragraph, Vincent provides this startling insight into matters on the home front:

"As for my family — on the occasion of my father's death — foreseeing that the misunderstanding with them could have gone on forever — I simply said for the sake of clarity — that as far as practical matters and way of life were concerned, my views were too different for us to able to agree in the long run. That I wanted to act entirely according to my own views, but only for myself. And that I relinquished my share of the inheritance..."

Once more we find ourselves face to face not with a broken or dysfunctional Vincent, but a resolute man, not afraid to dig in his heels when it came to living according to his views. It's also easy to take Vincent's words at face value. I'm not sure it felt as simple or as easy or even as practical as it turned out. If the bickering went on for three months, Vincent was outvoted, perhaps four siblings [and their mother] against one. He would have to accept their decision on the situation, quite humiliating for the eldest son, but better than nothing.

In Vincent's words, his habit of wasting money on women, or alcohol or charitable gestures is cast in a more respectable light. He shouldn't take his father's money, he admits, because he and his father didn't see eye to eye. That's already different to Theo's version, which was that the patriarch had devoted proportionately more to Vincent's education.

"...having been greatly at odds with my father in the last few years [which was true enough], I didn't consider that I had any right to nor did I have any wish for what was his. This cut short any further unpleasantness with my family, you'll admit. So that's finished, and for the rest I'm getting on very well with them."

Having more fully contextualised the financial situation as it stood in early 1889, and its steady evolution since Vincent's father's death in March 1885, I'm inclined to see the sense in having Vincent committed – for free – for an extended time. It meant Vincent's board and lodging were taken care of, and in a sense, so was he, and he could still continue painting. It was by no means an ideal situation, but it was a good platform from wish to attempt a gradual recovery, even if only a financial one. This also seems to explain how and why Vincent would voluntarily admit himself at Saint-Rémy. There he wasn't treated the way the other lunatics were treated. He could come and go, more or less, as he pleased, and he had the security that at least his accommodation was safe, and taken care of. In his own mind, he may also have calculated that over a year [sentencing himself effectively to purgatory] he could save the family, and Theo especially, from expense, and even make up for the financial haemorrhage that had flowed at the same time blood had gushed from where his ear used to be.

Does that make sense?

Gauguin came from privilege, Vincent did too in a sense, but he was also used to living without, and identifying with peasants, while Gauguin sought to take advantage of them. Gauguin saw easy money in scamming the Van Goghs, but like most people, he'd underestimated the depths of their resolve, and none more than Vincent's.

*Curiously, when Dr Felix Rey suggested to Theo that he transfer Vincent for treatment closer to Paris, he emphasized the point by noting he was coming to Paris to complete his doctorate. This meant, by inference, the doctor could chaperone his patient to Paris, and they could hit two birds with one stone [since the doctor needed to be in Paris anyway]. The doctor also remarks that Vincent's condition isn't a foregone conclusion.

This business has not gone so far that it cannot be stopped and for the commissioner to cancel his report. This is all the advice that I have to give you on your poor brother. Since I also have a brother I would be delighted to give you any news; also I have lived away from my family. In some months' time I will be going to Paris for my doctorate thesis; I would be glad if someone looked out for me during my ordeal.

It's interesting that the topic was raised, and dismissed, isn't it? The doctor saying "I would be glad if someone looked out for me during my ordeal" seems to be an effort to guilt-trip the younger brother into taking a keener interest in his sibling. The doctor seems aware, at least, that Theo exists, even if he seems not quite as involved as he could, or should be. Just days later, on January 2nd, 1889, the doctor's prognosis suddenly changes. Vincent isn't mad after all, just "overexcited", or to use another word, "intense."

I am happy to tell you that my predictions have been realized and that this over-excitement has only been temporary. I strongly feel that he [Vincent] will be himself in a few days. I have made a point of his writing to you himself, to tell you in his own words his condition.

To reiterate, any person capable of writing a letter, let alone a letter that's legible, comprehensible and sensible, can hardly be mad to begin with, can they? After several weeks of mostly silence from Theo, Vincent's situation, and his madness, worsened, and the rest is history.

The Third Van Gogh

"I think it's very logical of Cor to go there...it's possible that one might be happier far from our society." — Vincent van Gogh

The mainstream, the media and the PR surrounding Vincent van Gogh, which is a multi-million dollar industry today, are so preoccupied with his hundreds of letters to Theo, that the world is virtually unaware Vincent had *another* younger brother: Cor van Gogh.

Cor, born in 1867, fourteen years after Vincent, was the youngest brother and youngest of the six Van Gogh children. Vincent's correspondence with his family from 87 Hackford Road, in Brixton, a suburb of south London, quickly captured the imaginations of his two younger brothers. When Cor was a boy of six, the oldest surviving Van Gogh headed off to adventures in London, working for the London branch of Groupil & Co, a leading European multinational dealing in fine art. At the same time Theo followed in his older brother's footsteps, starting at the same company as Groupil & Co's youngest employee. Later he too transferred to the company's London office at 17 Southampton Street.

During the summer of 1886, when Cor, arguably the most handsome of the three brothers, was nineteen year old, Willemien van Gogh penned a letter to a girlfriend. The youngest sister, five years older than Cor, informed her friend:

"My father [Theodorus] was strict, and attached to all sorts of [Christion] conventions of which my brother [Vincent] never took any particular notice; needless to say, that often led to clashes and to words spoken in anger, which neither party [father or son] was quick to forget. So during the past eight years Vincent has been a bone of contention with many, and all too often one tended to forget all the good there was in him, the appearances to the contrary. During the past few years he has been working at home with us..."

We can see from this how the large family were often shaken not only by Vincent's conduct, but by the rows that erupted between the patriarch and his son. Since Vincent was living at home between 1881 and March 1886, it's easy to see how, under these circumstances, the majority of the family would side with their father, leaving Vincent on the outs.

The exception to this was clearly Theo, who shared after all Vincent's experience with other artists, and more than that – their lifestyle. Cor on the other hand was likely a teenager on the home front when a late twentysomething Vincent returned home from his luckless foray abroad. Vincent would have been able to share the rudiments of life in England with his youngest brother, but if this found fertile soil in Cor's mind, the family friction, ultimately ending in their father's death in 1885, couldn't have been easy to bear for the youngster.

The end of Willemien's letter from 1886 confirms as much:

"...after my father's death, Anna [the second oldest sibling, two years younger than Vincent] thought it would be more peaceful for Mother if [Vincent] stopped living at home, and saw to it that he left us."

We know Theodorus died in March 1885, and that Vincent left Nuenen to join his brother in Paris [without telling him he was], in March 1886. Thus, it was no simple request that Vincent leave, and then a quick exit, one has the impression that the whole family campaigned for months to get rid of him, and finally, he left.

He took that so badly that from then on [Vincent] has not been in touch with us, and it is only through Theo that we have news of him...

It's likely this forced exit from his home is not only the reason for the unusual closeness between the older brothers, but also the reason the two sisters and Cor hardly feature in Vincent's letters, and vice versa.

On 11 March 1887, Theo wrote Cor a letter about Vincent. Cor was about to earn his first salary check, so Theo congratulated his baby brother on taking his first step towards earning a living, which he was due to receive the next day. Interestingly, Theo admits "in letter writing I am no hero", a reference to his lack of communication with Cor "for a long while."

Theo also adds the following:

...make sure you can stand on your own feet, as being dependent is bad for oneself and others...It is also very pleasant for Mother to see you are looking after yourself...

After suggesting reading material to Cor [including Émile Zola's *Germinal*, published in 1885], Theo confides in Cor about trouble he's having with Vincent. In the same letter, Theo refers to an iron tower that's under construction in Paris.

It is a pity that [Vincent] has such a temperamental nature, for in the long run [he is] quite impossible to get along with....that does not make it too pleasant here at home and I am hoping for a change....Have you heard they are going to make an iron tower 300 meters high here? ...the designer tells us that ten years ago it would not have been possible to make...the necessary calculations [to keep the tower upright]...

When Cor came of age, he followed a different career path, but like his older siblings, headed to England to seek his fortune. Prior to the erection of the Eiffel Tower in 1887-1889 [by then Theo had transferred to Goupil's head office in Paris] Cor had studied engineering. Although some biographers claim he actually worked as a labourer on the tower, in fact he took his metalworking skills to Lincoln, a cathedral city 200 kilometers due north of London, in northeast England.

Lincoln was one of the epicentres of the steaming industrial revolution still sweeping the world at the time. In Lincoln steel locomotives were forged in fire, and eventually, the world's first tanks, just in time for the first World War.

In November 1904, Lincoln was struck by a major typhoid epidemic. Fortunately for Cor, he was out of the country, in fact in another hemisphere, long before then. On August 23rd, 1889, Cor boarded a Union Company steamship for a voyage bound for Cape Town, South Africa. In those giddy gold rush days it was a Dutch colony, and since the discovery of gold on the Witwatersrand three years earlier, the South African earth seemed to be filled with the egg-yellow ore. The colony wanted to get itself up and running, and that meant railways. The Nederlandsche Zuid-Afrikaansche Spoorwegmaatschappij [Netherlands-South African Railway Comnpany or NZASM] wanted to set up the Oosterlijn [East Line], a 562 kilometer [350 mile] railway track linking Pretoria to Delagoa Bay [modern day Maputo, in Mozambique] among many others. For such a major enterprise, they needed skilled labour – engineers, metal workers – and that's where Cor came into the picture.

It was a twenty day trip on the *Tartar* sailing from Southampton, to Lisbon, and then down Africa's west coast to Kaap de Goeie Hoop [the Cape of Good Hope] on the southern tip of Africa.

On September 5th, about halfway through his journey, Theo wrote to Vincent, informing him that their mother had received a letter from Cor who was "already far away" but in good health. Vincent replied, referring the grief of his departure gathering like "water in a swamp." After Cor's departure, the family have moved into smaller, more modest lodgings. Vincent had earlier communicated to his family:

I think it is very logical of Cor to go there [to Africa] instead of seeing one's vital forces...evaporate...it's possible one might be happier far from our society.

At about 19:00 on September 11th, 1889, Cor stepped off the *Tartar* and onto the dock at Cape Town harbour. Cor wrote that there was "nothing special" on this twenty-day journey, with the exception of their destination:

The arrival in South Africa was fine, very pleasant weather and a beautiful view of Table Mountain and Cape Town...

Cor took two full days to travel from Cape Town to Kimberley, which since 1867 [the year of his birth], had been caught up in a two-decades-long diamond-rush. *En route* Cor passed many whitewashed Cape Dutch homesteads. This gave him a sense of home, but the further he went north, the more the Dutch influence thinned, and until it seemed to wither and disappear entirely. Cor arrived in Johannesburg a few days later, probably near the end of the same month, September 1889.

Johannesburg is a place full of dust and gold. I enjoy my work...but for the rest here is no social life or amenities or entertainment of any sort. Our free time we spend lying reading; the city is ugly, without any neighborhoods...but one slowly gets used to everything.

While there seems to be a "glass-half full" attitude on the page from Cor, that didn't mean things in those dusty backwaters were easy or getting easier. In fact, Cor arrived at a particularly difficult and deteriorating time in the country's history. In the same letter he adds:

Everything is very expensive because of the drought, the people are talking of famine...On the way to Kimberley some oxen died because of lack of drinking water...

Cor would end his letters were a salutation invoking a "firm paw", a reference to a beloved dog that used to be his at home in Holland.

Vincent, at the time of these goings-on was living in the madhouse at Saint-Rémy. Although he didn't write to Cor directly, he received word from his mother and from Theo. On December 22nd, 1889, Theo wrote to Vincent about Cor's adventures.

Life down there [for Cor] can't be much fun. There are no plants or flowers...The Transvaal isn't to be recommended. Here the weather is abominable, cold and grey; almost everybody is ill.

Conditions were so bad, Cor began to set his sights on South America, which was experiencing it's own El Dorado, it's own gold rush [since 1883].

It's not the ambit of this narrative to deal in great detail with Cor van Gogh. The intention is merely to provide Cor's story in order to more thoroughly explicate the context of the other two brothers, and Vincent in particular.

So, jumping ahead to Vincent's death in 1890, when Cor finally wrote home in response to the news [in a letter dated October 8th, 1890], what's apparent is how little he has to say about his oldest brother:

Dear Jo and Theo

It is truly shameful that I have kept you waiting so long for a letter, but don't think I have forgotten you...I can't tell you how upset I was to hear the sad news about Vincent, I know it will be a terrible loss and emptiness for you, although I believe that it is better for him as things are...

Cor continues, recalling "happy days", but this has nothing to do with Vincent, and from there the letter returns to musings about local things like "coarse grass", the "terribly windy" weather and two banks that have collapsed. It seems incomprehensible on the face of it. It's particularly strange that though Cor uses the single word "upset" to communicate his feelings, and then has nothing further to say or ask. He seems to see it as a terrible loss and emptiness not for himself, but for them [Theo and Jo]. Worse still, Cor suggests his brother killing himself – being dead – is "better for him."

In 1897, after eight year in South Africa, Cor made the long trip home to visit his family, and meet his young nephew Vincent, who was seven-years-old at the time [by then both Vincent and Theo were dead]. He gave the boy some stamps, and spent a little time searching for a wife. There didn't seem to be anyone available, so Cor returned to the Transvaal and set about finding a wife in South Africa.

On February 16th 1898 Cor van Gogh married Anna Fuchs, a German and staunch Roman Catholic. She'd been living in the country twice as long as Cor. In October 1898, eight months after getting married, they divorced. It seems Anna left Cor, and not amicably.

A year later, the fortunes of Cor van Gogh, and indeed and entire subcontinent, took a turn for the worse. The Anglo-Boer War erupted on October 11th, 1899. At around this time, Cor went to see a lawyer to draw up his will, making sure to leave his assets to none but his mother, living in The Hague at the time.

Cor joined the Boer effort against the British, just as many other Hollanders did. Within months the war became one of the bloodiest and deadliest in human history. In January 1900 Britain sent its largest ever force overseas, 180 000 men initially, and then more reinforcements, until the combined strength of British forces numbered half a million men. The population of the country formerly known as Zuid-Afrikaanse Republiek, [and later Transvaal] was just 1.2 million. This meant for every two civilians there was one British soldier. The Empire meant sink its claws into the world's largest gold deposit.

The details of Cor's contribution to the Boer effort are not known. What is known is that in 1900 he fell ill with fever, and received treatment from the Transvaal Red Cross in a temporary hospital in Brandfort.* Brandfort then was an ugly, nothing little town in the middle of a tawny wilderness. Its only claim to fame then, arguably, was that it had once been the favored hunting ground of hominids from the Middle Stone Age.

My family owns a farm 45 kilometers south of Brandfort, and the old Brandfort road, a dirt track, passes the entrance gate to our farm on its way to the town. Having been there in person I can say with confidence that even today Brandfort remains a derelict shithole in the middle of nowhere.

As British forces advanced on the shitty little stronghold it was abandoned*, not only by able-bodied Boer forces, but by the inhabitants, and the few Dutch doctors and nurses that had been stationed there. Sick, vulnerable and as far from home as he could possibly be, Cor was an enemy combatant unable to escape.

Had he, in those long, lonely early days on the reef, ever gotten down to reading Zola, as Theo had suggested? Given that he said that's all there was to do, it seems likely.

Men were springing forth, a black avenging army, germinating slowly in the furrows, growing towards the harvests of the next century, and their germination would soon overturn the earth.— Émile Zola's Germinal, 1885 translation

Ominous words, given what was rolling across that southern country like a sickle, cutting men down like wheat. In those days Britain had stepped up a gear to contain the slippery Boer guerrillas. They'd initiated a scorched earth policy, which was exactly what it sounded like. Anything that could give sustenance, including fellow human beings, was burned or destroyed.

Wikipedia describes this process as a systematic drive, organised like a sporting shoot, to flush out Boer guerrillas. It was designed:

...to sweep the country bare of everything that could give sustenance to the guerrillas, including women and children ... It was the clearance of civilians—uprooting a whole nation—that would come to dominate the last phase of the war.

Cor had gone south to build a life, only to see it and the country go up in smoke. His brothers, he knew, had struggled too, and lost everything. Now it was his turn. With this monstrous machine of war*** bearing down on Brandfort, Cor gritted his teeth inside a baking hot tent. If he'd dodged a bullet by leaving Lincoln when he did, there was nowhere to hide now.

Finally he reached for his standard-issue Mauser, and killed himself. He was 32 years old. Comparing the years of their lives, Vincent lived longer than all his brothers.

*In 1977, Nelson Mandela's wife Winnie, was exiled to Brandfort. Even then the town had no running water or electricity.

**About eighty years after these events, my father began a large development in Bloemfontein, a medium-sized city 60 kilometers south. During excavations, he uncovered many incinerated Boer weapons, including pistols. These had also been abandoned and destroyed, so as not to allow the British use of them.

***Male prisoners of war were sent overseas by the British. It's not clear whether male prisoners stood a better chance of survival after capture. More than 26 000 women and children died in 45 British Boer War concentration camps.

FORWARDS

"I don't really have any friends except for you, and when I'm ill you're always in my thoughts." — Vincent van Gogh to Theo, from The Hague, 22 July 1883

Going Dutch

"I'm from Holland, and I'm used to rain." — Marianne Vos

Below the surface, the human body is awash with blood and buzzing with nervous energy. Capillaries, veins and arteries convey red liquid through the labyrinths of the brain, through purple, grey or brown organs, inside the rich galloping oxygenated meat that is human muscle. Throughout this system, electricity sparks and charges, conveying impulses, thoughts, feelings, emotions, warmth and pain, back and forth along salty corridors and across spinal thoroughfares. At the centre of the organism is a pump, which keeps the living system awash in glistening saline.

In Simon Schama's excellent tome *Landscape & Memory*, he quotes Plato and Barlow imagining:

"...that nature and our bodies were constructed according to the same mysterious...law of circulation [governing] all forms of vitality...to see a river was to be swept in a great current of myths and memories [a current] strong enough to carry us back to [our watery, elemental] existence in the womb. And along that stream were borne...the most intense passions...mysterious transmutations of blood and water; the vitality...of heroes [and] empires..."

Most of Holland [hollow land] is low, flat and wet. Much of the country is formed by the streams, tributaries and estuaries of three immense rivers. The southwest of the country is an enormous delta where masses of water discharge into the North Sea. Throughout the land an intricate system of enormous pumps, canals and dikes channel endless tides of water hither and thither, in an effort to sequestrate water from inundated *terra firma.**

Since only half of Holland's surface is more than a meter above sea level, it's hardly surprising that a quarter of its population lives below sea level, living on land that is "man-made".

In the 16th century, about 350 years before the birth of Vincent van Gogh, the Dutch set about creating artificial hydrological entities, fancy words for a simple, but difficult task: pushing back the sea and turning marshes and swamps into liveable plots of land called *polders.*

Long ago the iconic symbol for the Dutch, the windmill, powered the pumps that held back the sea. As these windmills turned, harnessing wind power, they could also be used to thresh [mill] harvested grain, or pound pulp into paper, or cocoa into chocolate [solid chocolate is a Dutch invention]. Sometimes people used these windmills for human habitation, or as a barn, or as a look-out post during periods of strife. In the case of the Zeddam tower mill, dating back to 1451, Canadian soldiers used the site as a safe house, and to set up a radio transmitter. Other mills, like the 33 meter high Molen de Noord, were used to make gin.

It's easy to see how the idiosyncratic [some might say crazy] determination to make a living where nature had decreed otherwise taught the Dutch to be entrepreneurs. It's difficult to imagine how a folk's capacities [creative, practical, intelligence] can be tested more than by trying to reroute water against the natural gravity and lie of the land, and yet, they succeeded.

With these initiatives came rewards. The windmill industry taught the Dutch excellent woodworking and carpentry skill, which translated to transforming another natural commodity – trees into planks, and planks into ships. The cloth used in windmill sails could also be used to build ship sails, ropes and masts.

Over the landscape, windmill sails could be swapped out to communicate messages to the farming community – such as weddings, warnings or welcomings. In the 17th century 9000 windmills dotted the Dutch countryside. With each new windmill the Dutch won more land, and more confidence. It's hardly surprising that windmills held a totemic sense of strength for Hollanders.

All this, real streams rushing one way, only to be sent another, ushered turbid streams of consciousness into being. People who were forced to think, and forced by the constant threat of water to think on their feet, became experts at the conquest of water. The Dutch came into their own in the 17th century. The Dutch Golden Age was an age of windmills and seafaring; if "ships" with large, slow, propellers lifted over the swamps to harness the winds and create farms, hundreds more were built to harness the oceans, and yield Dutch colonies.

By 1650, the Dutch had a fleet of some 16 000 merchant ships, the largest in the world, and the envy of other seafaring powers – the Portuguese, Spanish, French and British. With the same fevered enterprise on land, the Dutch set about creating outposts across the globe, establishing the Dutch East India and Dutch West India Companies, the world's first multinationals, complete with their own respective security forces. Colonies arose everywhere: North and South America, North and South Africa, Australia and New Zealand [named after Zeeland – sea land] and then in Asia, the near East [Indonesia] and the far East [Japan]. Having the world's first and largest capital concern soon led to the country becoming the world's first capitalist country, with the world's first stock exchange.

Where the Dutch went, others followed, and so they soon found themselves defending their sea routes [or shipping lanes] to the East and West. Initially the Dutch had to hold off the Spanish, as they did near Gibraltar in 1607, and Antwerp and the Flemish coast in 1648. In 1652, the same year a colony was formed in Cape Town, the Dutch battled the British to keep the channel they shared on either side, open for business and trade. Maritine warfare led to the more troublesome and expensive defense of terrestrial territories.

In 1672, the Dutch endured a *Rampjaar* [Disaster Year]. They found themselves at war with France, Germany and England simultaneously. Although the Dutch could still muster the maritime might to prevent French and English fleets from sailing to the western hemisphere, when their own tiny, waterlogged country came under direct attack from the

East, they found themselves vulnerable, and quickly lost territory to Germany. The Dutch were only able to stem the invasion by purposefully flooding their own territory.

In 1688, when an Anglo-French alliance appeared inevitable, the Dutch amassed their enormous navy and sailed to England, landing in Brixham, Devon. The enormous invasion went off without a sword unsheathed in anger. A Dutchman became the King of England, but when he failed to produce an heir, England automatically came under the authority of an English king, not through the rattling of sabers or the blast of a single ship's cannon, but through the law of succession.

From then on, Dutch colonies that had been set up were simply taken over by the English, from South Africa and Mauritius to North America, from New Zealand to Japan.

Back on home turf, the Dutch got back to work getting their windmills up and running, once again transforming the sea into soggy peat fields, and then to a substrate that could be occupied and farmed again.

Holland had lost its glittering golden glory. The Golden Age which had spawned so much, including dozens of Dutch masters in art, had seemingly been flushed away. It was into this sodden fabric of diminishing prestige and decline for the Dutch, that Vincent van Gogh was born, in the spring of 1853.

Dark Days

He came from a bleak world, born inside the stifling cloud of the Dutch Reformed Church on Markt 29, the main street of Zundert in Holland's wettest region, the far south. It was bleak because it was dark, wet and cold. One only needs look at the work of Dutch painters Vincent grew up to admire, to appreciate how dark this land below sea level could be.

Rembrandt's eponymous painting *The Mill*, executed in 1648 or thereabouts [when Holland was the peak of its powers], captures the tone and mood perfectly. It's mostly overcast, and there is so little light reality is little more than a silhouette. Colour is so diluted, it's difficult to distinguish textures, let alone tones. It's all so much grey and brown, broken by the glaze and occasional ripple of water. Figures in this haze are almost invisible, like soldiers lost in the smoke of war. The cows and the cottage are barely discernible, and the fact that there's some dispute about whether Rembrandt even painted *The Mill*, serves to emphasize its murkiness even more.

The windmill itself appears ragged and rickety despite a vague, golden tinge. Jozef Israëls, admired by Vincent, provides an interior view of the Dutch country in *Alone in the World*, painted in 1881, and into its mind-set in *We Grow Old*, painted in 1878. *Langs moeders graf* [Next to mother's grave] further illustrates the sense of a people crowded into a small country, trying to survive a Spartan life and avoid a watery grave through hard labour and rigorous morality.

The interiority of Charles de Groux, where one can practically feel the damp mould growing on the yellow walls, provides a claustrophobic sense of the Dutch tirelessly attempting to resist nature's efforts to drown their every hope in seawater.

One might imagine the *oeuvre* of the French artist who inspired Vincent, Jean-François Millet, to be both lighter and brighter, and it is, but just barely. Look at *The Sheepfold, The Sower, The Potato Harvest* and *The Angelus,* and they all seem like iterations of the same up-at-dawn, still-at-it-after dusk, bent-over, toil in a sunless shade. The main difference is Millet's work feels like it's set in a dryer, wider world. Even Millet's sunniest pictures, like *Shepherd Tending His Flock* and *The Coast of Gréville*, are grey, brown and sombre.

It's almost logical then that Vincent's early work was in this vein – dense, dreary, clotted, manure brown, as Schama describes it. He sullies his subjects in the colors of dusty potatoes, as Vincent himself once wrote, before they've been washed and peeled. Even Vincent's self-portraits start off in another world, a world without color or life, a world starved of light. These first portraits are hard to believe they were painted by the same man, let alone to reconcile with Vincent's final self-portrait.

If Vincent's foremost Dutch and French influences informed him that great art was dark, and that the world everywhere was the like the world he knew – watery and wet – imagine what a surprise it was for him to find, when he eventually did, that it was not so. This was no one-day wonder kind of surprise. It was wrenching. When you have lived to 35 years of age, and known the world a certain way, when you see it the realization isn't instant, human minds aren't wired that way. It takes years to unlearn what you have learned, to unsee what you've seen, to see a world lit in a hue you grew up not knowing.

Does that makes sense? Let me further illustrate the point – because it's an important one – by dipping into the art history of my own family.

Vincent came from Holland's waterlogged south; my family on my father's side came from the north, a village called Leek [pronounced Lake] in the Groningen province. The etymology even upcountry is associated with water, for there a leek is a brook, or creek, and near the village, lies a shallow lake.

My great grandfather painted for a time in the Royal Palace before he moved to Fishhoek Cape Town in 1920, almost 20 years after Cor van Gogh died in the Boer war. Like Vincent, my great grandfather studied the masters and painted typical Dutch farmyard scenes – the thatched houses, the barns, the windmills, the cows in the meadows.

In South Africa, my great grandfather, a landscape artists and portrait painter – like Vincent he also studied Rembrandt's artistic take on light and dark – but struggled to depict the bright blue of the South African sky and the vivid sunlight drenching the African fields.

Such is the level of darkness in Holland, even outside of it the idea of it remains. Thus, even when an artist *sees* the light of the New World first-hand, he struggles to shake off the training, all beneath the blanket of Holland's diffuse light. What's really happening when a painter is learning his *oeuvre*, is he's been taught to see and execute reality in a certain way. Now that a new reality is revealed, the old reality persists like a badly soiled reputation.

It takes time to learn, and it takes time to unlearn what he has learned. Not everything has to be unlearned, which presents a dilemma – what to keep, what to throw away. Where to find the new-born baby drowning in the bathwater? Not *everything* Vincent inherited from the Dutch masters was disposable, least of all the magisterial perspective they held of the material world. Vincent said as much when he wrote to Emile Bernard in July 1888, from Arles, while awaiting the arrival of Gauguin, and *his* imagination.

Those Dutchmen had hardly any imagination or fantasy, but their good taste and their scientific knowledge of composition were enormous.

The same principle of peeling away, and knowing what not to, applies to this narrative, which is why we need to spend so much time peeling away at each layer of Vincent's "post-truth". We must work delicately, more like a brain surgeon than a potato peeler, to counter the intricate webs of so-called knowledge, until we expose the softly sparking tissue at the bottom. There, if our eyes are open and ready, we can finally see Vincent's authentic, original reality as it really was.

I suppose the modern equivalent in a visual sense, is stepping out of a movie theatre, or from hours of video game play, into a bright, midday sun. One does not immediately see, let alone engage with the world. It takes a while to settle in. So too, when one leaves a family, a country and a philosophy that has nurtured your psychology, as Vincent did, the change was a lot more gradual than one might appreciate.

It takes years to develop the roots and anchors necessary to develop an entirely new identity, and even if successful, that process is fraught with existential crisis. Disconnected, rootless, the fear of death is far more evident, it's there because right beside it is the fear of life, the fear of the unknown. Our fear of the unknown is entirely rational, and it should be.

The all-too-real fear of exiting the world you know, comes about because of the knowledge that by entering some new world, one might never return. One may go in search of one's fortune and be doomed in the process. This is the real tragedy behind all three of the Van Gogh brothers, they dreamed and they dared, and when things turned sour, they persisted.

Instead of their bravery being rewarded, they were punished as can happen sometimes to birds when they take wing for the first time. The wonder of Vincent's life is that he transformed himself from a place of such watery gloom into such vivid, and electric warmth.

Coming from such a misty and malleable collective consciousness, we can clearly see how and why it could only be a Dutchman who could transform the way reality was expressed as vividly as Vincent would. What remains to be seen is the more personal journey he took. Who was he? We begin to answer this question, which is really the biggest question of all, by meeting Vincent's parents, starting with his mother Anna.

Understanding Anna

Anna Carbentus was the daughter of Willem Carbentus, the king's book binder. As such they were a prosperous family, Anna being one of eight children. In the 19th and early 20th century, large households were common in Holland, and around the world, including England and America. The idea was that the more children you had, the better the chance one of them might take care of you when you were old and frail. So a family of eight in 1850 was considered the "right" size, and children were seen as economic assets.

The Van Gogh family proved that a child, especially in a capitalist society facing imminent and ongoing decline, if unable to find or keep a job, could be a liability too. As such, family size has decreased dramatically since the 1920's with the average birth-rate in the European Union currently down to 1.6 children. [In Niger, currently, the fertility rate is about seven children per woman].

Still a spinster when she turned 30, Anna set about finding herself a husband. In March 1850, Anna's sister Cornelia, ten years younger, became engaged to an affluent print dealer – Vincent van Gogh, the uncle-to-be of the unborn artist. Three months about Cornelia's wedding, Anna asked her sister to introduce her to Vincent's younger brother, Theodorus, a preacher, and a meeting was arranged. Soon after the meeting, since both were eager to marry, that's what they did on May 21st, 1851.

By all accounts, Anna was a good [in the traditional sense] subservient wife. She supported her husband in his work, doing the rounds with him as he visited parishioners throughout Zundert. Vincent inherited his expressive and energetic personality, as well as his propensity for letter-writing, from his mother.

Unfortunately, Anna was a somewhat cold parent. Instead of showing warmth she communicated feelings through words. This too, Vincent may have inherited, and may explain why he struggled to maintain intimate relationships with the opposite sex, and why he tried as hard as he did to express himself so profoundly. It was Anna's philosophy that happiness could only be found in the home, and that in the bosom of family one found one's ultimate refuge. It's also apparent that Anna infected her brood with a degree of separation anxiety. Separations were treated as a family crisis, somewhat contradicting the idea of instilling independence in one's offspring. For this reason we can understand Vincent struggling more than an ordinary person when he'd waited for Gauguin, prepared for his arrival and then struggled to come to terms with Gauguin leaving as soon as he did.

Although all three her sons subscribed to the same philosophy, only Theo glimpsed the happiness of the family home. As an unsuccessful young man Vincent would return home in search of succour, only to find his parents resentful of his return. So much for the happiness of home!

Vincent's parents were both history buffs, and would regale their children with after-dinner stories about the adventures of Dutch heroes triumphing on land, and at sea. Having fallen so recently from such dizzy heights, one can understand the nostalgia and sentiment attached to Holland's recent history. These were stories of Empire coming into being, and dying.

During the day, Anna invested her efforts into developing the local arcadia. Her fondness for nature, and gardening in particular, was also keenly felt by Vincent until his last days. In fact, it's likely the very last sketch he did was of a garden in Auvers.

If we are to trace Vincent's exceptional archive of letters, and letters filled with sketches, this surely started with Anna's family's service to the king, and taking a few leaves out of his notes and illustration. We also know that her in-laws were involved in a print dealership. All of this would have imbued Vincent with a deeply ingrained sense of using both words and forms to communicate. Anna herself sketched plants and flowers, filling her notebooks with them. We can see in this the root of his sunflower series, and his interest in floral forms.

In October 1888, while awaiting Gauguin's arrival in Arles, Vincent painted a portrait of his mother, giving her a vivid green background, sombre attire and a slight smile. Anna outlived her husband and all three of her sons. She died in 1907, when she was 87-years-old.

Living Under Theodorus's Whip

Theodorus' family was even larger than Anna's. They were eleven children. Theodorus was the only one to follow in his father's footsteps. Like his father, he decided to be a pastor [and Vincent's initial career choice was to follow in Theodorus' footsteps], and when he graduated, Theodorus' father confirmed him into the Dutch Reformed ministry. At that stage Theodorus [and Anna for that matter] lived in Utrecht, approximately in central Holland.

From Utrecht Theodorus was sent, with his new wife, to do mission work in Zundert. There Vincent was born.

Unlike Vincent, his father was known as a handsome man with strong spiritual values, and unlike Anna, he was the more loving [at least initially] of Vincent's parents. If Theodorus was good-looking, perhaps this made up for his mediocre sermons. Over time, Theodorus served a succession of small congregations in small towns, including Etten and Nuenen.

What he lacked in charm, as a pastor, he made up for in his dedication to his flock, and the model he presented of upright respectability. The Van Goghs wanted to look the part of the ideal Dutch family, or at least, that was the plan.

In reality, things went awry from the get go. Their first child was stillborn. It was into this bleak household environment, of parents still grieving their first, lost lamb, that Vincent II came into the world.

To aggravate the omens even more, the dead firstborn [who was also called Vincent] was born – and died – *exactly a year* before Vincent II came into the world. Thanks to Vincent II, the impressions the faithful flock had of the pious Van Goghs would remain skewed and not quite right for an extended period.

Between them Theodorus and Anna would eventually produce three sons and three daughters. Only half their brood would survive into middle age, and beyond.

Back at the ranch, if Vincent's mother was cold, his father was tense, certainly in response to the intensity of Vincent II. If Vincent didn't inherit his father's looks, his mediocre sermons or his money, what he did inherit was his temperament. Who knows what his parents muttered to one another in frustration, as their dreamy, distracted, hair-trigger child cast from one flight of fancy to the next.

Met molentjes lopen…Vincent's walking with windmills again [which means to be crazy]

*A klap van de molen hebben…*Vincent's been hit by the windmill again [he's gone crazy again]

Theodorus couldn't understand why the boy was so short-tempered and so argumentative. It's likely that at least some of that flashy temper had been kindled while his parents had been unavailable emotionally to Vincent as an infant, as they continued to grieve for his ghost brother. It's also possible his parents were rigid-to-the-rules and emotionally unavailable in general, period. This conjecture is dramatized to some extent in *Loving Vincent*, so it appears to be well founded.

This unavailability stoked the fires of insecurity and inadequacy, making the boy overcompensate in his efforts to express himself, to get and keep hold of the attention of his parents. Vincent's parents probably took some time to see the Vincent as he was on his own terms, and not Vincent as a sort of reminder of another idealized Vincent who'd been lost to the world. By the time they did see Vincent, he also saw what it was they saw, in Technicolor clarity. He wasn't who they'd intended as their firstborn. He didn't measure up. He wasn't good enough. It wasn't an easy pill to swallow, but he did.

In another epic letter penned in January 1882, Vincent responds to Theo over the course of 2800+words, making his case against his parents point by point. Below are just two of them.

#2 That expression that I contrive to make Pa and Ma's life miserable is actually not yours, I've known it for a long time…I told Pa and Ma that I considered it a Jesuitism and didn't take the slightest notice of it. Pa regularly comes up with some such saying [like] 'you'll be the death of me', while calmly reading the newspaper and smoking his pipe. So I take such expressions at their face value.

I hope it's clear from this, that Vincent felt unfairly persecuted by his parents [plural] above all, and yet he stood his ground regardless [in the sense that he didn't change his behaviour, and when an ultimatum was set, he left.] We see here Vincent's propensity for endurance when it came to insult and injury. That's not to say he's thick-skinned, or insensitive, quite the opposite. Simply that he was his own man, and in possession of his own mind, the sort of man whose stubbornness could resist the paths of water, in other words.

#6. I felt a great deal of remorse and sorrow, and tormented myself because things were going so badly between Pa and Ma and me. But now that it's come to this, well, so be it, and to tell you the truth I'm no longer sorry but can't help feeling relieved. If I realize later that I did the wrong thing, yes, then of course I'll regret it, but I still don't exactly see how it would have been possible to act otherwise.

As much as Vincent wants the support of his family, he doesn't need it. What he believes and knows about himself, he feels, is sufficient.

"When someone tells me in no uncertain terms, 'leave my house, the sooner the better, within the half-hour rather than the hour', well, old chap, then I'm out in less than a quarter of an hour, and won't come back again either…now that they and not I said 'go away', well, the path I must take is clear enough…"

In the same emotional missive, Vincent describes his father as "very easily hurt and irritable and full of obstinacies in domestic life and is used to getting his way." It's likely Vincent was the same way in a sense, particularly his obstinacy in regards his art and choice of lifestyle.

So we see, Vincent was first a failure and a disappointment in the eyes of his own father.

I've known it for a long time…

I didn't take the slightest notice of it

…it would not have been possible to act otherwise…

the path I must take is clear enough

This psychological curse had been there right from the start, with Pa, living with him, haunting him like a spectre under the same roof. If it wasn't the cold shoulder of his mother, it was the hot displeasure of his father, and soon, most of his siblings too. Here was the most important person in his world, who not only disagreed with him, but *disapproved* of him.

This disapproval is often cited through Vincent's "shaggy dog" reference, from a letter to Theo written on Saturday, December 15th, 1883:

"There's a similar reluctance about taking me into the house as there would be about having a large, shaggy dog in the house. He'll come into the room with wet paws — and then…he'll get in everyone's way. And he barks so loudly. In short — it's a dirty animal. Very well — but the animal has a human history and, although it's a dog, a human soul…able to feel what people think about him, which an ordinary dog can't do.

And I, admitting that I am a sort of dog, accept them as they are."

It's obvious that in 1883, seven years before his death, Vincent accepts the way his kin see him, as unflattering as it is. What's more, he's able to communicate and convey this unflattering portrait of himself with a lot of self-deprecating detail. He's *immersed* in their disapproval.

A year earlier, in another oft-quoted excerpt, Vincent wrote to Theo on Friday July 21st, 1882, once again demonstrating the degree to which he'd internalised his sense of alienation – from his family, and the world.

"What am I in the eyes of most people? A nonentity or an oddity or a disagreeable person — someone who has and will have no position in society, in short the lowest of the low. Very well — assuming that everything is indeed like that, then through my work I'd like to show what there is in the heart of such an oddity, such a nobody."

Could it be any clearer that he has no truck what society thinks of him. His answer will come from his art. His art will be his declaration of intent.

"This is my ambition, which is based less on resentment than on love in spite of everything, based more on a feeling of serenity than on passion."

Vincent's not doing this out of reactionary zeal, or pig-headedness, but out of a sense of personal passion, a sense of a real identity rooted in the creative process. He feels – he knows – he has something valuable, something of worth to contribute, and by gum, he does, and he has.

These self-effacing assertions are enormously significant, because it provides us with the first clues to the depths of Vincent's emotional deprivation, and also, just how firmly imbedded, how deeply dug was his resilience, and how far it had to have evolved since then. It all started in Zundert! And the fact that Theodorus died relatively young, at 63, before Vincent could prove or redeem himself, meant the project of becoming an artist of some repute became a lifelong one, welded to Vincent's identity, part of his very being as an artist.

Now, after his father's death, having committed so much, invested so much and lost so much, Vincent had to see it through to the end. He would paint on, tirelessly. He wouldn't quit until he'd received the redemption of the world. He wouldn't stop until he could repair the myriad financial confidences of his brother, and perhaps someday, he would live to feel the blessing of the sun once more upon his derelict shoulders.

Only now do we see how far it went back, the scale of that gritty determination, the scope involved in attempting to turn the turbid waters of Pa's disapproval around. Just as his parents saw ghosts, so did Vincent with his father gone. He was trying to win back the forgiveness of an eternally absent father; he was trying to transform the cruel silence of the wheat fields into something approximating *a man living in sunny harmony with the world.*

In point of fact, Vincent had become inured to rejection by the time he reached his thirties. If he'd absorbed it from his parents, what did it matter what anyone else thought? It wasn't that it didn't *bother* him, he'd simply relocated his locus to some infinite creative reservoir sparking deep inside of himself, and there it could burn bright and hot, far from the madding crowds, unfettered by fashions and the shifting tides of fickle spectators.

This was Vincent transforming his inner countryside, just as it had come naturally to Dutch sensibilities for centuries. It was steering streams of consciousness towards a different way of expressing the world, and oneself in it. If bodies of water could be shifted, just as bodies of blood could be harnessed, so could the faculties of the mind, and of art, if they were allowed to be liquid enough. The ocean itself could be turned on its back, and borne on bright new beaches of glistening consciousness.

And through all this, Vincent imbued the electricity of life, the fear, the pain, the disappointment, and also the joy, as it flowed into the world, as it flowed into him, like carpets of electric flame, transferred to canvas.

*In current day South Africa, where the Cape Colony was a former Dutch colonial outpost, modern efforts are the opposite to those in Holland. If water is still being sequestrated and channelled out of Holland, Cape Town has run out of fresh water, the first major city to experience this catastrophe. Residents have seized on an ingenious solution to the fresh water crisis: to tow water in the form of dislodged icebergs to Cape Town. Since some of these dislodged icebergs have already drifted two-thirds of the distance to Cape Town from the edge of the Antarctic ice shelf, and given how ice-cold surface ocean water is around the Cape Peninsula, the proposal is hardly as farcical as it seems at face value.

"Overzealous" – 1873 - 1878

"One must work and dare if one really wants to live."—Vincent Van Gogh

There's zealous and overzealous. Zealous is the right amount of energy, passion and motivation. Overzealous is the wrong amount, more specifically, too much. Overzealous can also mean:

Fervent

Fanatical

Obsessive

Manic

Overenthusiastic

More words that come to mind are overcompensating, and to over-deliver. In one sense, these traits can be too much in a person we regard as too intense. For the father of expressionism, they're all the ingredients we'd expect. We *expect* to see intensity, vivid color, vital expression, profound feeling.

In order to touch effectively on Vincent's fanatical personality [he wasn't only fervent in his art], let's briefly review Vincent's career choices while simultaneously highlighting the loves of his life during those particular junctures.

Worth playing for?

1873

#1 Art Dealer with Groupil in London/Eugénie Loyer

Family connections set Vincent up in his first gig, as an art dealer for Groupil in Holland. When Vincent completed his internship at twenty years of age, he was transferred to Groupil's branch in London, from The Hague.

It was quite an eye-opener, London was, it was the world's largest city, twice the size of Paris, according to Naifeh-Smith, and very likely an "inconceivable immensity" for a kid used to small-town Holland.

During his first year in Dickensian London, Vincent's earnings eclipsed those of his father. Jo van Gogh, Theo's wife, would later describe this as the best year of Vincent's life. It's unclear what she meant or whether Vincent himself would agree – did best mean successful? Did best mean the year he made the most financially?

In January 1874, Vincent had this to say, to Theo, in a letter from London:

Things are going well for me here, I have a wonderful home and it's a great pleasure for me to observe London and the English way of life and the English themselves, and I also have

nature and art and poetry, and if that isn't enough, what is? Yet I haven't forgotten Holland... We're busy in the office, we're occupied with the inventory...I hope you had a nice Christmas, just as I did...regards to everyone in the office and anyone else who asks after me, particularly...the Haanebeeks.*

In terms of other pursuits, it clearly *wasn't* Vincent's best year. He falls in love with his landlady's daughter, Eugénie Loyer [pronounced "Loyeh", unless corrupted by the English to "lawyer"]. Vincent is so besotted he actually proposes to Eugénie. But she turns him down, in part because she's already engaged to the previous tenant, Samuel Plowman, an engineer. Vincent, fanatical, obsessive, stubborn, refuses to be brushed off and tries to seduce red-haired Eugénie, a young woman who is Vincent's mirror image in not-so good looks, but more important, in temperament.

Eugénie's daughter would describe her mother subsequently as difficult and short-tempered, but witty, an independent woman with a sparkling intelligence. In other words, she could have been Vincent's sister. Eugénie's mother – the landlady, a 58-year-old window, the daughter of a long dead ship captain – isn't impressed by Vincent's lechery, and boots Vincent out of his lodgings.

In April 2014, the *Guardian* covered this aspect of Vincent's adventures in London.

[Vincent] moved in with a widowed landlady, Ursula Loyer, (whose husband had been a French languages professor) and her 19-year-old daughter, Eugénie. The two women ran a school for little boys. And it was in their house that Van Gogh fell in love for the first time.

...in 1914, Van Gogh's sister-in-law, Jo, revealed: "Vincent felt great sympathy for the mother, fell in love with the daughter, Ursula." This slip of the pen (the daughter, remember, was Eugénie) created biographical confusion...

Whether Vincent tried his luck with Ursula, who was gaunt with suffering eyes, or Eugénie, who had a big mouth and even bigger nose, the *Guardian* notes:

Neither woman....is an obvious choice for a sexual obsession. And yet... by 30 March, his 21st birthday, something was wrong. Van Gogh's family sent a box to 87 Hackford Road, containing cake, chocolate and six pairs of cufflinks, on receipt of which he scribbled uncharacteristically brief thanks. The tenancy was ending in mysterious difficulty...

There's no doubt Vincent had a thing for the daughter, but based on what came about after, it's understandable that people would wonder. They do now, despite the facts, but then it was a great deal worse. Vincent's sister Anna also visited London and took piano lessons in the Loyer home; it's through her that we get absolute clarity on the target of Vincent's focused but unfortunate first infatuation.

The *Guardian* continues:

After his departure, his family reported that his mood was sombre. His mother told Theo on 15 August 1874: "Vincent will also not have had it easy at the Loyers's...he will surely have been disappointed by them and his illusions will not have been realised – real life is different from what one imagines." His sister [Anna] goes further, saying that whenever people fail to live up to [Vincent's] illusions, he is so disappointed that he "throws them away like a bouquet of wilted flowers".

We too may be inclined to brush these anecdotes aside, to throw them away like an unwanted bouquet. What we see here is the very earliest indication of Vincent's raw idealism. Unused to the world, especially now the world's capital, he sees the world as simpler and better than it is, and himself as more idealized than he is, and others better than they are. Imagination meets reality and the young man is sorely disappointed with the real world. It's all so...*Dickensian*, isn't it? Reality is disappointing. The people who occupy it are disappointing too. Things don't unfold as he imagines. So he turns to books for inspiration. Vincent does a lot of reading, immersing himself in the fabric of Dickens – not just the words, but the illustrations. It's here, perhaps, that Vincent is inspired to write and illustrate, this is the seed of those hundreds of letters to Theo: Dickens.

A good story may be a solace, an escape from real life [just as a good work of art may be]. But real life doesn't work as it does in fiction, or on the canvas of the Impressionist – it's uglier, it doesn't obey the rules, it doesn't do as it's told. Things don't necessary go your way, or end well. Unknown things go on beyond the safe perspective of the frame.

Vincent's disillusionment at home in London soon infects his work. He soon finds himself critical of the manner in which Groupil commodifies art. It's unclear why; perhaps it was the mass production of certain works into prints, or cards. Whatever it was, Vincent found it soulless, even if he was earning a handsome packet from participating in it. And here again we see his idealism burning through, making the angry young man inclined to throw away his work like yet another irritating bouquet.

I know when I visited London for the first time, I was surprised by how secular it was, that in spite of its many magnificent cathedrals, many were empty, and people I encountered had no need of it. I too found this secularism disheartening, initially at any rate. According to the Guardian, in 1950 Arthur and Marjorie Smith bought the house that was once Vincent's home. Even today it's dark and damp setting, but in his letters, Vincent clearly approved of his first digs.

"I now have a room such as I always longed for without a slanting ceiling and without blue paper with a green border."

Well, in Auvers, at the end of his life, he'd be back under a slanting attic ceiling once more, and he'd die under it.

I stand at the top of the house and try to imagine him immersed in English literature as Olde Wolbers tells me he was reading George Eliot and Keats [and Dickens] and beginning to form his delicately complicated view of love: "What kind of love did I feel when I was 20... my physical passions were very weak then, perhaps because of a few years of great poverty and hard work. But my intellectual passions were strong, meaning that without wanting any pity, I wanted only to give, but not to receive. Foolish, wrong, exaggerated, proud, rash – for in love one must not only give, but also take."

In this too, Vincent reveals how he martyred himself not only in art, but also in love, and not only in love, but in life. Besides this, he describes his passion in his early 20's as being more intellectual than physical. That's saying something about his intellectual interests and pursuits. If we're not sure exactly what it means, well, Vincent cared so much about intellectual things, he allowed himself to be booted out of the best job he'd ever have soon after being booted out of his home for daring to love.

There is much more to say about this opening chapter, the opening salvo effectively in Vincent's battle to find his place in the world. He had just seventeen years to make his mark, and he did, but this first mark well and truly set the tone. It really deserves its own narrative, a distinct *Portrait of the Artist as a Young Man*, standing apart so as to fully explicate** the mysterious *Who* of Vincent van Gogh. Perhaps, if this narrative does its duty, such a narrative will follow. Otherwise, the reader is advised to browse Naifeh-Smith's *Van Gogh: The Life,* focusing on chapters six to twenty-nine.

Meanwhile, let's move on.

April 1876

#2 Supply Teacher [Unpaid]/Ramsgate & Isleworth

In 1875 Theodorus and Cent, Vincent's uncle, sensing a decline in his work [besides the fact that Vincent hadn't written home in two months] had the young man transferred against his wishes to Groupil's Paris office, a path Theo would follow nine years later. Vincent was furious. Such meddling! His father replied that Cent had approached *him* with the idea, not the other way round.

Less than a year later, Vincent was fired. The reason? In his loneliness and woundedness, he'd found solace in religion. His spending the busy Christmas season at home was given as the official reason for his dismissal, effective on April 1st.

That Vincent surfed his victimhood all the way back to London, provides some idea of how invested he was in London to begin with. He arrived back in England in mid-April 1876, happy to take on the lowly position of volunteer supply teacher offered by one William Stokes at a small boarding school in the English seaside town, population 12 000, of Ramsgate.

Once there he posted Theo a sliver of seaweed. By the end of May Vincent seemed to be seeing color in his world:

The sea was yellowish, especially close to the shore. On the horizon a streak of light and above it immensely large dark grey clouds…[and] rain coming down in slanting streaks. The wind blew the dust from the little white path among the rocks…and shook the hawthorn bushes in bloom…To the right, fields of young green corn, and in the distance the town…with its towers, mills, slate roofs… I watched the sea last Sunday night as well. Everything was dark grey, but on the horizon the day was beginning to break. It was still very early and yet a skylark was already singing…

One has the impression when the weather cleared, and the sun basked the sands of Ramsgate, Vincent saw himself holidaying with the English, putting on bathing suits and plunging into the summer surf with them, just as he did with Eugénie and Anna, during their summer holidays together.

But that paradise was well and truly lost. The reality was that in Ramsgate, Vincent was living in a moth-eaten house with rotten floorboards and broken windows. Perfectly Dickensian!

In June, at the height of summer, Vincent's school uprooted and moved to London. Well, perhaps Vincent hoped to find his way back to his city of dreams. On several occasions he'd walked 50 miles [80 kilometers, that's two marathons back to back] from Ramsgate to London, and presumably back again, treks Naifeh-Smith describe as "the longest…journeys [during] his time in England".

Vincent called these treks "quite a stroll" when he wrote about them to Theo.

When another friend – whom he'd met in Paris through Groupil, an oddball and an outcast with the strangely affirmative name of Gladwell – lost his seventeen-year-old sister in a horse-riding fall, Vincent walked from Isleworth [a London suburb] to Lewisham [18.6 miles/30 kilometers] on the day of the funeral.

To appreciate what was happening in Vincent's inner world just then, his letter to Theo from Isleworth on August 18th, 1876, only four months into his new career, provides ample evidence of his newfound religious zeal. The letter refers to the horse-riding incident and the funeral, but then, more troublingly, luxuriates – marinates – in a kind of "blessed" mournfulness.

They had all just come back from the funeral, it was a real house of mourning and it did me good to be there. I had feelings of embarrassment and shame at seeing that deep, admirable grief…Blessed are they that mourn, blessed are they that are 'sorrowful, yet always rejoicing', blessed are the pure in heart, for God comforts the simple. Blessed are they that find Love on their path, who are bound intimately with one another by God…

And so it goes on, eventually entire letters to his family [impatiently discarded like unwanted bouquets] will be devoted to sermonising. But in this one is a warning about who Vincent wants to be, and how he sees himself. He wants to set himself up as a saviour, as a comforter, not to the avant-garde or even the bourgeois, but to the everyman.

...it must be good to be the brother of the man I saw so sorrowful yesterday, I mean that it must 'be blessed to mourn' with manly sorrow, how I'd have liked to comfort the Father, but I was embarrassed... There was something hallowed in that house yesterday.

When Stokes, William's boss, proposed a transfer to Isleworth, board and lodging but without pay, Vincent baulked. He decided to pursue something in the line of a clergyman, but beggars can't be choosers, and in July, Vincent ended up at *another* school in Isleworth, and moved house again, this time to Holme court. His new employer was one Reverend Thomas Slade-Jones.

Slade-Jones wanted Vincent to travel extramurally, into London to tutor sick children, and children whose parents had fallen behind in their school fees – it was perfect! This took Vincent through some of the poorest, the most Dickensian parts of London. His route, incidentally, would also take him through the world's largest agglomeration of street workers [hookers].

Vincent would later write of this time trudging the sweaty alleys by day, the gas lit streets of the world's capital by night, as a time of great shame, inadequacy and unworthiness. As young as he was, he wished to cleanse himself of the sins of his youth. In the misery of his self-flagellating long walks, he wandered the psychological road of the martyr. This was his self-inflicted purgatory, his punishment for being as unworthy as he was, and his road to Damascus, and the light.

Vincent hated his life, and felt tremendous guilt. But he wasn't a tortured man, and he wouldn't become a tortured artist because he was mad. He was tortured for a more terrible reason – he was unloved, and felt himself unlovable.

We may cast about for reasons, but they're right in front of us. Vincent's rejection of himself was simply an expansion of the rejection he felt in his own home, under the cold Calvinist doctrine of his own parents. His repeated attempts to initiate impossible relationships, to embark on doomed relationships with women who'd already given their hearts to others, were an effort to heal that childhood trauma, to overturn that immense burden of not being worthy of love. Could he prove that he was? If he could change the heart or mind of one woman who didn't care for him, would that save him? More than likely, the moment a woman did accept him, he'd reject her, because what he wanted was the same cycle, the same overturning of the burden until the world had deemed him lovable, or he'd deemed himself a lovable asset to the world.

The psychologist and author, David Hosier, provides prescient insight into this well-known condition, at childhoodtraumarecovery.com:

It has been hypothesized (originally by Freud, but also by much more recent researchers) that if we suffer a terrible trauma in childhood, such as parental rejection, we will (on an unconscious level) be compelled to put ourselves through similar experiences in adulthood...by engineering situations in which we are bound to be rejected again...or by behaving in such a manner that forces the other person to reject us. Why should we be unconsciously driven to behave in such a self-destructive and [despairing] manner? A leading theory (again, originating from Freud but endorsed by later researchers) is that we are unconsciously attempting to gain mastery over such trauma.

By mastery Hosier means we want to get over ourselves, or rather, over the pain of our past selves. And so we gravitate back to crisis, to recreate and to transform ourselves through catharsis. The more we repeat this cycle, the more the original pain. From this we can see that it was profoundly painful for Vincent, who within the blink of an eye, went from having the world at his feet, to losing it, and really, he only had himself to blame, which only made the narrative – Vincent's self-styled cross – harder to bear.

July 1876

#3 Assistant Clergyman/Isleworth

Soon after attending the reception of the Gladwell funeral in August, Vincent spent the remaining five months of the year working as an assistant to a Methodist minister. During this time he was immersed in the works of, and inspired by, George Eliot [AKA Mary Anne Evans]. Eliot/Evans wrote about social outsiders in a rural setting, and the value and beauty to be found in the mundane details of country living, and peasant societies.

Eliot's *Felix Holt* presents the heroic model of a man of privilege who abandons his legacy to preach among the working class. In this, the hero alchemises the popular idea of failure. It's heroism as a self-sacrificing martyr.

Naifeh-Smith hit the nail on the head in their psychological assessment of Vincent at this juncture, in their assessment that "no one…needed the balm of religion more than Vincent." And that where Vincent recognized the "longing" among the folks eeking a living in the gutters of the world's capital, it was a mirror to his own longing, and his own trips through the same gutters.

But Naifeh-Smith are also missing the point, and perhaps mishitting the nail. If Vincent needed balm, it wasn't that of religion he needed, but self-discovery. Religion can contrive to place a barrier between young men and experience, and young men and the world, and young men and women, and Vincent had had enough of barriers, strings, conscriptions and rules, although he didn't know it then, and he didn't know which barriers were depriving him of life per se. All he knew was the reality of his deprivation.

What he wanted was salvation, a way through, a way to save himself, a way to redeem himself, but more than that, to *find* himself, and to do that he would need to *escape* himself, or rather, *find his way away* from the indoctrinated self, to his authentic self.

That may sound easy, but it's a little like being in Holland surrounding by water, and murk, and being given just a glimpse of somewhere drier and brighter, but that's all. Getting there isn't going to be easy; adapting to an entirely new way of "seeing the light" when you've grown up in the dark, well that's well-nigh impossible.

Vincent was hardly an original in his religious zeal in 1876. London was awash with it, and Vincent simply got swept up by the tide.

Vincent was sketching a little at the time, though his efforts of the churches at Petersham and Turnham Green were amateurish, and pun intended, nothing to write home about.

On October 31st, Vincent wrote to Theo regaling his brother with news of his first sermon. Oddly enough, Vincent described this experience, of preaching, as similar to "someone emerging from a dark vault underground into the friendly light of day…"

It wasn't the light of the Lord that was shining in his heart, however, it was the newfound sense of personal mission, and even more, Vincent's sense of significance, that had made his world into a brighter place. Insignificance is humiliating, it's the opposite of life, and love. Insignificance is withdrawal, contraction, a shrinking away from life. It's a living death. No wonder the pulpit felt like he was coming alive, and living again. This was a breakthrough in that Vincent had found his calling in life – not so much to preach in a church, but to express deeply held feeling, to reach out to strangers, and effect to touch and be touched by them.

He wasn't a tortured man because he was mad. He was tortured, driven mad, because he was unloved.

January 1877

#4 Working in a Bookshop/Dordrecht

Vincent visited his parents that Christmas. They'd moved from Zundert, in the far south, near the coast, about 100 miles [170 kilometers] inland to the tiny hamlet of Etten, on the Eastern border with Germany.

Naifeh-Smith suggest Vincent may have returned home under the illusion that he was the Prodigal Son who still expect to enjoy the good graces of his kin. Instead they "reproached" him. To outsiders this may seem a logical response, but if one recalls Vincent's own father was a pastor, and now his son showed real interest in the same vocation, the family's disapproval seems somewhat hypocritical, doesn't it? Surely there was a sense of conflictedness in them, *shouldn't* they support Vincent in his religious fervour?

Naifeh-Smith describe Vincent and his family spending Christmas Day with Uncle Cent that year, the same uncle that had set him up at Groupil months earlier. That had to have been awkward. Far from returning to a hero's welcome, Vincent was now very much the black sheep of the family; the disgraced first born unable to find his way in life.

For reasons unknown, Vincent's father simply couldn't imagine his shy, anti-social son following in his own footsteps. That may be because he suspected Vincent didn't have the work ethic for the job [in terms of the eight years of study required, for starters], or perhaps

Theodorus guessed that Vincent lacked the conviction. It may be that Theodorus didn't want his son besmirching his own spotless reputation, thereby contaminating his congregations, and so preferred his son to seek his fortune elsewhere. Such as…in a bookstore in Dordrecht.

Incredibly, that's exactly what Vincent did. In spite of his overzealous attitude to serving God and the destitute, Vincent was convinced by his family to cast aside his foolish pursuits, and head to Dordrecht to begin a new life doing the relatively safe work of book selling, in the relative safety of a town that placed Vincent simultaneously at an arm's length from the Van Gogh's, and close enough to be supervised [that is, controlled and kept in check].

Naifeh-Smith describe Vincent accepting his parents' new instructions not to return to England, and to give up his religious calling with "uncharacteristic meekness"; adding that guilt lay behind his quick turnaround. It also indicates how shallow Vincent's sense of self was, and perhaps why that was: his parents told him what to do, and what to think, and so his identity was very poorly formed. His propensity to shrink from the world into books, and into religion, didn't improve his experience of the world either, let alone his prospects of finding his place in the world.

We see here how his parents, in their efforts to control him, were also frustrating him in his effort to find his way. By setting him up yet again in a job they found suitable, [Uncle Cent was involved in this career choice too] Vincent wasn't learning to find his own way, he was, like a lost stream of water flowing somewhere through Holland, he was being recollected and *shown* the way. He was being given a role by society, and he was expected to fulfil it.

Naifeh-Smith choose the apposite term for this phase of Vincent's life – *dutifulness*. Although it's the last word we'd associate with Vincent on this side of history, that's a mistake. He *was* a dutiful son, and even in his religious work to follow, as he was in his art work, he remained a dutiful, conscientious type of person. Think about that word in the context of his letters to Theo, and preparing a room years later for Gauguin, and for admitting himself into an asylum.

Just days after Christmas, Vincent headed off to embark on yet another "new life", this time, back in Holland, at the *Blussé & Van Braam Booksellers* on Dordrecht's busy market square. Since his possessions were still in England, Vincent had to have the trunk sent to his new address, a boarding house just across from the square where he worked. From there he also had to write to Slade-Jones to explain why he wasn't returning. It served as an explanation to himself as well.

In March 8th, Vincent wrote to his uncle expressing gratitude.

It was a wonderful day when Pa was here recently; we took a walk together and also went to the museum to see the paintings by Scheffer. I'm doing well here, at the beginning of the year there's a lot of work in the shop, so I'm there until 12 or 1 o'clock at night. I'm happy to be back in Holland, only I loved the work over there – even with all the trouble and deep disappointment connected with it – and continue to do so, and the disappointment and, for once, relative failure make me deeply attached to it.

He also refers to Anna looking for and finding work.

If it's all right with you that Theo and I come next Sunday...

Your loving nephew

Vincent

But if it seemed Vincent was settled, and about to live happily ever after, he wasn't. In his boarding house he lived like a recluse, spending all his time translating the Bible, and becoming even more pious. Soon his piety began to affect his diet and lifestyle, as Vincent avoided meat and lived a life of thrift, a habit that would serve him well till his dying day.

April 1877

#5 Failure as a missionary student/Amsterdam

One can see why working in a bookstore made sense. Vincent was a bookworm. He loved to read and for that matter, write. And yet, despite the all-is-well tone in the letter to his uncle, Vincent wanted more out of life. He wanted to be more, do more, give more. It didn't take long for the opportunity to jump the bookseller ship to present itself.

Four months after starting work at *Blussé & Van Braam*, Vincent borrowed money from his boarding-house mate Paulus van Görlitz, to attend a funeral with his father in Zundert. Vincent's return to Zundert for the funeral coincided with a trip through the memory lanes of his own childhood. He visited with the former servants of their household, and in speaking to them, found his long-dead memories resurrected, and vivid.

Just as the Gladwell funeral had a profound and life-changing impact, so did the death of an old farmer, a former member of Theodorus's church flock. Seeing his father minister to the grieving family, a tower of strength and comfort, authoritative and kind, providing solace, and all this happening over Easter [in terms of Resurrection, the most symbolic event on the Christian calendar] it steered Vincent back towards resurrecting himself, and reviving his sense of mission, a return to the intensity of life-and-death meaningfulness, and so, yes, back to God.

This time, witnessing the impact of a grieving family and the graveyard on his son, Theodorus elected to support Vincent. He was allowed to quit his work at the bookstore and move in with his uncle, Johannes Stricker, who was a theologian based in Amsterdam.

With his family's blessing, Vincent was all-in. He prepared for the University of Amsterdam's entrance exam in theology. He was going to be his father's son after all, following in his footsteps. Except, Vincent failed the exams. His family had been right all along – he wasn't cut out to be a pastor, he especially wasn't cut out for the training required to become one.

In July 1878 Vincent moved out of Uncle Stricker's home, but if his family had lost confidence in him, or his quest, he hadn't. If his ego was shaken, and it was, his mind turned to comforting, reinforcing preoccupations. The symbolism of reaping and sowing, of planting and harvesting, of soulful investment and everlasting fruitfulness. Vincent had grown up on a household where troubles could be cured through prayer, so why not solve his real world issues the same way?

Except the troubles persisted, and along with it, the humiliating guilt. By August, feeling he deserved punishment for his failure, he did what all fervent believers do – he punished *himself* [another word being 'martyred' himself] by eating only bread, and consuming coffee and tobacco. Occasionally he left his quarters to sleep in a shed on the ground. All this self-imposed deprivation and mental anguish led to a mental breakdown, his first.

His letters show clear signs of mental disturbance as well, far more than those written from Saint-Rémy ten years later.

He also wrote, on August 18th, of breakfasting on beer and bread as a remedy against suicide, at least, according to Charles Dickens.

...got up early and [saw] the workers arriving at the dockyard with the sun shining wonderfully... [painting] the curious sight...of black figures...streaming into the narrow street into which the sun shines only briefly and later at the yard. Had breakfast afterwards, a piece of dry bread and a glass of beer – that is a remedy Dickens recommends to those on the verge of committing suicide...and being effective at ridding them of that intention, for a while at least.

Well, it was a remedy that evidently worked for him in the late summer of 1877. What's abundantly clear here, is Vincent's propensity to punish himself for falling short. But he does so not through actual self-harm, not through inflicting a blade against his flesh, but through toil, through hardship, through suffering. What's more, he communicates his intentions around these disturbing issues to his family.

Late 1878

#6 Failure as a missionary student/Laken

Vincent did a three-month course at a Protestant missionary school in Laken, not far from Brussels, the Belgian capital. Vincent, 24 years old at the time, failed that too. He failed to sow the seeds of his own idealism, and so, there was nothing to reap in the desert of the real.

In just five years Vincent had squandered virtually all his family's faith in him, including that of his extended family. It had also cost the family dearly to finance Vincent's various career changes, never mind endure the embarrassment of his failure to take flight, to finally launch his life force into the world.

These failures were important, because they gave Vincent exactly what he'd needed all along, the possibility of self-determination. Through this, Vincent would fail even more spectacularly, and then, he'd only have himself to blame.

There's critical insight to examine right here: when Vincent felt supremely guilty for winning the trust of his family, and then squandering it, he was in the habit of imposing on himself an adequate punishment. Thus we see in this twin failures, in 1877, and 1878, Vincent not only taking on the role of martyr, but also, *getting used to* the idea of failure and the experience of misery, including that of self-imposed suffering. If we are to understand the events, and Vincent's reactions, in Arles in 1880, and Auvers, in 1890, we have our psychological precedent right here.

Sidenote from South Africa, circa 1991 - 2000

I identify deeply with this phase of Vincent's life, because I lived it too, almost 120 years later, in South Africa. It's a period where, as Naifeh-Smith put it, one's terror of failure exists side-by-side with a desperation to succeed. One battles illusions, delusions, shifting perceptions and reality, including – and especially – of oneself, simultaneously.

In my case I *knew* I wasn't sure what I wanted to do, or be, and this translated to my studies. What I wanted to do during my first year out of school, two years after my mother's suicide, and immediately following my military service, was to take a year out travelling and just get settled psychologically. My inner reservoirs had been depleted not just by her death, but by years of bullying during high school. I needed my own space and a little time to recharge, to return my capacities and capabilities to a healthy level. I needed to become a happier person again.

My father thought by telling me what to do, I'd find direction, but what I really needed was the opposite – more experience with the world, and in the world, to find out who I was and what I wanted, and to extricate myself from a compromised state. Clearly, some people can be shown a door, or a path, and they can go through it and walk on it for the rest of their lives. I wasn't one of those people.

Since my father was holding the purse strings, and wouldn't allow a year off, goofing around, I suddenly had to make a rush choice. Which university course should I do? I had about two months to submit my application.

My first choice was law, inspired by American depictions on television, and in John Grisham's books, of justice as heroic, charming, challenging and even glamorous, this in spite of the fact that in Apartheid South Africa, the law seemed more a hypothetical concept than something one could, or would want to, really invest oneself in.

Incidentally, my interest in law, as a concept, and my disinterest in law within the South African context remains pretty much the same now as it was then. In the same way, Vincent's first choice, to study as an art dealer, was ultimately the right path for him, certainly better than the paths that diverted afterward, but if it was right, it wasn't *quite* right.

Art was the right area, creating art was how he needed to execute his interest within that area. In my case, law was the right area, but how I needed to execute my interest within that area in a way that was viable, was to write about it through true crime narratives directed towards an overseas audience.

Drilling down into the details, I suppose on my journey to self-actualisation, like Vincent, I struggled in most areas, persisted in others, and thrived in very few. During my first five years at university I went from law, to increasingly what my father demanded I do – Quantity Surveying – and then back to what seemed practical, a commercial degree. It was a constant pendulum swing trying to find a workable solution and trying not to waste time, money or anyone's patience. Over each passing year, the credit I had with my own family, especially my father, diminished, just as Vincent's evaporated with his. Each year of failure conveyed me towards a better, stronger position in terms of knowing what I didn't want, or couldn't do. Of course, to everyone else it appeared the other way round – that you increasingly don't seem to know what you're doing.

With law, although I enjoyed it, I couldn't master Latin*** [a subject that's since been struck from the syllabus]. I'm not bad at languages, but unlike my fellow students, I didn't have Latin at school, and to be fair, if I had more time to choose my direction, I'd probably have found a way to avoid a course with Latin. It wasn't just Latin though. Although I enjoyed Law, there was a lingering sense from lawyers I spoke to during my first year, that they *hated* their work, and hated who they had become because of it. Books like John Grisham's *The Rainmaker* seemed to confirm this sense that an idealistic lawyer had no place in the real world of lawyering, especially not in the legal black comedy that is South Africa.

Besides Latin, I *enjoyed* studying law, and the idea of it, but when I quit the course at the end of the year, having passed almost all the subjects, my father once again baulked at the idea of travelling to set my mind right. Even then, I felt I needed a timeout to figure things out. But he knew better; he basically frogmarched me into studying what he studied, Quantity Surveying. The course load was crippling, one of the toughest university degrees after medicine. This time the rogue subject I couldn't hack was accounting. Like Latin, it wasn't necessarily difficult, just stupendously dull. I was 20-years-old; I decided it was time to grow-up and *apply myself*, and that included applying myself to things I had no aptitude for, and no interest in. Work is work, I reasoned, you can use what you earn for play. Work shouldn't be enjoyable, and one could find areas of fulfilment in it, didn't everyone?

Just apply yourself...

I "applied" myself to Quantity Surveying for three long years. I did fairly well, just not in accounting or the main subject itself. I loved, for example, the History of Architecture and

Commercial Law, I enjoyed Marketing, even became quite interested in Economics, Physics and Statistics. I made stuttering progress in Applied Maths.

My father showed very little interest in me during this period, which surprised me. Like my older brother and younger sister, I thought I was being set-up to work in the building industry, in which he'd established a strong reputation and a successful business. Eventually I saw the light and announced another change, if I was going to be a businessman it clearly wasn't going to happen in the construction industry.

The good news was, my massive course load in QS had earned me a bunch of credits I could put to good use in a slew of other, alternative degrees. Unfortunately, changing to a B.COM meant dragging accounting with it.

Just apply yourself...

But no amount of tutoring, or focus could slay the accounting dragon. In the end, to extricate myself from its curse, I made one more, final change, to a B.ECON. That's the degree I eventually got, along with a few distinctions, but not before leaving the country for two years, for the same place Vincent visited – London.

When I returned I knew who I was and who I wanted to be. I'd been healed, heartbroken and rehabilitated into the world, all at the same time. It was the baptism of fire I needed. When I returned, in the same year I got my degree [and more distinctions] I also got a post graduate diploma in marketing. That was a revelation; I sailed through the course, effortlessly eclipsing my peers in creative and strategic thinking, and amazed myself that I was actually good for something in the academic sense. At the end of the year I was given something of an accolade, I interned at The Jupiter Drawing Room, South Africa's most creative advertising agency in Cape Town.

None of it mattered, though, because by 2000 if you had a white skin, were male, and had an Afrikaans sounding name, you weren't going to be offered a job in Post-Apartheid South Africa [and that remains true 20 years later]. Besides that, I worked through a small fortune in family money spent on a decades-long education [equivalent, arguably, to a doctorate].

I'd also used up all my credit at home. And there was little goodwill left, I found, in my South African countrymen. So I headed back overseas, and worked for almost five years teaching English in South Korea. There I started blogging, and then started committing acts of journalism and progressively, photojournalism.

So much for the conscientious pursuit of law, or the ideal of working alongside your father and conquering the world, or getting a business degree, or working in advertising and everything else. When my last contract ended in South Korea, I did not renew it. I'd had enough. I wanted to do something more meaningful and challenging than teach English as a second language for the rest of my life. But I did not want to return to South Africa either, fearing continued unemployment.

Eventually, and this is cutting the original story very short, I found a way to employing myself fulltime, as a writer, writing about criminal law, and mountaineering, and occasionally art, from the rich literal substrate of one of the most corrupt, unequal and tragic society's in the world. Like Holland several centuries earlier, South Africa today is drowning, but not in seawater, in its own bitterness and uneducated ignorance and nonsense. Instead of constructing windmills to channel water out, the people here build dams to drown its people in it.

Yet in another sense, South Africa is like anywhere else in the world, either you adapt, or you die. When the world, or one's country, feels turned against you, it's a precarious life, and very easy to sink in it, to drown in it. Sink or swim. Over the years, as a fulltime writer, I've nearly drowned many times in the interminable wash and rinse of this country, as it seeks to wring itself dry from the past. Each attempt to avoid its history comes with a fresh deluge of guilt and blame, so the struggle to keep one's head above water is ongoing.

As I say, I identify deeply with Vincent's tragic story. I hope it's clear that sharing my story is more than mere self-indulgence, it illustrates the complex of fluctuating motives and intentions a young person may face as they seek to find their first, firm foothold in the world.

Primary among these for me, as it was for Vincent, was establishing an identity. It's important to understand that the individual, the family, the community and society are complicit in this failure. It takes a village to raise a child, but it also takes a village to fail in this enterprise. Vincent's identity had been usurped by domineering parents and a culture of rules and roles. The artist as a young man had also given up the project of "finding himself", through repeated escapes into books, including the bible.

The only way to know the world, and your place in it, is by stepping in it. And so, when he was 25, Vincent did exactly that, but this time, with no safety net.

*This reference to the Haanebeeks is not incidental. Vincent had stayed with the family during his work for Groupil at The Hague. It's commonly believed Vincent was in love with Carolina Haanebeek – she married Willem van Stockum that same year [1873]. Interestingly, Theo soon after fell in love with Carolina's sister Annet [who died in 1875], causing much grief, or as Vincent put it 'melancholy', for Theo.

**In the penultimate chapter, *Finding Vincent*, an additional titbit from Vincent's formative year in the world's largest city, with the Loyer family, is provided to further fine-tune this sketch of the artist's fundamental psychology.

***Vincent couldn't master Greek during his preparations for his theology entrance exams. He prayed for deliverance, but somehow, was still allowed to fail. Naifeh-Smith describe Vincent "lamenting" his decision then, to abandon his work at Groupil. "If I had only given all my strength to it [being an art dealer at Groupil] before…"

Into the Borinage, then on to Antwerp – 1879 - 1887

"I wish they would only take me as I am." —Vincent Van Gogh

1880 – Autumn – The House at Cuesmes

What Vincent needed to find his way, to become his own man, was to be allowed the time and space to make his own mistakes. We learn by doing, and we learn quickly and urgently when what we do is blunder spectacularly, as Vincent was about to do.

Sometimes when we blunder a little, we can recover the little ground we've lost. But Vincent didn't want that, he wanted to dare greatly, to risk all. Blundering badly early on in life can lead to lifelong catastrophe, and for Vincent, it did. What he was about to lose, the world would eventually gain, through the gift of his art, a legacy of sublime revelation, or even transcendence.

Transcendence is word seldom used, and seldom understood. Even in hindsight, we need to spend some time familiarising ourselves with the innards of toil and hardship, to understand how Vincent transcended these. Significantly, we begin this journey towards a state of grace, otherworldliness, wholeness, a state of perfection, by entering the world at its bleakest, dirties and hardest: we must venture with Vincent down into the coal mines, joining him in his purifying fellowship with the sooty faced mineworkers of the Borinage.

January 1879

#7 Lay preacher/Borinage, Belgium

In 1879 and 1880, Vincent's ruin basically ran its course. During this period, essentially Vincent's 7th career change in five years, Vincent – now a lay missionary ministering to sick and injured miners – wrote letters from Petit-Wasmes to Theo, occasionally sketching the scenes underground.

None of these drawings were art, or really part of his archive, *per se*, but it did serve as Vincent's psychological training ground. His letters during this period were also barely readable, because Vincent had become so consumed by religious fervor. But if Vincent was becoming lost in one sense, he was transforming in another. He was being *trained to endure* what would be his last ten years of remaining life, but more significantly, he was being prepared to *see the world in a different way* – the world at night, the world inside a mine, the world of blood, sweat and unseen tears, the world inside the world…

In February 2015, the *Washington Post* provided deeper, and darker insight into this period of Vincent's life.

In a letter to Theo, Vincent wrote: "I went on a very interesting excursion not long ago; the fact is, I spent six hours in a mine, in one of the oldest and most dangerous mines in the area, no less." And on this winter day in the 125th anniversary year of the great artist's death, I'm gaping at the mine's remains, listening to a recording of the letter.

Vincent enjoys the fact, as some young men do, of danger and adventure, in his work. There is excitement in his going down a dark road, literally, and allowing himself to face his fears, and the all fearsomeness the world has in store for him. He *wants* exposure to it. He wants a first-hand experience of the dirt of the world on his skin, the company of people bent over in physical toil, rubbing against his own shoulders. He wants to feel alive in a living world, a world made all the more alive by the threat of disease and death.

...my guide through Belgium's Borinage region, less than 60 miles southwest of Brussels, adjusts his audio player as the recorded voice cuts through the stillness with Vincent's words...

Just as the reporter in 2015 was on a journey of exploration, fascinated by the devastation wreaked on a life, Vincent in 1879 was on a similar journey towards reality, captivated by the holocaust that was the daily grind for these unfortunate peasants.

"At first sight everything around it has something dismal and deathly about it. The workers are emaciated and pale due to fever, and they look exhausted and haggard, weather-beaten and prematurely old...All around the mine are poor miners' dwellings with a couple of dead trees, completely black from the smoke, and thorn-hedges, dung-heaps and rubbish dumps, mountains of unusable coal and Maris would make a beautiful painting of it." (Vincent was referring to the Dutch painter Jacob Maris.)

In the Borinage, Vincent drifted through cauldrons of subterranean grief, and soon recognized the need for solace, a need that resonated so deeply, it became permanently etched into him.

While Vincent's heart bled for the peasants, so much so that he gave up his comfortable accommodations and possessions to live like them, and amongst them. But starchy church officials didn't see it that way. Vincent wasn't a character in a Charles Dickens book, or part of some elegant, affirming plot by George Eliot. They saw him as a smelly, homeless person no better than those labouring in squalid conditions. He was fired for undermining the dignity of his profession. Vincent walked 47 miles [75 kilometers] to Brussels, and eventually, due to mounting pressure from his parents, returned home once again under the vast thundercloud of disgrace.

Interestingly, during Vincent's sojourn at home in Etten, Vincent's father suggested he be committed to an asylum. This set the precedent in everyone's mind, including Vincent's, that he wasn't merely overzealous or troubled, he was mad. Within eight years, Vincent would take his father's diagnosis to heart.

Whatever Theodorus said, or threatened, however, Vincent didn't go to the asylum. Instead, he did what had started to come naturally now, and something even Theo had begun to encourage: Vincent began to draw and then paint.

August 1880

#8 Amateur artist/Cuesmes

In Simon Schama's *Power of Art*, he mentions Vincent "picking up a brush for the first time" at about 30 years of age, and then going on to produce incredible art. Strictly speaking, that's not entirely accurate. Vincent had been drawing on-and-off for years, first as a youth, encouraged by his mother, then, through the course of many letters, encouraged by his brother. It was something he seemed to do naturally, for fun, impulsively.

From 1880 onwards, Vincent's art would become a compulsion, like everything else. Given what Vincent had gone through, and what he expected of himself, and what his family expected of him, his intensity is more the stuff of a dutiful son trying to redeem himself, than a madman.

So it's not true that Vincent picked up a paint brush and basically executed masterpieces from the get go. After making a complete mess of life and career through his early and mid-twenties, Vincent spent five years training, applying himself, to become a professional artist. At the end of that period, shortly after his father's death in 1885, he produced his first masterpiece: *The Potato Eaters*. The point is it took Vincent five years of study to do it. It wasn't that Vincent couldn't apply himself, he, like most people, just needed to find something he was good at, and that was art.

At the end of 1880, Theo persuaded Vincent to study under the mentorship of Willem Roelofs, a Dutch artist. Vincent was opposed to art as a formal discipline, but he was maturing in his passionate view of the world, and Theo was able to talk his older brother into attending classes on anatomy, modelling and perspective at the Académie Royale des Beaux-Arts, an art school in Brussels.

Even so, mastery didn't come easy; it never does, not even to masters. In 1881, and for the foreseeable future, Vincent was stuck in the dark Dutch mentality, executing art in varying shades of manure brown and unpeeled potato yellow. It was a pointless education in the age of Impressionism, but in another sense, no failure is entirely pointless, and if anyone could turn the waters of failure into wine, and change the ocean of consciousness, Vincent could, because he was living it.

April 1881

#9 Amateur artist/Etten/Cornelia "Kee" Vos-Stricker

Now, for the umpteenth time, Vincent returned home to pick himself up by his bootstraps and make something of himself. This was hard to do given the low opinion his parents, and family, had of him at this stage. Cloaked in failure as he was after eight years of struggle, everything he did seemed to be a bad idea, but who could blame them for thinking that?

In August of that year, as if to rub it in everyone's noses, Vincent fell in love with his cousin Kee Vos, the newly divorced daughter of his pastor Uncle, Johannes Stricker. Kee

Vos was a single-mother with an eight-year-old son. She was also in her mid-thirties, seven years older than Vincent. He didn't have a hope of maintaining her, let alone her son.

Vincent's infatuation didn't go down well with anyone, including Kee Vos herself. When Vincent went so far as to propose marriage, she replied: "Nooit, neen, nimmer."

Her father was galled by Vincent's cheek, and so were his parents. It was all anyone could do to keep Vincent's lovelorn exploits from scandalising the family, by gossiping congregants.

November 1881

#10 Internship Anton Mauve/Amsterdam/Clasina Maria "Sien" Hoornik

With Kee Vos, Vincent didn't simply take no for an answer. Well, he was overzealous wasn't he, through and through. He continued to send her letters, causing her parents, the Strickers to write to the Van Goghs, chastising young Vincent for his disgusting persistence.

When Kee Vos went to Amsterdam, Vincent followed. She had no wish to see him. This led to the story where, in desperation, Vincent offered to put his hand in the flame of a lamp. He should be allowed to see her at least as long as he could hold his hand against the flame, at least, that's how the story goes. It's difficult what to make of this story. It appears to have been a written scenario, rather than an actual situation lived by them.

Like the ear narrative, it's been dramatized as evidence of Vincent as a madman, or incurable romantic. But it was just persistence. Vincent's persistence now turned to his art, and his second cousin, Anton Mauve who was a fulltime artist. What's more, he was successful, and Vincent, aware that the Strickers had rejected his advances on the basis of his inability to support her financially, finally saw the incentive to make his own money. To be worthy of love! And so this was primarily what drove him to get serious about art, at the direction of Mauve, who was also an example that it was achievable.

Mauve introduced young Vincent to watercolors, and mentored him in his efforts in other mediums, like pastels and charcoal. After a month, Mauve and Vincent clashed. Mauve drew from plaster cast models of humanity, whereas Vincent wanted real models.

Over this period Vincent and his father quarrelled more, and Vincent, who'd been so resolute in his faith, now refused to attend church.

Mauve evidently had good reason to disapprove of Vincent paying street models to sit for him; they were invariably prostitutes, and if they were paid to sit, he [Vincent] might as well sleep with them when he was done.

In 1882 themes of fatigue, sorrow and distress manifest in Vincent works, few more memorable than *Worn Out,* a pencil sketch executed on watercolor paper. Vincent executed the same image in paint, *At Eternity's Gate*, months before his death. The despairing theme and more pertinently, the desolate name, meant this artwork was believed by some to be his last painting before his death, but it isn't. As you can see, he'd been painting the despairing theme for *eight years* by then.

Now, in the summer of 1882, Vincent was hospitalised for three weeks with a sexually transmitted disease. Some records say he'd contracted gonorrhoea, others venereal disease, and still others, syphilis. Shortly after his discharge from hospital, Vincent went into high gear, painting in oils using money provided by Theo, and probably, now that he had a taste for it, sleeping with his models.

By March 1882 he'd invited one of them, Sien Hoornik, to live with him. Sien wasn't just a prostitute, but an alcoholic, mother to a five-year-old girl and a mother-to-be. On July 2nd, Sien gave birth to a baby boy, her fourth child. Willem would later come to believe, rightly or wrongly, that Vincent was his father. Sien gave up both surviving children, her daughter to her mother, and her new-born son to her brother, and resumed prostitution while Vincent's father forbade his son to see her.

In 1904, fourteen years after Vincent's death, she committed suicide by drowning herself in the River Scheldt.

December 1883

#11 Emerging artist/Nuenen/Margot Begemann

Now Vincent was 30-years-old, and the Van Gogh clan were getting used to the cloud that hung permanently over his head. When Vincent returned home, penniless and without prospects of any kind [including love], Vincent's family took him in out of duty, but little else.

The cold shoulders he got from family, sent Vincent out with his canvas and paints for most of the day, a habit he'd hold onto throughout his art career, especially in Arles and Auvers. In Nuenen Vincent focused on the work of weavers, and on depicting their thatched cottages.

It was here, watching the weavers, that Vincent first noticed the power of colour on fabric, and how certain colors side-by-side, could create particular textures, tones and patterns when seen from a distance. Vincent didn't know it then, but these months exposed at close quarters to the bustle of the weavers, would give his own work a threaded, dappled pattern which from a distance, would turn into stars, and threaded wheat fields, and throbbing suns.

While this was going on, the neighbor's daughter, Margot Begemann, fell in love with Vincent. Once again, it was a woman of inappropriate age, she was ten years older, and once again, the marriage bells were rung. Both families opposed the union and poor Margot, as I mentioned earlier, attempted to poison herself.

We can see in these many personal crisis, Vincent gradually coming into his own, slowly coming to a point of self-possession. He becomes used to disappointing his family, and being as disappointed in love as in life. He becomes used to struggle and failure in the eyes of virtually everyone. Over time, he develops consistency in his art, and soon his art becomes both a source of escape from the world, and somewhere to anchor himself, in a world where reality, and everything in it, seems to shift.

Right here, when the artist was 32-years-old, and finally finding himself, we come upon a contradiction. When his father died, Vincent had no profound revelation, doubtless because for the first time, Vincent knew his father as a real person, inside and out, balls to bones. The unfortunate devolution of their relationship, meant by the time Theodorus died, he'd transformed from a heroic saviour to a controlling, oppressive, undermining presence in the life of his son.

That Vincent didn't even stop painting during his father's passing shows to some extent Vincent's newfound maturity, and his consistency, in the face of overwhelming emotion. And also the extent to which he'd become invested no longer in his family or even God, but in his art.

Vincent's *Still Life with Open Bible*, painted at the time of his father's death [just as The Potato Eaters was], still has the manure brown of typical Dutch art in place. The symbolism is simple: the legacy of the great book lifted against an overwhelming black background with an extinguished candle beside it. In the great bible, Vincent represents the size and weight of his father's influence, and in the small yellow book by Emile Zola, almost invisible in context, Vincent gets the last word in their ongoing quarrel; He finds a place for himself on the table, and in his own way, gives himself permission to have his say.

Six months after his father's death, one of Vincent's young peasant sitters fell pregnant. It was September 1885, eighteen months into Vincent's latest and last sojourn at home. This time Vincent was accused of forcing himself on the sitter. The rumor had some substance to it, apparently, because the village pastor, in the absence of Theodorus, forbade his congregants to model for the budding artist.

November 1885

#12 Antwerp Academy of Arts/Treated for syphilis

At the beginning of winter in the year of his father's death, about a month after the "rape" scandal, Vincent moved [not voluntarily] to Antwerp. There he occupied a small room above an art dealer's house. Once again, he seemed to punish himself for his sins, electing to eat only bread, drink coffee, and consume tobacco as he had in his lay preacher days in Amsterdam, seven years earlier.

By February the following year, Vincent admitted to his brother that he'd only eaten six hot meals in nine months. In Antwerp, still inspired by the weavers no doubt, and maybe Theo had advised Vincent about the colourful trends of the Impressionists, sweeping the art market, Vincent began to experiment with color. He visited museums and became an ardent student of the craft.

By now, Paris was calling. If Vincent was serious about making it as an artist, he had a final stop to make before he could truly graduate into the craft. To that end, Vincent undertook admission exams for a course at the Academy of Fine Arts in Antwerp. Where he had failed twice in theology, he succeeded [to a point], in the academia of art.

Vincent attended art classes at the Antwerp Academy while battling various illnesses that winter. True to form, Vincent argued with the director of the Academy, Charles Verlat, who criticised his unconventional style. Then Vincent quarrelled with Franz Finck, the drawing class instructor. When Eugène Siberdt asked his students to reproduce the contours of plaster casts, Vincent repeated the same defiance he'd shown to Mauve, his second cousin. Why paints plaster casts when one could paint the real human form, in all its naked glory?

When Siberdt saw Vincent's effort of a headless, limbless but voluptuous peasant torso, he was incensed by Vincent's open rebellion. Siberdt made such violent corrections in crayon, he tore the paper. According to Naifeh-Smith, Vincent shouted angrily at his professor in response:

"You clearly don't know what a young woman is like…she must have hips that can carry a baby!"

This clearly suggests how familiar Vincent was with the female form by then; perhaps too familiar for his own good. It also adds fuel to the fire around the suggestion that he'd made Sien pregnant after all, and *might* have been Willem's father, and what's more, had potentially forced himself on that peasant model in Nuenen.

During this period preparing himself for Paris while in Antwerp, Vincent drank heavily and painted obsessively. He was motivated despite poor health. Vincent received follow-up treatment in hospital sometime in February or March for syphilis. It's clear, despite the lack of indisputable forensic evidence, that Vincent's sexual exploits in 1885 were sufficient to sicken him, but also that the sickness was insufficient to deter him, not from work or from carnal expressions of love.

We can see, therefore, that Vincent, as early as 1882 and 1886, was infected with physical disease, and yet he was able to persevere – to endure – regardless. His ability to walk more than 40 miles at the drop of a hat speaks of his stamina, though admitted, this fluctuated as his circumstances did. More important than Vincent's physical strength, his mental resilience, demonstrated over time, provides us with powerful psychological tools to counter his seeming weakmindedness that suddenly manifested in December 1888, and again in the days prior to his murder in July 1890.

March 1886

#13 Fernand Cormon's studio/Paris

The final leg of Vincent's five-year internship as an artist, was in Paris, the world's art capital. For the first time, the artist would encounter real heads of state, and have his sense of identity *as an artist*, tested against other artists. Was he deluding himself as an artist as well, or *was there something there*, something of real worth, this time?

Vincent moved to Paris in March 1886. He didn't tell his brother he was coming, probably because he'd once again left under a cloud of disgrace, this time for failing his first year at the Antwerp Academy of Arts.

With Vincent already in Paris, he didn't have much choice, but to dutifully take him into his apartment in Montmartre. Thus Vincent began another internship, this time at the studio of the French master, Fernand Cormon. At Cormon's studio Vincent would encounter other important artists, like Henri de Toulouse-Lautrec, Louis Anquetin, Eugène Boch, Paul Tampier and Émile Bernard. Vincent had no idea he would eventually eclipse all of them.

Yellow Paint

"It is better to be high-spirited even though one makes more mistakes, than to be narrow-minded and all too prudent." —Vincent Van Gogh

1888 – Still Life with Flowers

It's important not to drown in the detail of the last two chapters recounting Vincent's rise as an "overzealous" artist. What matters is that through these many years of trials – physical and emotion suffering, sickness, feeling himself humiliated by other artists [which we'll deal with imminently],those close to him, by lovers and even by society – we get a sense of Vincent's emerging identity and his resilience. He's not weak, he's tough. He's someone with the capacity to love, and he dearly wants to be loved [and married] in return. He's not mad or without purpose, he's motivated and committed by the time he arrives in Paris, and even more so, when he leaves.

If anything, he's more aware than ever of the importance of money, of earning a living, to be a person of worth, and thus a person worth being attached to, in the romantic and sexual sense, over the long term. Vincent wants a relationship with the world, and wants the world to want him back. Thus far, the world still needs convincing, but Vincent's determined that with enough effort, it will.

Émile Bernard testified about Vincent's already frenetic work rate at Cormon's studio:

"[Vincent] would make three studies each session, getting bogged down in impastos, constantly starting all over again on new canvases, painting the model from all sides, while the pathetic students who laughed at him behind his back took eight days to make an idiotic copy of a foot."

So we see the senior statesman of the class suffering ridicule, but he's also the one working the hardest to distinguish himself. Another student described Vincent as being serious, with a terrifying temper.

One of the few works that survived this period, was *Nude Study of a Little Girl, Seated,* which shows somewhat disturbingly, that even children performed in those days, as models for painters.

When Vincent stopped going to Cormon's *atelier* after three months, he wrote a letter to one Horace Livens, an Englishman he knew from the Antwerp Academy. The letter from sometime in the fall of 1886, paints an intimate portrait of the artist in Paris. We get a sense of how Vincent felt he *could* compete with his fellow artists. There are touches of generosity mixed into the ambition, color and passion interposed with hardship, enthusiasm combined with early thoughts of escape to the south…

"….with much energy… I would say an artist can get on here notwithstanding the many obstructions. And I intend remaining here still longer. There is much to be seen here – for instance Delacroix to name only one master. In Antwerp I did not even know what the

Impressionists were, now I have seen them and though not being one of the club, yet I have much admired certain Impressionist pictures..."

Vincent rattles off a few names and their works, including Degas and Monet. Then he relates to Livens, details regarding his own artistic efforts.

"And now for what regards what I myself have been doing, I have lacked money for paying models...but I have made a series of colour studies in painting simply flowers, red poppies, blue corn flowers....white roses, yellow chrysanthemums – seeking oppositions of blue with orange, red and green, yellow and violet...trying to render intense COLOUR and not a grey harmony."

We can see Vincent's internal intensity is already established, and is brewing, bubbling under, almost ready to burst onto his canvases. Despite hinting to Livens that he might stay on a little longer, in the same letter, as a postscript, Vincent adds temperamentally:

"I have been in Cormon's studio for three or four months but did not find that as useful as I had expected it to be."

Perhaps the jeering and pranks from some of his fellow students was getting to him; perhaps he sought moral support. That may be why Vincent extends the following invitation in the same letter to Livens:

"I will, if you like, share my lodgings and studio with you so long as I have any. In spring – say February or even sooner – I may be going to the south of France, the land of the blue tones and gay colors...since I saw the Impressionists I assure you that neither your colour nor mine...is exactly the same as their theories but...we have a good chance...of finding friends."

Vincent adds that his health, since arriving in Paris, has improved, admitting he was "low down in health" in Antwerp. Showing a keen arithmetic for the art market, and how to woo it, Vincent writes of the "slow" trade in the art market, where only the masters can command, and get away with what he calls "exorbitant" prices. He describes the dealers [Theo by inference] doing "little or nothing" for young artists.

Meanwhile the next tier of dealers, Vincent points out, do sell the works of young artists but at cutthroat prices. Vincent professes to have faith in colour, believing that the market would eventually catch up, pricewise, "in the longer run." How right he was, but even he had no idea how right he was. This was his reality:

"...for the present things are awfully hard, therefore let anyone who risks [coming] over here [to Paris], consider there is no laying on roses at all ['Paris is no bed of roses']."

February 1888

#14 Yellow House Studio/Arles/"Rachel"

Two years after Vincent's letter to Livens, he finally did as he said he would. He took the train south. Vincent and Theo had been arguing, but this time, Vincent left without being forced out, or kicked out, pretty much for the first time in his life. What's more, he travelled to Arles fuelled by inspiration rather than resentments, with the bright sun of Provence blazing optimistically overhead. That had to be a first as well. Gone was the dark thundercloud he seemed to drag with him whenever he left someplace.

It's no surprise then that Vincent's efforts in Arles, where he found himself comfortable in his skin, and fully embracing his identity as an artist for the first time in his life, produced the works that eventually made him world famous. It happened then, because that's when Vincent really became who he was.

During his ten or eleven months in Arles, two with Gauguin, mostly without, did Vincent fall in love with anyone? I believe he did, but he didn't let it interfere with his work. Vincent also became the picture of physical and mental health, in his numerous long walks through the countryside, before Gauguin arrived.

Late May 1890

#15 Ravoux Inn/Auvers/Marguerite Gachet

In all, Vincent went through about 15 separate "reinventions" of himself. By that I mean, career changes, often involving a change not only of craft, but also of place. That's a lot of trial and error, and obviously, the second half involved Vincent finding his way as an artist, not only in *oeuvre*, but in terms of place. If he knew who he was, the next matter was finding out where to be, where to do, where the world would accept him, and then love him.

Financial constraints meant Vincent wasn't free to go exactly where he pleased, yet there was a certain amount of freedom wherever he was. Vincent occupied that freedom with hard work, almost regimenting his efforts.

He was becoming the dutiful son again, but this time, through the persona he knew best, the artist. It was within this blossoming of self-actualisation that Vincent fell in love with chrome yellow, sapphire blue and emerald green. It was an artist coming into his abundant best, creatively speaking, absorbing and reflecting the superabundance of the natural world, all its verdant and organic forms, all its vertiginous swirls, clouds of white mixing with the mad delights of the tallest trees.

And it was this person, this fiery, yellow minded man who encountered Marguerite Gachet in Auvers in the dreamy summer of 1890. She was shy and inexperienced in the world, as she sat by the piano, and in her, Vincent recognized himself, and a plight he had once faced, and finally emerged from. If there was anyone in Auvers who could take Marguerite's hand and guide her, emotionally, psychologically, spiritually, it was Vincent.

For the first time, Vincent was worthy of real love, and what's more, about to be seen as worthy, by the rest of the world. As Schama declares, when he opens his episode dedicated to

Vincent *in Power of Art*, by the summer of 1890 Vincent had just sold his first painting. An art critic had hailed him as a genius of the future. In the final flourish of that summer, Vincent produced several masterpieces, including Wheat field with Crows.

As Schama intones:

> *"Just for once, [in the summer of 1890] everything was going right for Vincent van Gogh..."*

So why would he want to kill himself?

New Theories

"They are vast fields of wheat under troubled skies, and I did not need to go out of my way to try to express sadness and extreme loneliness. I hope you see them soon – for I hope to bring them to see you in Paris as soon as possible, since I almost think that these canvases will tell you what I cannot say in words, the health and restorative forces that I see in the country."
— Vincent van Gogh

1890 – Summer – Tree Roots

Simon Schama does offer an explanation at the end of *Power of Art*, for why Vincent killed himself. Trouble is, although it may satisfy art historians, it's nowhere near acceptable as explanations go, in the annals of true crime.

It's all too easy to imagine that when suicides occur, motive is irrelevant, or worse, meaningless. If the greatest theme in the arts is who am I, then right up there with that, is why one of the greatest artist of our species would chose nonexistence over life? If the public don't know or care, it expresses the precarious state of the human condition in this corner of the cosmos. It shows the extent of how lost we are, and in some sense, purposefully lost in an ocean of purposeful oblivion.

When someone kills themselves, it's still murder. It's the murder of self. When the murderer of self is alleged to be the father of expressionism, then we fully expect the artist to leave clues to his mental condition, either in his autumn forest of letters, or in his archive of art, and probably both. We expect him to be explicit about his motives, even if he didn't mean to be. When someone is as intense as Vincent van Gogh, how can he not mean to be explicit about his motives, on life and death, when he's been explicit about everything else through the course of his life?

With the enormous archive of expression at our disposal, a daily diary of carefully, conscientiously and concisely handwritten thoughts and emotions, how can we not fathom the artist's interiority, and his motives, in vivid, sparkling detail?

So, of course, we can, we are and we will.

We begin this process by looking at what the mainstream believe to be Vincent's final painting, and what the evidence shows was his last effort at expressionism. Then we interrogate the mainstream's view of Vincent's idiosyncratic use of yellow. We follow this by examining the artist's physical and mental health, then another review of the ear narrative, using the same mainstream versus evidence construct. And finally, we look at Vincent's death narrative.

By juxtaposing the last painting, with the conventional and alternate theories regarding his favorite color, his health, ear and death narratives, we should *expect* to see a pattern linking the conventional narratives together.

Now, if I have done my work, we should also expect to intuit a pattern linking the counter narrative to itself. Does it hold together? How strongly does it hold itself together? With both narratives firmly established by now, the mainstream and my counter narrative, we can at last place them side by side, and ask:

Which one *works* better?

Which one *integrates* the most, and seems *truer* to the artist, now that we know more about his history, and who he is, in his own words?

Are you sure you want you want to hear this?

1. Last Painting?

It's a simple question. What was Vincent's last painting? In true crime, when dealing with an innocent witness, one often hears information volunteered along the lines of: "That was the last thing she said before she died." Or, "That was the last time I saw him…" From this disclosures were often form an intimate portrait of the final moments of a particular person's life. These first-hand details, whether someone was smiling, or in a rush, introspective or optimistic, oblivious or anxious, are invaluable pieces of the psychological puzzle. With them, we can confidently place the motive piece in a context that fits, without forcing it to fit.

When dealing with a crime, especially murder, and especially from the murderer at the scene, the last thing we'd expect to hear is what the murderer really saw, heard and felt in terms of his victim. That changes when dealing with a suicide. Then we do expect to see aberrations in thoughts, behaviour, feeling and expressions, whether written on paper or painted on canvas.

Vincent's last painting is important for precisely this reason. If he meant to murder himself, what were the last things he saw, and felt and said [if only to himself]? It's a mistake to assume an artist painting a picture isn't disclosing any information about himself, let alone an expressionist trying to withhold his raw authenticity at the denouement.

Since there is no suicide note, and since there is this persistent suicide narrative, we have to look for a suicide note in his work and his behaviour if we are to find any real meat to this story. We find a few scraps clinging to the bone in *Wheat field with Crows*. The rumor started early, by Adeline Ravoux, which explains its sticky persistence.

I continue therefore the account of the confidences that Vincent Van Gogh made to Father in the course of the night of Sunday to Monday that he spent with him. [On the day he was shot] Vincent had gone to the wheat field where he had painted previously…

In *The Letters of Vincent van Gogh*, a book edited by Ronald van Leeuw [the director of the Van Gogh Museum from 1986, and employed at the Rijksmuseum until 2008] and including translations by former South African Arnold Pomerans, the authors confidently state that "Van Gogh shot himself at the scene of his last painting, the foreboding Cornfields with Flight of Birds…"

It's unequivocal. a) He shot himself. b) He shot himself in a wheat field where he painted *Wheat field with Crows*. c) *Wheat field with Crows* is his last painting, which he presumably carried from the wheat field where he shot himself, after putting a bullet in his stomach.

It's all very convenient that the director of the museum who is making these bold contentions has the artwork in question on the wall of his museum. So we can see how Van Leeuw is incentivised to talk up the whole suicide in a wheat field scenario, as well as the "last painting" narrative.

If one could be allowed to make-up history after the fact, *Wheat field with Crows* is an excellent choice for a last painting, which is why Schama's episode in *Power of Art* opens and closes with it. Indeed, the episode itself is titled *Wheat field with Crows*. Schama calls this artwork, supposedly Vincent's last, the one that "begins" modern art. It's as if Vincent purposefully spent his life martyring himself, and then, in his last painting, wrung the last and best drops of his life force from his body, mind and soul, and splattered them onto the canvas for our pleasure. As though he'd shot himself standing in front of the canvas, and *Wheat field with Crows* was the result.

In the end-credits to Schama's excellent documentary, after crediting himself and the actor, Andry Serkis, the first thanks expressed are to the Van Gogh Museum, in Amsterdam; the purveyors of the suicide/wheat field/last painting narrative, and the benefactors of it. How do they benefit? By making themselves, their museum, this picture, the centrepiece of the one of humanity's great and most valuable artists. Through their books, fundraising and merchandise also.

Wheat fields with Crows works because it was painted in Auvers, and it was painted in the final year, the final month, the final weeks of Vincent's life. So whether it was Vincent's final painting or one of his last, it's still a significant work, it's still a "revolutionary masterpiece", as Schama calls it. For our purposes, being vague about it isn't good enough. We want to know exactly when it was painted, because we're trying to build a scenario, and a context, to whatever was Vincent's "last word" on canvas.

Although Schama balances his praise of *Wheat field with Crows* by saying "it says nothing about Vincent's frailty," I'm not so sure. If it seems I'm shooting my own argument in the foot, I'm not. Schama's right that it's *not* a suicide note. But it doesn't say nothing. It does say something, and *it does say something about frailty*.

The mere idea of a summer field with a large flock of birds says something about the field being vulnerable to the sky and clouds, and the elements of nature. The fact that Vincent paints this many birds, and they're black, at this time of his life, hardly seems purely coincidental. Is there any other painting with so many animals or birds in them? The closest to the busy-ness of *Wheat field with Crows* is the only painting Vincent sold in his life, *The Red Vineyard*, painted while Gauguin was staying with him in Arles.

Instead of birds rising into the sky, perspective is provided by grape-pickers receding into a field, and behind them, a row of trees disappearing towards a long sickle-shaped horizon.

It's undeniable that the black crows *are* a symptom of the artist's moodiness in July. If *The Red Vineyard* evokes the tones of Autumn, and the impending chill of winter, *Wheat field with Crows* is brighter, filled with the quivering energy and radiance of summer, at high noon. And looking closer at the painting, despite its brightness, you can see there is a blackness threaded through the blue vault spanning the yellow field. What seems to be happening is the crows are either flying down out of this black vault, or flying up, into it. Either interpretation is somewhat ominous. It seems to suggest a world contaminated by its connections to itself.

At the same time, stepping back and considering the full palette, the vivid yellow, puffs of white, the bright blue and fertile brown, the splashes of green altogether contrive to create a sunny scene. The crows provide connection and contrast, opposition to the lightness, sure, but not to overwhelm lightness, but to reveal it. It's a kind of harmony, like a pattern woven into fabric not to define it, but to highlight it, to provide finishing touches. This is Vincent's daylight version of *Starry Night Over the Rhône.* Instead of stars coming down to Earth through the reflections of street lights [blurring the boundary between heaven and Earth], the crows are the stars of the midday heat.

If we are going to look at the color black as a key indicator for suicidal thoughts, then we must compare Vincent's use of black in *Starry Night Over the Rhône* and *The Red Vineyard* too. *The Red Vineyard* has a dark, bristly, brackish foreground, even the figures are clothed in black skirts. In the background the sky is a vivid yellow. In other words, it's an inversion, palette-wise, of *Wheat field with Crows*.

In *Starry Night Over the Rhône* we see three separate horizontal sweeps of black – at the very top, through the centre, and along the edge of pier. These sweeps are meant to provide perspective and contrast, just as the roads and hues are meant to in *Wheat field with Crows*. If we are going to quibble about black as symbolic of death, or suicide, then *Starry Night Over the Rhône* is an ever better choice, it's one of Vincent's darkest pictures, but any imbecile can see that the darkness is there to reveal the light. If he'd called the picture *Couple Have Just Dumped Their Offspring into the Rhône,* even that couldn't shake us from the sparkling merriment of the scene.

The strongest case for an ominous narrative around Wheat field with Crows is of course, the crows. In 2017, on the ten year anniversary of the death/disappearance of Madeleine McCann, I wrote a trilogy casting aspersions on the culpability of the little girl's appearance by using the raven as a motif, a harbinger – of death, and truth. It's clear that crows and ravens are well-established in human history, heraldry and art as symbols. In Norse mythology, ravens had a supernatural ability to tell the future.

In this sense, if *Wheat field with Crows* was the last painting by Vincent, we'd certainly have to wonder if he wasn't trying to use symbolism to suggest something. But the fact is, it's not the last painting. It was probably completed about two weeks before Vincent's death, and he painted a bunch of other paintings afterwards, including the whimsical *Town Hall at Auvers* on July 14th, and *Daubigny's Garden* subsequently. In one of Vincent's last letters, written on July 23rd [he was shot on the 24th], he mentions Daubigny's Garden.

"Perhaps you'll take a look at this sketch of Daubigny's garden – it is one of my most carefully thought-out canvases."

In fact there are *three versions of the garden*, and a sketch of it, in Vincent's final letter. In the final section of this narrative, in the *Last Train to Paris* chapter, I deal with the symbolic import of the garden, though I'm sure the inferences to be made are already quite clear by now.

Another fake contender for Vincent's last painting is *Sorrowing Old Man At Eternity's Gate*. Once again, it's easy to see why. The despairing man, the title of the painting, and the date it was painted [May 1890], all make for a good case that a suicidal Vincent painted this as a definitive statement of his mental state, and intentions. It's all very compelling, except Vincent painted this while he was still at Saint-Rémy, and as I've mentioned earlier, he'd executed various iterations of the same portrait *eight years* earlier, and wrote about it on November 24th, 1882, to Theo:

"Today and yesterday I drew two figures of an old man with his elbows on his knees and his head in his hands. I...always kept the drawing, because I wanted to do it better another time...What a fine sight an old working man makes, in his patched bombazine suit with his bald head."

It's clear from Vincent's own description that he's not painting a self-portrait. The figure in 1882 doesn't even look like him, and for that matter, there's no resemblance in May 1890. In fact it's identified as Adrianus Zuyderland an old pensioner and war veteran from The Hague.

Another site that perpetuates the Wheat fields with Crows/depression/suicide narrative is the authoritative sounding vangoghstudio.com. Here's an excerpt.

It's long been thought that Wheat Field with Crows was Vincent van Gogh's last painting. This could be because of the neat way it fits into the Van Gogh story and his narrative of falling deep into a depression that pushed him to suicide.

The website cleverly suggests reinforcing information for why *Wheat field with Crows* is the last painting. It seems to set itself up as an informed, authoritative source. It continues:

The art work [Wheat field with Crows] is full of loneliness and intensity, a dark and brooding sky with a path that is cut off, and crows flying toward or away from the viewer, it is hard to tell.

So far so good, and the loneliness aspect is a nice touch, especially the combination of loneliness with intensity, and "dark and brooding". Having set the tension nicely, the next step is this:

The elements at play in this painting seem to point toward the end for Van Gogh and has been both used in the films Lust for Life and Vincent and Theo as his last painting for dramatic effect.

The site is saying something without explicitly saying it, but one thing is clear, Wheat field with Crows is highlighted repeatedly as the last painting, even though we know it wasn't. The site shoots itself in the foot [though is unaware of it] when they write of Vincent's "remarkable output" despite the obvious "depression" he was suffering from in the last days of his life.

His final series of paintings were all based on the wheat fields. He was also aware of the mood of these paintings...

"They are vast fields of wheat under troubled skies, and I did not need to go out of my way to try to express sadness and extreme loneliness..."

It's easy to get the impression from this that Vincent's last works were wheat fields. Going through the last hundred or so of Vincent paintings, there's hardly a single consistent theme that sticks out. If anything, it's the combination of themes that strikes the researcher: flowers, faces, fields, haystacks, houses, vineyards, blossoming, growing, gardening, ears of wheat, children, churches, farms, village streets... This was Vincent's mindscape in the last days of his life.

Of course, there's a method to both the museum and vangoghstudio.com peddling the Wheat fields narrative. It's clearer in the latter, where at the very end of the page, the website offers hand painted reproductions of "Van Gogh's last painting" at the bargain price of € 480,00. The product is described as "a vibrant work somewhere between death and dramatic rebirth." There's a financial incentive in pretending both that Vincent was mentally disturbed, and by holding up Wheat field with Crows as an exhibit of that disturbance, but trumpeting it as the "last painting", the incentive to purchase it also increases. This is simply post-truth in the service of capitalism, of greed, which is why it's hardly surprising the story around the world's most expensive artist, even around simple issues, is as opaque as it is.

Authoritative news sites like bbc.com do no better, but occasionally, they have their moments. This is dramatic but unhelpful:

On 27 July 1890, Vincent van Gogh walked into a wheat field behind the chateau in the French village of Auvers-sur-Oise, a few miles north of Paris, and shot himself in the chest.

This is equally misleading:

This letter...found by the independent researcher Bernadette Murphy...proves without doubt that the artist cut off his entire ear.

This, on the other hand, is useful:

When I visited [the Van Gogh Museum] recently, though, something else caught my attention: an unfinished painting, a metre across, called Tree Roots (1890). Van Gogh worked on it during the morning of 27 July, a few hours before he tried to kill himself. It is the last painting he ever made.

Well, it could be. An unsigned painting could be recent, though some artists abandon their works and allow them to stew in time and entropy for years, if not indefinitely. But an artwork painted in late July and unsigned, by an artist who at that stage, only been living in Auvers for two months, and had upped his output to a painting a day, certainly suggests that he was – indeed – busy with it, finishing it, finalising it, and about to sign it when he died. If true, then Vincent's mind in his last days, perhaps the last day itself, were on roots. It also adds unexpected credibility to Adeline Ravoux's contention that Vincent spent his last day behind the chateaux [because there were large trees there, with large roots, which would be exposed by the deep gouging path]. Here it is again:

Vincent had gone to the wheat field where he had painted previously, it was situated behind the Auvers chateau...The chateau was more than a half-kilometer from our house. It was reached by going up a steep hill, shaded by large trees...

The writer isn't sure what to make of it. What do *roots* mean? Are roots also harbingers of death, even more so than crows, he gasps?

Fortunately he turns to the curator, Nienke Bakker, for guidance. One must be careful treating any source as definitive, but Bakker sounds like she has her head screwed on right.

[She] urges caution. "There is a lot of emotional agitation in works from the last weeks of Van Gogh's life, such as Wheat field with Crows and Wheat field under Thunderclouds," [Bakker] says. "It's clear he was trying to express his own emotional state of mind."

Well, he was trying to express himself, and what was around him, and his emotional state. Every execution clearly wasn't simply about Vincent trying to express his own state of mind. If that were the case he could have drawn self-portraits all day.

"Yet Tree Roots is also very vigorous and full of life. It's very adventurous. It's hard to believe that somebody who painted this in the morning would take his own life at the end of the day. For me, it's hard to say that Van Gogh painted it intentionally as a farewell..."

You can see how the narrative shifts from the idea of an emotional mind agitated by disturbance, to an expressive person sharing his sense of vigor and plucky audacity with the world. Only a sick soul would wish to pervert neutral terms like vigor and adventurous into suicide. And yet the suicide narrative requires people to find evidence in his expressive final works. It's precisely why the suicide narrative is so harmful, and why it must be done away with, because people are looking for something that isn't there, but their imaginations are reminding them something must be there.

"All of these tortured, gnarled roots make Tree Roots a very hectic, emotional painting," she says. "But it's not a painting created by a crazy mind. He knew very well what he was doing. Until the end, Van Gogh painted in spite of his illness, not because of it. It's important to remember that."

There you have the curator of the Van Gogh Museum, scotching the rumor that Vincent's last painting, whatever it was, was a suicide note of any kind.

He knew very well what he was doing.

What's clear is his art in his last days wasn't darker than before, if anything, it was lighter and brighter.

In sum: the mainstream narrative regarding Vincent's last painting is bogus, but there is money to be made by those perpetuating. My contention is that the last painting was *Tree Roots*, and if this painting said anything, it spoke of Vincent's need to anchor himself to his work, and to anchor his identity to something tangible – a person, a place, a philosophy, a work ethic. Once again, that psychology is completely at odds with someone intend on doing the opposite, cutting their anchors and yielding to entropy and oblivion.

2. Seeing Yellow

Much has been made of Vincent's fondness, some might say obsession, for yellow. It's true, Vincent sucked poisonous chrome yellow paint from a tube while at the asylum in Saint-Rémy, but then, he also ate dirt, smeared his face with coal and drank paraffin.

In July 2013, the *British Journal of General Practice* prognosticated expertly on this strange subject. Did Vincent's "yellow vision" reveal something sinister about what was going on his mind? Did have defective vision, or a psychological disturbance? Was mental illness the reason Vincent cast the world repeatedly in yellow?

It's far-fetched but hardly farcical. It turns out that some people are afflicted by a tendency to see the world through yellow-tinted glasses. It's called Xanthopsia. The author refers to victims suffering from an "overriding yellow bias in vision", which can be provoked by multiple disorders besides cataracts [which Monet famously suffered from]. Remember, there were no dark glasses to shield artist's from the glare in the France of the 1890's.

Now, according to the *Journal*:

Over 150 physicians have ventured a perplexing variety of diagnoses, ranging from bipolar disorder, schizophrenia, neurosyphilis, interictal dysphoric disorder [a kind of mood disorder associated with epilepsy], sunstroke, acute intermittent porphyria, temporal lobe epilepsy precipitated by the use of absinthe in the presence of an early limbic lesion, to

Ménière's disease. Whatever van Gogh's exact diagnosis may have been, it is highly likely that after admission to the asylum at Saint-Rémy in 1889, his physician [in Auvers], Dr Paul Gachet, prescribed digitalis, which is why medical historiography strongly supports the hypothesis of van Gogh having suffered from digitalis-induced Xanthopsia. In Portrait of Dr Gachet, 1890, the foxglove plant is presented in front of Dr Gachet; digitalis is extracted from foxglove plants.

From this we can see why the story of Vincent's life is so difficult to disentangle. Even medical experts are bewitched and befuddled. You can't solve a true crime case with a stethoscope or a scalpel, you need a far more integrated approach. Nevertheless, the medical view is worth brief consideration, especially a review of neurosyphilis, epilepsy and bipolar disorder. We'll deal with these under the next heading.

Digitalis or foxglove, a poison, is invoked as evidence relating to our prime suspect. Vincent's *Portrait of Dr. Gachet* captures this flower, so it had to be of some significance. We also know that after he was shot, Vincent appeared as if he might recover. Dr. Gachet treated Vincent's wounds, and Vincent suddenly declined. With what did Gachet treat his wounds?

The use of digitalis at the time was undoubtedly widespread. Indeed, Samuel Hahnemann, the father of homeopathy, listed 73 indications for treatment with digitalis, including melancholic thoughts...mental illness...nausea..."

The *Journal* goes on to dismiss Vincent's prediction for chrome yellow as a stylistic choice, not a sign of any medical or depressive affliction, adding several facts to support this conclusion.

First, it is unlikely that Dr Gachet indeed overdosed van Gogh with digitalis. Well aware of the potential lethal side effects of the drug, he used homeopathic doses and wrote in an unpublished treatise:

'We understand the physiologic effects of this plant well enough today to be afraid of its dangers, and strongly advise against its use, since it can produce syncope by slowing the heartbeat and it can cause paralysis of that organ.'

I'd like to offer a correction to the above. It's unlikely that Gachet mistakenly overdosed [poisoned] Vincent with *digitalis*. The fact that this point is raised at all, given Gachet's profile as prime murder suspect, is significant. We can also see, Gachet was, by his own admission, an expert in the physiological effects of this plant. The plant is inextricably linked to Vincent's narrative because Vincent associates it with Gachet directly. Moreover, we see Dr. Gachet warning against the dangers of using *digitalis* in medical prescriptions. If *digitalis* was in widespread use in 19th century France, and Gachet was a homeopath expressly hired to treat Vincent's melancholia, then it's entirely possible either that he:

1) Mistakenly poisoned Vincent, perhaps causing Vincent to wish to shoot himself at the site of his pain – his stomach.

2) Purposefully poisoned Vincent, perhaps while pretending to treat him, and after shooting him, to speed him on his exit out of this world.

But the *Journal* adds:

...it is doubtful that van Gogh would have outlasted extended periods of digitalis levels high enough to induce Xanthopsia. As with absinthe, by the time he had reached toxic levels, he would have been unable to paint.

Well, we know he was unable to paint during his last hours of life. Was that entirely due to the bullet wound? Probably, but possibly, *digitalis* was also a factor.

Now the Journal does in the medicinal sense, to prove its case, what I've just done in the psychological sense in the previous heading. It refers to Vincent's archive of art to prove his "yellow vision" didn't afflict him spontaneously as a symptom of madness.

Second, van Gogh's paintings prior to 1889 already showed a preference for yellow. Therefore, his 'yellow vision' was evident in various paintings, such as his iconic 'Sunflowers' and many others, cannot be attributed to his alleged treatment with digitalis at Saint-Rémy...it becomes clear that van Gogh's colour scheme was always deliberate and not linked to any visual impairment. The study of his paintings should remind the audience to not merely reflect on what they see, but also to consider what the artist saw during the creative process.

It's not clear whether the *Journal* is mistaken, in that reference to *digitalis* treatment at Saint-Rémy. If correct, it certainly goes some way to explain why Vincent's mental health suffered episodic attacks while in the asylum. It also explains the halo effect around points of light in *Starry Night*, which Vincent executed from his hospital room window.

According to the *Guardian* as recently as August 2017, the symptoms of *digitalis* poisoning include that:

Occasionally, points of light may appear to have coloured halos around them.

Wikipedia describes the entire plant – roots, leaves and flowers – as toxic, and provides the following list of side-effects.

...the victim may suffer various cerebral disturbances, especially of a visual nature...with objects appearing yellowish to green, and blue halos around lights, convulsions, and deadly disturbances of the heart... Vincent van Gogh's "Yellow Period" may have been influenced by digitalis therapy which, at the time, was thought to control seizures.

If his treatment for a phantom condition amounted to intermittent poisoning and recovery, then we have an alternative explanation for his sudden onset of madness.

In sum: Vincent's preoccupation with yellow is yet another misleading mainstream narrative festooned with murky subtext. It contrives to create the false impression of the mad or tortured artist. It mischievously suggests not an artist who knew what he was doing, but one simply suffering from a series of chemical reactions that amounted to poisoning and mental illness. My contention is that Vincent's fondness for yellow was part of his idiosyncratic intensity. It was his way of expressing the life force, and the way to depict the divine energy flowing through the world.

He knew very well what he was doing...and he painted in spite of his illness.

What matters here isn't the narrative of yellow, but the link between Vincent's dodgy physician and his access to a poison whose effects he was clearly familiar with. We also have an innocent explanation for Vincent's erratic behaviour during his purgatory at Saint-Rémy.

3. Health

Vincent suffered from syphilis as early as 1882, and we know his younger brother died from the disease, meaning he was in the fatal tertiary stages of it. Vincent probably was too, and if he knew it, this could have played into suicidal thoughts. Once again, Vincent had been living with syphilis for several years by the summer of 1890, and if his physical health was ailing, it didn't look like it. He was up each day, active, walking and working. None of that sounds like someone who is suffering from any physical or mental malaise.

That's not to say Vincent was the picture of health, even if his paintings were trying to be. We have our best clue into Vincent's medical status in the last moments of his life: the fact that after suffering a bullet wound, he was able to stumble to his room, and lived for another 30 hours. A difficult question to answer is: would anyone else have survived the same thing? Would they have survived longer? Without having an autopsy verifying organ damage and blood loss, we can't be sure. Since Dr. Gachet chose to paint Vincent's face, and not record the wound, we're not better off. Essentially we have some medical history at the beginning, and at intervals, some more around the ear incident, more from the asylum, and then his last moments.

We also have Vincent and Theo's letters which suggest lucidity – mental health – at the very least. But I wonder if neurosyphilis was *starting* to become a factor in the late 1880's, for both brothers.

Neurosyphilis is difficult to predict. It can manifest anywhere from three to 25 years after the initial infection. The symptoms include abnormal gait, confusion, disorientation, sudden personality changes, changes in mental stability, memory problems, moodiness, irritability and seizures.

Vincent spoke of suffering attacks, but also, that the best antidote for staving them off was – not suicide – but work. Multiple attacks leading to memory loss could also be epilepsy, but what makes that narrative problematic, was the confusing tendency of French doctors at the time to describe a variety of mental disturbances as epilepsy. In other words, epilepsy was epilepsy, and it wasn't.

If Vincent had an epileptic seizure while intoxicated, during Gauguin's visit, the Frenchman may well have misinterpreted this as madness, seeing Vincent as a raving lunatic and overreacted, perhaps lashing out with a sword to defend himself. It's possible, but it's too colourful a contention to be probable.

What we know for certain is that Vincent associated excessively in his youth with prostitutes, was hospitalised numerous times as a result, but significantly, was able to recover his health and strength. His habit of walking, regular exercise in other words, was one way to flush out the sickness.

We also know that in the 19th century, syphilis was one of the largest public health hazards in Europe. Everybody seemed to have it, but its association with prostitutes [especially for sons of a respected pastor] meant it was a taboo subject. A respectable community finding out someone was wandering around with syphilis, was likely to cast such a person out. That may have happened in Arles, and Gauguin, behind the scenes, may have made sure it did. Calling a fellow artist "mad" may have been a polite code, at least in people's mind, for something far less respectable.

Once again, the syphilis and neurosyphilis narrative are neatly excised from Vincent's legacy. He was mad, he was brilliant, he shacked up with an old prostitute as a gesture of pious generosity. In reality, Vincent and his brother both had syphilis, and this had a real impact on their physical and mental health. Did Vincent know his brother had syphilis, and this news was too much to bear? That's unlikely, if he had syphilis himself, and seemed to be doing okay in spite of it.

In sum: The mainstream narrative regarding Vincent's physical health is absent. It's all focused on his mental health. The opposite was true, his physical health fluctuated and could have brought on seizures, especially when he was highly stressed, anxious or in poor condition due to insomnia, exhaustion or poor nutrition. My contention is that Vincent's sickness had been with him for years. He'd been with others who were sick, he'd endured his own, and so by 1890 it was merely more of the same. He'd learned to live with it, he was able to endure it. If anything, Vincent was in reasonably good health after spending a year convalescing. Since the doctors treated him almost as an outpatient in 1889 and early 1890, not as poorly afflicted as others in asylum, we have enough to know that his condition was slightly compromised, but he was still quite functional. This narrative also counters the suggestion that Vincent was depressed and suicidal. On the contrary, he was healthy, motivated and eager for life, and living.

4. Ear

If Vincent's immunity was severely compromised when the ear incident happened, he would have suffered an infection and died. Instead, he recovered his health fairly quickly, and soon was back to painting, starting with portraits of himself sans ear.

By the same token, when the ear was sliced off, if Vincent wasn't healthy, he would not have had the strength to flee the scene on foot, and hand over his ear. Interestingly, in both the ear incident and the shooting, Vincent propels himself away from the crime scene on foot. It makes sense, he was a frequent walker, so his strength as a pedestrian was likely more than average. By the same token, if he'd been attacked, he was likely fitter and more capable of fleeing both his attackers [in Arles and Auvers] on foot. We know for certain that Vincent walked while wounded, which speaks volumes about his will to survive, not his intention to die.

What's also worth bearing in mind, when dealing with the ear incident, is that Vincent was an argumentative guy. When he lived at home, he argued with his parents. When he lived with Theo, they argued. When he trained in Antwerp, he argued with his teachers and instructors. So when Gauguin moves in with him, didn't they argue? Two artists, very different attitudes, philosophies and personalities, why wouldn't they argue?

When Vincent describes their lives discussions as batteries discharging, he's being kind. He's casting the narrative in friendly terms for Gauguin's and his brother's benefit. Gauguin is there to vindicate Vincent, so Vincent – whether they agree behind doors or not – wants to be a supportive voice for Gauguin.

Except Gauguin is a selfish scallywag, perhaps feels a sense of envy and competition with Vincent, perhaps raw jealousy. If that's the case, he has no intention of singing Vincent's praises, but he means to emerge from the equation ahead, somehow.

Conveniently for Gauguin, the instant he exits the scene, Vincent goes mad.

In reality, Vincent goes to hospital. There doctor Felix Rey, a young intern, is on duty while everyone else is enjoying Christmas. Rey, with his limited experience, tries to treat Vincent's ear.

While Vincent is indisposed at Hotel Dieu Hospital in Arles, recovering from severe blood loss, Gauguin has plenty of time to spin his version of events. He does so to Theo, on the train ride back to Paris. Given Gauguin's critical acclaim of late, and Theo's interests in making sure it stays that way [not only does he wish to hold onto his cash cow, he want to hold onto his fiancé], one can see how and why the younger brother may have been duped by the more senior artist.

Gauguin soon tells Bernard the same story, and the newspapers do the rest, recycling it through the four corners of France. And with no other witnesses for the time being, the local newspapers in Arles fall in line as well, printing Gauguin's version of events, such as it is.

While Vincent convalesces, the story catches on like wildfire on two fronts – in Arles and in Paris. Even Theo, having drunk Gauguin's Kool-Aid first hand, emerges as a credible early witness. If the younger brother Theo says it's true, who's to doubt it?

Imagine what it was like for poor Vincent, coming out of the hospital sans ear, with nothing but his bloody, semi-ransacked apartment waiting for him, like a particularly macabre Christmas gift. Meanwhile, the ether is filled with the great Gauguin's version of events. Was there any point in him – a down-on-his-luck Johnny-come-lately, a nobody – disputing any of it?

In sum: Vincent is sketched by the mainstream narrative as a tortured artist. That's the reason he sliced off his ear. There's rarely any context to this, other than that Gauguin and Rachel are witnesses in some way. There's also no reason why Gauguin abandons Vincent when he's supposedly at his most desperate, or indeed, why Vincent gives Rachel his ear. The explanation is plucked out of the ether – Vincent's madness is why he cut off his ear. My contention, when one trawls through Vincent's history as a young man, he's an argumentative, difficult type, but that doesn't mean he's not sensitive and intelligent, especially in his letters. In all of Vincent's quarrels, whether with his father, his brother, his instructors, there's no indication that he was ever violent; quite the opposite. We see a man committed to his fellow-man, often more than himself. In Gauguin we see the opposite. The madness explanation raises far more questions, whereas a violent altercation between Vincent and Gauguin settles them. Further, it makes more sense, both that Gauguin is the perpetrator and Vincent the victim, than the other way round, because before and after the incident, that's what Gauguin was and went on to become, and the same applies to Vincent. Gauguin left many of his friends in tatters, just as he did to Vincent. One could argue Vincent did the same, except that what Vincent wrought was shame, on himself and his family, whereas Gauguin had no shame. Gauguin even abandoned his own wife and children, whereas Vincent repeatedly returned home to his, and wished to help people, and wanted to be part of families.

In fact, throughout his life Vincent attached himself to at least seven families, the Haanebeeks in The Hague, the Gladwells of Lewisham, the Loyers in London, the Strickers in Amsterdam, the Roulins in Arles, the Ravouxs in Auvers, and the Gachets. At the time of his death, he was hoping to be part of yet another emerging family – Theo, Jo and baby Vincent. Far from being threatened by these developments, near the end of his life, I believe he was warmed and soothed by them.

In addition, I believe Dr. Paul took great exception to Vincent's predatory attentions towards his twenty-year-old daughter, and that wouldn't be the first time Vincent's infatuations would be deemed inappropriate, and too close to home. How many incidents are there, taking place under similar circumstances? Eugénie Loyer – whom he was sharing his boarding house in London. This caused her mother the landlady to disapprove of Vincent's attentions and he was kicked out. Vincent's cousin Kee Vos, once again causing a rift with his family and the Strickers, the canny observation:

His persistence is disgusting.

Sien Hoornik – another rift. Margot Begemann – the neighbor's daughter at Nuenen. Both sets of parents are upset by this and Margot tries to kill herself. Every time Vincent falls in love it's wildly inappropriate and everyone, especially him, feels humiliated. Isn't that what happened in Auvers? Yet another ill-advised and alliance. We have no idea whether Gauguin and Vincent argued over a woman in Arles, but why not – two artists, both single, both regulars at houses of ill repute, both with syphilis, and both clearly had an eye for the ladies. So why wouldn't Gauguin swoop in and perhaps try to hijack someone that meant something to Vincent. He'd fallen in love with prostitutes before. When Vincent confronted Gauguin, Gauguin exploded.

In both scenarios, in Arles and Auvers, Vincent doesn't harm others, *he's the victim*, and both perpetrators, in Arles and in Auvers, happily used Vincent's dodgy social prestige to get the better of him, and for their own temporary benefit. Ironically these myths only served to bolster Vincent's legend and his legacy as the poster child for tortured artists.

5. Death

I'm not spending much time on this aspect, because I deal with at length in the final chapters, but it's important to contextualise the mainstream narratives regarding Vincent's Last Painting, the myths surrounding his Yellow Vision and his Health, the ridiculous theory around the current version of the Ear Incident, and the even shakier ground surrounding Vincent's so-called suicide and/or accidental shooting.

We see what we expect to see – in all of these narratives – is that the mainstream view in each instance is seriously misinformed and at odds with who Vincent really was. Why is that?

The various narratives surrounding these incidents don't hold together. Vincent is mad when he cuts his ear off, and when he commits suicide, otherwise he seems rational. How does that make sense? What does mad even mean – insane? Mentally ill? Tortured?

Throughout the mainstream narrative, Vincent's art and circumstances are opportunistically, and casually, introduced as "evidence" for his deteriorating state of mind, but are used with slapdash convenience rather than a reasonable, or historically accurate argument. What's more, we can see a profit motive returning repeatedly as the real force driving, perpetuating these myths, which explains why they're still in play today.

In 2018, at the time of writing, we have the technology tools and apparatus to quickly assemble a large archive of research, and test, evaluate and analyse great volumes of easily accessible and verifiable data. We can browse our way quickly to an approximately complete chronological archive of his original works, and have them wash over us first-hand, the colors, the themes, the sights and sounds he knew, and saw.

At the same time we can wade through the thick forests of Vincent's correspondence, and place all of that consciousness and experience, into historical context. What happens when we meticulously do that? The mainstream narrative shifts into something else. Into something new. It shouldn't, but it does.

As such it's *unconscionable* that in matters of great import such as this, where a narrative of such inestimable value to the human story is at stake, that the mainstream should continue to be purposefully misled and bamboozled about the circumstances surrounding the life and death of the world's greatest artist. Are we sheep that deserve to be deceived, or do humans deserve better stories from those in the know, who ought to know better?

Perhaps there is a sense that only with a fake story, or that only with some strategically placed *fake emphasis*, can Vincent van Gogh be truly regarded as one of the world's great artists, and monetised accordingly. In my view, the truth vindicates his work more than the threadbare mainstream myths do, but the authentic narrative of who he truly was also humanises and personalises him. It allows us to see ourselves in him, and he in us, which makes his art even more lively and soothing, urgent and accessible. The mainstream mythology reduces him to a cartoon character whose madness is given credit for his art, not his humanity or his creativity.

In sum: In the last section I will tie these loose ends together, and provide not only a reason why Gachet murdered Vincent, but how his family benefitted from the most brazen heist in the history of art.

The Most Popular Museum in Holland

"This innocent-looking young woman with a little baby on her arm, nobody took her seriously, so that kind of kept the collection together for a longer time than if Theo was still alive, I think. She was able, still in 1906, to show a complete set of Van Gogh works." — Wouter van der Veen on why Vincent van Gogh art became so valuable

In 1882, at the beginning of Vincent's campaign to woo the art world, Vincent described himself in a letter to Theo as "a nobody, a non-entity, an unpleasant person. Someone who as not, and never will have, any position in society, in short the lowest of the low."

Eight years later, Vincent's art had come a long way, and in a sense, so had Vincent, who'd become a master painter. Yet in the eyes of society, Vincent was just as much a nobody in 1890 as he was in 1882. In fact, as a 37-year-old, homeless, earless, fresh out of the madhouse, with no family of his own, and no income, he was arguably even lower than he was in 1890.

I've already made the case that by then, Vincent was inured to his failure and sense of struggle. He hadn't given up, but he'd cast off the desperation to sell his work, and in its place, he'd developed something else. Maturity. Mastery. Resolve.

That's all good and fine, but how was it the failing nonentity was transfigured into the sparkling success story [however real or fake it may be] we know today? How did it happen?

Schama in *Power of Art* notes that Vincent died at the exact moment of his vindication. Even Theo knew his brother was on the verge of greatness. He was, but I wonder, if Theo had whispered into his brother's good ear, as he was dying, what would eventually transpire, how would Vincent react? Would there be anger at how his words and works would be distorted behind his back? How his name would be taken in vain? Would there be tears of gratitude?

Or would it simply be impossible for either of them to believe, from this sweaty deathbed floating in bright, scarlet failure, that Vincent's name *would* eventually be attached to a museum in Holland, and that that museum, the Van Gogh Museum, would become the most popular in Holland?

If we are to begin to answer this difficult question, we must start by asking an easier one, or two. How *did* Vincent's work become world famous, and how long did it take? *Who* was the major player in bringing his work to the world? How did Vincent's art achieve *real* value?

Let's start with the first question.

1. **How long did Vincent's art incubate before it burst on the world scene?**

Vincent's art stewed for a long time before it was ready to hatch in all its golden, yolky glory. That's because Vincent first became famous not through his art, but through his letters. His writing made him famous.

Vincent's letters to Theo were originally published in three volumes in 1914. Who worked silently in the background to make this happen? Theo's widow Jo. Jo had plenty of incentives too. She was a single mother trying to raise a little boy, Vincent', Theo's son. Jo was an unusual woman for her time, she was college educated, and could speak English, which made her a key player not only in getting Vincent's and Theo's letters out there, but getting them edited and translated, and thus opening Vincent's legend to the English-speaking world.

It took Jo almost a quarter of a century to get the first works published, and it didn't do Vincent's work any harm that her second-marriage was to a Dutch painter, or that her brother Andries was also an art dealer, although to be fair, Andries was initially indifferent about Vincent's work.

Since Vincent's mother was the daughter of a book binder to the Dutch king, and Uncle Stricker had links to booksellers like the one in Dordrecht, and the extended Van Gogh family had links to Groupil's, it's not hard to see how Vincent's art machine was set in motion, and why it gathered so much momentum when it did.

What's incontrovertible is that for 25 years after Vincent's death, his art was basically forgotten, though not for lack of trying. Six weeks after his death, Theo organized memorial exhibitions in Paris, Brussels, Antwerp, The Hague and Antwerp. These were followed by a retrospective exhibition in Brussels in 1891 and another one, arranged by Émile Bernard and Julien Tanguy, in Paris. In the same year, as if the run of bad luck plaguing the Van Gogh's couldn't get any worse, Albert Aurier, the only art critic to express any enthusiasm in Vincent's work died of typhoid fever. In the space of two years Vincent's two best champions and supporters were out of the equation as well.

In April 1894 the art world stirred a little. The Durand-Rue Gallery in Paris eventually went along with a deal where they acquired ten paintings from the Van Gogh estate on consignment. In other words, the works weren't bought, exactly, they were simply put on the market without anyone paying for that to happen. Once the works sold, proceeds were distributed back to the original seller, and the gallery of course took their cut.

Interestingly, Gauguin wasn't interested in assisting in the promotion of Vincent's work, although Gauguin would later credit himself for being a key influence on the artist [a very dubious claim] during their fateful two months cohabiting in Arles. By disassociating himself the way he did, Gauguin managed to shoot his own prospects in the foot, and assured himself of ending his career as a penniless, failed artist, in a far worse state than Vincent when he died.

In 1901, a year after Cor van Gogh's death, and eleven years after Vincent's, another retrospective was held in Paris, this time a large one. Then a decade passed during which virtually nothing happened. Seeds had been planted but would they – *could* they – germinate?

Then, gradually, there was *some kind of emergence* everywhere but in Paris. A few of Vincent's paintings appeared in Cologne, Germany in 1912. A few more at a group exhibition in New York in 1913. A few pundits began to emerge who started talking about the Dutch artist, like the Dutch artist and art critic Henk Bremmer. Then, Jo published Vincent's letters and he immediately shot to fame – though not in France, in Austria and Germany. But right then, evidence that the curse was still by no means lifted, the First World War happened, and all the interest that had been generated was swept away. The world completely forgot about art for several years as they cast about in massive tides of destruction. Lincoln, England, Cor van Gogh's former home, now emerged as a key supplier of weapons of war, chiefly tanks and armoured trains.

For almost a decade following the end of the First World War, amnesia remained in place. It took Irvine Stone's book *Lust for Life* in 1934 to revive interest in Vincent, though once again literature was leading the way to Vincent's fame, not the art itself. *Lust for Life* was based more on Vincent's *letters* than his art. The film adaptation in 1956 inverted the narrative from words to pictures once again, and so, for the first time, international audiences especially in America, got to see the artist – but far more important, his art – and in some kind of narrative context.

Effectively it was the film then that was the game changer, combining letters, the narrative set out in Stone's book and the actual paintings into a newly cohesive, integrated narrative for the first time. This film of Vincent's life captured the popular imagination when the art world had remained mostly indifferent to it.

So how long did it take? 66 years. And once it did take, no more World War loomed on the horizon to eclipse it all again. The curse had been lifted!

2. Who was the major player?

Without Jo, clearly, Vincent's legacy would have disappeared. Jo's son also played an important role in passing on the baton, and keeping it intact and the momentum of his story ticking along, while he occupied himself in other things.

Vincent van Gogh II [we'll use this nomenclature to differentiate Theo's son from the original artist] inherited the Van Gogh estate in 1925 when Jo died. Vincent II's mother was relatively young, just 62 years of age, when she died . Vincent II was 34-years-old at the time, the same age when his own father had died of syphilis.

Since Vincent II was born virtually fatherless, it was really up to him to make something of his life, and he did. Like his late uncle Cor, Vincent II studied mechanical engineering and worked as an engineer around the world, including Japan, France and the United States.

Vincent II, like his forebears, was an hard-working, conscientious and enterprising fellow. He started Holland's first management consultancy. Vincent II also arranged for the republication of his uncle letters, this time with no world wars on the horizon. As his famous uncle's renown grew, Vincent II became known increasingly, and somewhat more anonymously, as "the engineer."

Vincent II's contribution to Vincent's art is both dubious and valuable. Dubious because Vincent II in his early years didn't seem much interested in art, much less the value of his late uncle's work. But his contribution was clearly valuable because like all the Van Gogh's [especially Theo, Vincent and Jo], Vincent II was able to at least keep the collection [art as well as letters] together, intact, and in a safe, secure state.

In 1962, Vincent II transferred the entire family legacy to the state of Holland, via the Vincent van Gogh Foundation. The Rijksmuseum took until 1973 to exhibit Vincent's work, that's 120 years after Vincent's birth, and more than 80 years after his death. When the museum opened, by far the majority of visitors weren't from Holland, they came from elsewhere.

What's that saying about a prophet, who is never accepted in his hometown?

3. How did Vincent's work become so valuable?

It may seem as if we've more than answered this question by now, but actually, we haven't. It took Vincent's letters to bring his art into the world, and a kind of growing external popularity to boomerang back, for the Dutch state to eventually say, "Okay, we'll build a damn museum for him."

But neither of these factors *completely* explain why or exactly how Vincent's work became so valuable. So *who* was responsible for leveraging his worth?

Are you sure you want to hear this?

The narrative around this artist set the tone for the art. The chicken thus came before the egg. As such we can see how the narrative itself – the tone and quality of it – may enhance or impinge on the perception, and the perceived value, of the art.

Who set the narrative in motion initially? It wasn't Theo, or Jo, it was Dr. Gachet, and it all started at Vincent's funeral in Auvers. It started with suicide, and who better to pontificate on Vincent's madness than his doctor, murderer and benefactor.

Of course, it didn't end there. In the same way that Jo carried the baton of Vincent's legacy after Theo's death, and Vincent II carried it further after Jo's death, there's another dimension of baton carrying mirroring this one. The Gachets.

Guess which Vincent van Gogh painting was the first to really crack the whip in the art ~~scheme~~ scene? This one. Of all the controversy surrounding Vincent's work, the most fevered surrounds his portraits [plural] of Dr. Gachet.

Twenty years ago at the time of writing, the *Independent* published an article on this controversy titled *No cachet in a Gachet.* It's a clever play on words, cachet, meaning prestige, status, respect or distinction. The article was unambiguously stating in 1999 that there was no credibility in a Gachet, implying the art works, and perhaps more than that.

The article refers to Vincent's death as a "botched" suicide. Whenever I see that word in the context of true crime, my eyebrows shoot up, and then lower with the weight of cynicism. The following true crime cases are associated with "botched" crimes: Madeleine McCann – "botched" burglary. Oscar Pistorius – "botched" burglary [imagined]. Amanda Knox/Murder of Meredith Kercher – "botched" burglary. JonBenét Ramsey – "botched" burglary/kidnapping. Murder of Laci Peterson – ""botched" burglary/kidnapping.

Returning to the matter at hand, from the *Independent*:

In the past two years [1997-1999], several art journalists and scholars have revived another explanation for Van Gogh's extraordinary production during the final 10 weeks of his life in Auvers-sur-Oise...he didn't paint them all. Several of the Auvers paintings, they suggest, are fakes, painted, most probably, by Dr Paul Gachet...

But it wasn't just the doctor who'd been implicated. At around the same time as the Independent covered the story, so did the *New York Times.*

...questions arose because of the behavior of the son [Paul-Louis], a recluse who spent his life (he died in 1962, at 89) tending his father's legacy with pathological and paranoid zeal. He preserved everything in the family house as if it were a shrine.

To put that in perspective, Gachet's son, who was perhaps better known by his pseudonym Paul-Louis van Ryssel, than by his real name, [Gachet himself also used the pseudonym Paul van Ryssel to further confuse matters] spent his life preserving his father's artistic legacy, which is to say, his connections to Vincent van Gogh. What did that mean? Well it meant father and son spent a lot of time copying Vincent's art work, the art Gachet had seized when Vincent died in lieu of payment for his services [his failures] in treating him, and over many years, it no longer became clear what was the original, and what was copied.

Only rarely did Paul-Louis let visitors see the collection, [even] preventing photographs of it. Its contents didn't become known until the 1950's, when, having discreetly sold off parts of the collection, Paul bequeathed what remained of it to France.

The Gachet's held onto Vincent's art for 60 years, knowing that an artist's worth increases immediately after his death. The critical word here is "discreetly". Why was it necessary to be discreet about selling Vincent's art? Everyone else was trying to make a fanfare about it, so why were the Gachet's doing the opposite? Did they have something to hide? Well, evidently they did.

People inevitably asked what, if anything, he had been hiding all those years. The present exhibition is considerably absorbed by these questions. The heart of it consists of paintings...which until now had never left the country, supplemented by other works once in the Gachets' possession...doubts have been expressed about several of the other pictures on view, among them a spectacularly awful scene of cows [supposedly] by van Gogh and a clunky still life by Cezanne. The curators [unsurprisingly] argue sensibly for authenticity: they say Paul's secretive nature provoked unnecessary suspicions, that good painters have bad days and that some of the pictures are simply bad, not fraudulent.

The *New York Times* goes on to point out that the point of the 1999 exhibition in the Metropolitan Museum was expressly to attempt to disprove the rumors of deception and fakery regarding Gachet's collection.

When the show opened in Paris a few months ago it prompted another spate of [cynical] newspaper articles. Did Gachet or his son, who was also named Paul and was also a painter of sorts, forge pictures? Did they...capitalize on the public's sudden enthusiasm for previously neglected masters, in this case Cezanne and van Gogh?

Then we discover that Gachet was so obsessed with Vincent post mortem, he intended writing a book about him.

As part of a book about van Gogh that Dr. Gachet intended to write, additional copies of the collection were made by a woman named Blanche Derrouse, a family friend. These are in the exhibition, too, with artifacts like van Gogh's palette and vases and silverware that were the basis of several van Goghs and Cezannes in the show. Like all relics, they have an extraordinary talismanic appeal that often exceeds the attraction of the pictures on view.

What we're seeing here is a sort of black market effect, in the sense that alongside the Van Gogh Estate, was the parallel Gachet Collection, with himself as its centrepiece. As Vincent's reputation gradually grew, the Gachet made their own quiet, calculated efforts to make their collection work for them. But the devil is in the details. Do you see it?

...These are in the exhibition, too...artifacts like van Gogh's palette...

I have noted previously that on the day Vincent was shot, he was seen by the Ravouxs to have gone out with his painting equipment, just like he did every other day. This is dramatized [poorly] in *Lust for Life*. When Vincent returned that evening, he was bent over, clutching his side, bleeding from a bullet wound. His painting equipment – easel, paint box, brushes, palette – were abandoned, wherever he left them. After his death, these artefacts disappeared, along with the pistol he'd supposedly used to shoot himself.

Ever since those incidents, mystery has surrounded where Vincent shot himself. Was it halfway between the Ravoux Inn and Gachet's home, or closer, in the wheat field beside Gachet's home, or closer? It only makes sense for Vincent's art equipment to disappear if he died somewhere that would point the finger of suspicion to someone who lived where he died. That house, we know for a fact, had a pistol, of the type associated with Vincent's death. We know it belonged to Gachet, and that he kept it in a drawer in his office.

And now we know, after 60 years of secrecy, when there was no one left to remember [Theo was gone, Jo was gone, and Vincent II was too young to remember], Vincent's palette resurfaces. It's a very personal possession, one of Vincent's most personal. It doesn't surface as part of the Van Gogh estate, but discreetly, as part of the sly doctor's.

A third publication, the *Guardian*, also expressed reservations about the authenticity of the second portrait in 1999.

But did Van Gogh actually paint that famous portrait of Dr Gachet posing gloomily beside the foxgloves and digitalis with which he treated the artist? Of the two versions that exist, the authenticity of one, signed, is beyond doubt – which is just as well, since it set a new record for a work of art when it was sold at Christie's, New York, for £49.7 million in 1990.

The origins of the other, owned by the Musee d'Orsay, are murkier. It may even, some dare suggest, have been painted by the good doctor himself, or by his son Paul, both keen and prolific amateur artists. Partly in a bid to clear up the confusion, the first important exhibition devoted to the remarkable Dr Gachet opens this Saturday in the Grand Palais in Paris.

Returning again to the *Independent*, we get a stronger sense of agitation and discord about both the efforts of the curators to twist the arms of disbelieving art critics, and the irate art experts, many of whom are unanimous in their assessment, that sinister attempts are being made to bamboozle the art industry, as well as an unsuspecting public.

At issue – what is real about Vincent's work, and what isn't, with Gachet's hand front and center in this mess?

...which are the Van Ryssels and which are the Van Goghs? The show has been put together by the chief curator at the Musee d'Orsay....and the Van Gogh Foundation in Amsterdam. By hanging the Van Goghs and the Van Ryssels (Gachets) side by side, the curators hope to prove the first part of their argument. The disputed pictures - especially the "second" portrait of Dr Gachet - may be below the quality of the artist's best work but are infinitely superior to anything attempted by the doctor or his son.

The curators admit the second portrait is dodgy, and subpar, yet they insist it's superior to the Gachet's [father and son's] shoddy work. Well, they had decades to improve – surely they did, in their obsessive copying?

Now we see just how desperate the stakes were to force the perception that the second Gachet was irrevocably authentic:

Furthermore, the curators say, both the Van Goghs and the known Gachet paintings have been subjected to 12 months of the most minute and rigorous chemical and X-ray analysis. These investigations reveal that the amateur, and amateurish, Gachets always drew the outlines of their subjects and filled in the colors later, like a child painting by numbers. The disputed Van Goghs and Cezannes were not painted in this way. They were painted directly on to the canvas.

Ah, that settles it then! The amateurs never painted directly on to the canvas…well, so they say. No one knows because whatever they did, happened behind closed doors. See the dilemma?

"The X-rays showed no signs of touching up. It showed a strong, firm line in Van Gogh's manner and a background filled in with large brushstrokes, crossing over one another, as in most of his paintings," reported Daniele Giraudy, head of the contemporary arts laboratory at the French museums directorate.

It's pretty incredible, this flowery sounding artistic jargon. You don't need X-Rays to see how different the portraits of Gachet actually are. One of them is entirely missing Vincent's signature dabs of color. One of them, as I've mentioned before, prefers a lighter eye-color for the doctor, a clear suggestion the subject was very personally involved, and very clear on his eye-color. How ironic that his selfish narcissism is what gives him away!

[The] French critic, Jean-Marie Tasset, says the exhibition shoots itself in the foot. By hanging two unimpeachable Van Goghs - The Church at Auvers and a self-portrait - close to the disputed painting, they have exposed the "second" Gachet portrait as "a lifeless, clumsy, soulless composition". On the contrary, says Mr Van Tilborgh of the Amsterdam Van Gogh Foundation, the portrait is a "moving work", well beyond the capacity of either of the Gachets...

Despite the official narratives of the museums and foundations, now thoroughly infected with the bogus narrative, the *Independent* appears to agree that the curator's so-called "proof" is poppycock. *Convincing proof? Not in the least, say the doubters. "The star canvas of the exhibition [the portrait of Dr Gachet] is a cuckoo's egg," said Benoit Landais, the French art critic and Van Gogh specialist. He points to the letters sent by Van Gogh to his brother in June and July 1890, which gave detailed accounts of all his work in Auvers but made no mention of a second portrait of the doctor. Landais says that the painting is manifestly a fake, probably copied from a photograph of the original.*

All this makes and sham even darker. The fact that *Portrait of Dr Gachet* sold for a record $80 million plus, reveals just how high the stakes were in winning the PR war, and how far back the fidgeting in dark actually went. But they pulled it off. The Gachets won. Vincent, his authentic story and his authentic art, lost.

Does it matter though? If Gachet made a copy, or sold a copy, if mistakes were made, does it really matter?

The *New York Times* that same year, posed the same question, and answered many of them with elegant prescience.

In particular there's something about the authenticity of these objects [a reference to Vincent's art equipment] – their direct contact with the artist – that inevitably returns a visitor to the question of the authenticity of the pictures. Whether the authenticity of the Gachets' collection will be resolved to everyone's satisfaction will depend on whether someone someday steps forward with irrefutable evidence. Many fakers have become known because the faker confessed, sometimes even having to overcome experts who refuse to believe the confession.

Twenty years later, no one has stepped forward to dispute Gachet's contribution to the messy mainstream narrative. At least, no one has come forward that has changed that narrative. Until now. In 1999, the *New York Times* vacillated with issues we have yet to resolve to satisfaction.

The ultimate question is...what difference does it make? If a picture is admired before it is revealed to be a fake, isn't it still admirable afterward?...isn't the esthetic value of a work finally independent of who made it?

In other words, is Vincent disposable? Does it matter if it's Gachet's work, or Gachet benefitting from usurping it? Of course it matters!

No matter how much we think art can be judged purely in visual terms, it's a commodity. Authenticity is a measure of market value, a peculiarly Western idea that we impose even on works from other cultures...originality...in our marketplace...value is nonetheless based on standards of invention, individuality, authenticity and so on. This is our way of measuring quality. And quality is about faith. We value a Van Gogh to the extent that we may trust it is by him. For good reason, fakery is sometimes likened to sex: admiring a fake, it's said, is akin to making love in the dark to someone who turns out to be the wrong person. That is, art appreciation, on a basic level, is transactional and not simply esthetic. It demands trust.

Given what we have to deal with in this murder investigation, the sex analogy is doubly significant. The analogy of trusting a Van Gogh work of art, versus doctor Gachet's trustworthiness, versus Vincent's record of inappropriate conduct with women. What was happening in the dark places, the barns and behind the haystacks, on that fateful July day? Was Vincent trustworthy with Marguerite? Was Marguerite a good and faithful daughter?

Fakes loosen our foothold in reality because they mix with true objects to infect the historical record. Sometimes, in the case of forged documents, they can actually change history itself...

And there we are, at full circle. Since the reality of this story has been changed, since the historical record has been infected, since our foothold in the reality of Vincent's story has been loosened, in spite of his letters, in spite of his art, we must turn to the source of these infections, the fakery and all these slippery changes.

In the powerful postscript provided by the *New York Times*, the allegory turns from sex to poison. The subconscious train of thought rumbles out of the yawning abyss and into the gleaming, ghostly station of cold, dry, empty, and yet hard-won reality.

[A philosopher]...once compared the relationship between a genuine painting and a forgery with that between an edible mushroom and a poisonous one. To think that the

difference is merely esthetic or superficial is to be dangerously ignorant. "We can either look harder for the difference, or avoid paintings and mushrooms entirely." If the Gachet show tells us anything, it's that even mediocre paintings have a purpose, which is to give us a firmer grasp of genuine greatness.

And now we have a firm grasp of the true villain in this story.

STARRY NIGHT

"That desire [for marriage] has left me, though the mental suffering of it remains." — Vincent van Gogh

View of the Sea at Scheveningen

"A good picture is equivalent to a good deed." —Vincent Van Gogh

We've arrived at the train station of the dark subconscious. This could be Arles, Auvers or Paris a hundred-and-some years ago. It could be anywhere. Wherever we are, we're not quite ready to disembark, we have to have our ticket clipped first by the train man – our murder suspect.

He's on his way to our present subtext, but he's not quite at the cabin. Sitting quietly on the seat opposite is Vincent, blinding in the blackness, a man we've gotten to know quite well by now. Out there, floating beyond the polished coal-black of the station, Vincent's art will stew for decades before it becomes worth anything. Poor Vincent doesn't know it yet, but we do.

With our unclipped tickets we can hear the sound of shuffling through the inky interior, as the train man approaches. We may understand Vincent, but do we understand the criminal mind, and its approach to art?

In order to prepare for this final leg of our journey, we must project out of our physical form, and penetrate the darkness. We must float through the ether, moving like ghosts through the fog to the beach at Scheveningen, on the Dutch coast. It's lighter here, on the North Coast, but not much brighter. It's the year 1882, August 22. A great grey storm is billowing, sweeping the clouds, the sea and the sand into curtains of swirling murk.

Vincent is struggling with his easel, painting *en plein air*, and scrambling every now and then to catch his canvas as it tears off, and cartwheels along the strand. Each time he brushes off crystals of sand, curses, and throws more paint as it, working at a frenetic pace. The wind howls louder until it shrieks, and the curtain closes over the scene.

Four days later Vincent wrote the following to Theo:

All this week we've had gales, storms and rain here, and I've been to Scheveningen many times to see it. And came back with two small seascapes. There's already a lot of sand in the one, but with the second, when there really was a storm and the sea came very close to the dunes, I had to scrape everything off twice because of the thick layer of sand completely covering it. The wind was so strong that I could barely stay on my feet and barely see through the clouds of sand. I tried to get it down anyway by immediately painting it again in a small inn behind the dunes, after first scraping it all off, and then going out to take another look from there. So I have a couple of souvenirs after all...

Now we drift 45 miles across the muddle of time and place, landscape and memory, on a north east track. Vincent will return home where this early impressionist work will eventually be forgotten in the attic of the family home. When the family move out of the house in Breda, the painting is left behind; another lost relic.

Somehow, over the passage of the first twenty years, the painting passed into various hands, first a carpenter's, who sold it as part of a "rubbish" sale in 1902. Then a tobacco importer bought it from an art shop for 2500 guilders, more than twice the going rate for Van Gogh's at the time. Then the tobacco merchant's daughter, Liesbeth Peletier inherited it.

In 1989, when Liesbeth died, she donated it to the state, and so it came into the possession of the Van Gogh Museum 107 years after Vincent had executed it.

As Scheveningen in the late summer of the year 1882, and all its memories, grows smaller behind us, the horizon before us gradually sparkles as Amsterdam appears in mid-winter, a miserable Saturday in December 2002. It's 120 years later, and it's almost 08:00. *Beach at Scheveningen in Stormy Weather* has been in this austere museum for thirteen uneventful years. But that's about to change.

Two figures emerge out of a van, and onto a freezing wet, deserted street. They hoist a ladder against one of the walls of the Van Gogh Museum. Working quickly, one of them – Octave "Okkie" Durham – scales the fortress-like walls of the museum and smashes a window with a hammer. Okkie's sidekick follows seconds later. While the alarms go off, both thieves sprint through the museum's interior, and both thieves drop their hats on their way out, which is down a rope attached to a flag pole.

As one of them rappels down, he falls and the painting under his arm crunches sickeningly against the ground. One of them leaves a black beanie, the other dislodges his black cap. Inside, DNA will be used to positively identify Okkie. Three minutes and 40 seconds later, two small works, *Beach at Scheveningen in Stormy Weather* and *Congregation Leaving the Reformed Church in Nuenen* disappear into the dark, wet morning, along with Okkie and his sidekick. Both paintings will disappear into the underworld for the next fourteen years.

Following Okkie, through the subterranean streets of the underworld, we hear him putting the word out. We see Okkie meeting with a kidnapper, Cor van Hout, convicted of kidnapping Freddy Heineken, a beer magnate. They make a deal, but two months after the heist, on the day Okkie's supposed to hand over *Beach at Scheveningen in Stormy Weather*, Cor is assasinated. The same thing happens to another prospective buyer.

Okkie doesn't give up, and eventually he finds a low-level Mafioso who offers him about €350,000 for both paintings. In reality they're worth 100 times as much on the legal market, closer to $30 million [and currently worth $100 million]. And that's exactly the point. Raffaele Imperiale, the buyer [who also ran a coffee shop in Amsterdam at the time], isn't interested in the art, or the value of the art, just in how much value society puts in it. Why? The art's not for decorative purposes, Imperiale couldn't care less about that. It's an insurance policy. If someone in his network is caught, and faces trial, one or both of these paintings can be used as a massive bargaining chip. Their value, traded against the value the authorities place in bringing certain top level criminals to justice.

And so, floating through the years 2003 to 2016, we find our way to a house over 1000 miles south east of Amsterdam, halfway down Italy, in the city of Naples. The name of the house is *Castellammare di stabia.* Vincent's paintings aren't on a wall, or even in a cupboard. They're wrapped in cloth, hidden in the floorboards of a kitchen, in the home of Imperiale's father, waiting for a rainy day.

How did the authorities find the art works? Well, when Imperiale was arrested, and Italy's drug trafficking Camorra clan had been overturned, he *told* the police where they were.

According to ganstersinc.com:

Imperiale had used the paintings as a bargaining chip to shave years off his prison sentence for narcotics trafficking. In a signed letter to Italian authorities, Imperiale admitted running a drug ring and gave the location of the stolen Van Goghs. In return his sentence (in absentia) was lowered from 20 years to 12. He continues to reside in Dubai as a fugitive.

When art experts at the Van Gogh Museum evaluated them, both paintings were in poor shape. *Beach at Scheveningen in Stormy Weather* had a chunk of old paint chipped out of it. But grains of sand from Scheveningen were still embedded inside the thick paint, where they'd been trapped for 135 years or more. It was clearly the real thing. From grains of sand, to stars in the sky.

In March 2017, both of the retrieved paintings reappeared in the Van Gogh Museum. However, since they'd gone on adventures together, their value compared to all the other art works still sitting there, had quadrupled. Why? Because of the *story* around these paintings. And because in some strange turn of fate, the psychology of the criminal underworld, in attaching their own commodity value to these particular worlds, their real value had also increased. That's how value works. What we decide is valuable, *is* valuable, as long as the underlying artwork is authentic.

This is how reality shape shifts around art. It's not the art that's changing, it's the reality that's changing around the art.

Now, we can return through the ether of the present, through the gleaming, lunar station house and into the coach where we are sitting with our still unclipped tickets. A shadow scuffles into the cabin, and holds out a small silver ticket clipper. The train man grunts, and Vincent offers his ticket. The shadow, looming over the blinking man, still seated, takes the ticket and punctures it. In that moment the ticket loses all of its value.

When the train man approaches me, I flick a switch on my torch.

"Who are you?" I ask.

But the light of the torch in the dark subconscious can do nothing to change the light. Vincent's clear liquid eyes glint towards me. The spoken words hang in my mind, but in the dark subconscious, nothing that can be spoken can be heard. The dark shadow lingers, his hand outstretched, his clipper ready to puncture my ticket.

"I think that we must not count on Dr. Gachet at all. First of all, he is sicker than I am…now when one blind man leads another blind man, don't they both fall into the ditch?"

Issues with Animation and Schama's Van Gogh

"There is no blue without yellow and without orange." —Vincent Van Gogh

True crime is a lot like Monet's attitude to the pond in the garden of Giverny. You can look at something, but to appreciate what it really is, you must see it again and again, in different colors, on different days and in various contexts. What does summer say about a particular scene? How does an image of reality hold up in winter, or spring? How is the light different at dusk, or dawn, or after the rain? It may seem silly, but by revisiting the same thing over and over again, while reality washes in its various forms around it, you get a real sense of what something is, and for what something isn't.

In a sense, every narrative about Vincent van Gogh, is like revisiting the pond. Sometimes there are new leaves, buzzing insects, a few ducks, or what looks like a path. Other times, with more information, what is part and parcel of the scene remains, and is reinforced. The structure of the scene becomes increasingly concrete, and colors change. Some things are revealed with time, other things hidden, that must be uncovered.

When we cross-reference some of the popular documentaries, films and books about Vincent van Gogh, we come across patterns in the narrative, like ripples in the water. Have these been recycled, or are they self-evident? Were they always there, or added later?

Each new visit from a new author, a new visionary, a new art historian or researcher, provides a slightly different sketch. It's not the prerogative of true crime to be just another narrative, true crime is too important to be left in the realm of another entertaining poke at something. And so, true crime research must evaluate all these narratives and find a way to filter through them, to get to the source of those ripples. Is it the wind, or a tree branch, fish, or birds taking flight? Some of what is collected and discarded is based on evidence, and some, admittedly, is based on intuition.

What's discarded in true crime is never destroyed, it's archived in case it may be needed later, even if only to disprove a recently resuscitated myth. What's collected and synthesised, are all those things that together, add up to a cogent whole. If the pattern is strengthened, and it connects to a source, and the source resonates, then all these elements of the narrative must be carefully assembled and preserved. In this way, all the other narratives become building blocks in their various capacities, almost like dabs of paint on a canvas. Individually of little value, collectively they help form the final picture; they're useful as supports for one super arching narrative, the definitive explanation that integrates all possibilities in the first, best, cogent whole.

I have endeavoured to do that here. Is it worth anything? Let's test how far we've come by revisiting a fraction of this filtering process; let's swim quickly through two visual narratives, to see what sticks, and what doesn't.

We'll revisit the recent animated film of 2017, and Schama's documentary of 2007. We are now far enough in this investigation to be *au fait* with Vincent's story, to know how other narratives and interpretations stack up against it [or distract from it], aren't we?

So, before we clip our tickets, let's see how well our well-informed antenna do the job of filtering the narrative wheat from the chaff, starting with the animation's version of this story.

1. *Loving Vincent* – a vivid reimaging or a set-up?

Loving Vincent pretends to deal with Dr. Gachet, pretends to have the resolve to interrogate him as a suspect, but when it comes down to it, the character offers the same dog-eared version as the Van Gogh Museum: Vincent committed suicide because he didn't want to be a *burden* to his brother Theo.

This explanation suggests a very poor understanding of suicide to begin with. Suicide isn't about being a burden to others, but to oneself. That's understating it to a significant degree. People who commit suicide do so because they can't face something regarding themselves. They simply can't acknowledge it, and if or when reality intrudes, they can't live with it.

Now it may seem, superficially at least, that Vincent couldn't face being a failure as an artist, or that he couldn't acknowledge his struggles as a painter, or that the birth of his nephew, and the fate that awaited his brother's new family, was a kind of terrifying reality for Vincent. The contention works because the logic, broadly, holds. If we were in a similar situation, unemployed, relying on a sibling, and that sibling suddenly started a new family, we'd find ourselves similarly burdensome, wouldn't we?

But though there is truth to the burden narrative, it has very limited import when it comes to Vincent's story. Vincent had been a burden since those early days in London, with the Loyers, as 20-year-old, way back in 1873. When he discovered Eugénie was engaged, Vincent thought nothing of burdening her with his persistent pursuit of her, even less of burdening her mother with his lechery.

I hope it's clear by now that Vincent was a burden to most of his family, his neighbors, his bosses, his art instructors, in one way or another to *everyone* who knew him, for most of his life. He'd been a burden to Theo, financially and emotionally, for years before the events at Auvers.

As for Vincent not being able to acknowledge his struggles as a painter, he'd been living the painter's life for almost a decade when he died. It wasn't as if he'd intimated about giving it up. Instead, at the time of his death his output was as industrious as ever. If anything, he was finally being vindicated – Vincent knew it, Theo knew it, Albert Aurier saw it, and Anna Boch bought *The Red Vineyard* at the Les XX expedition for 400 francs [about $1600], between January 18th and February 23rd, 1890. If anything, Vincent in 1890, five months after selling his first painting, was on the verge – for the first time – of being *less* of a burden.

Finally, the idea that Gachet could simply *tell* Vincent something about his brother, presumes Vincent didn't already know. Vincent and Theo had been corresponding almost daily for years, and besides that, had similar appetites when it came to brothels and women. Vincent himself had syphilis, so why would it upset the apple cart if he found out Theo did?

Ultimately, when we trawl back and forth through Vincent's back story, we see that he was a tough nut to crack, whether in terms of his work [his ability to persist despite ongoing failure] or as a burden to his family [he didn't mind being a burden to his own parents for years, and was not above saddling them repeatedly in embarrassment and disgrace].

Even in the symbology of the story as *Loving Vincent* presents it, Dr. Gachet nevertheless kills Vincent, instead of curing him. The character says as much: "I killed him…" [because I told him his brother had syphilis]. So even in the contrivance of the animation, their version is that Gachet is *in a sense* responsible for Vincent's death. Not criminally responsible, but indirectly a factor. Close, but not close enough, and not nearly a convincing explanation.

All of this is a pity because so much besides the Gachet narrative in *Loving Vincent* is based on fact. It's hard not to when the film animates Vincent's art the way it does, and so, it must be wedded deeply into the artist's life and psychology.

On the plus side, *Loving Vincent* is one of very few narratives that suggests, quite courageously, that a dalliance between the artist and Marguerite Gachet was not only possible, but probable. This is dangled like a carrot, but then neutralized – not completely, but significantly – by the character herself denying any romantic goings-on. Once again, the narrative sets itself before shooting itself in the foot, and ends up being a kind of also-ran in the archive of neither-here-nor-there narratives about the artist.

2. How Courageous, how Powerful, is Schama's Wheat field with Crows Really?

Why is Schama so effective in his depiction of Vincent? Part of it, undoubtedly, is due to an effective beginning, and a powerful, evocative ending. Schama himself, one of the most eloquent and intuitive of modern art commentators, is – true to form – the star of the show. Vincent is too, but what exhilarates here is Schama's success not only in connecting the audience to the art, but the artist.

His narration begins with a contradiction. "Just for once, everything was going right for Vincent van Gogh…"

Surely, the thread of Vincent's life was a torturous, pride-swallowing siege from womb to tomb? Wasn't that why he committed suicide? Schama repeatedly reveals "another" Vincent van Gogh, someone gifted, not deranged, someone dogged, who persisted valiantly, heroically, not madly.

Schama also bravely introduces us to the raw, earthy qualities of Vincent as they really were. He refers to "spermatic" moments, Vincent's thick paint as "ejaculations" on the canvas, and most authentic of all, refers to the Dutchman's habitual "fucking", expressly using that term. What this does is humanize the man, while the accomplished music composer David Julyan [responsible for composing a slew of memorable scores for Christopher Nolan flicks, including *Memento*, *Insomnia* and *The Prestige*], does the rest.

Schama succeeds in making an emotional connection to Vincent, and his story. For my own part, while researching Schama's interpretation and exposed to Julyan's lyrical anthem to his art, I was moved to tears. Somehow one is dazzled inwardly by the same tragic and triumphant rush of life Vincent must have felt. Schama refers to it as a "consolation for our mortality". And that's what it is. When Vincent arrived in Provence – like the sunflowers he painted – he turned his face to the nourishing light, and "felt the Life Force stirring". When we look at Vincent's art, the same thing happens to us. Julyan's deep violins convey the depth of this feeling, the richness of the light, and the Life Force, and it's impossible not to be moved by it.

But not all of it is sunflowers. Schama's episode was made prior to Bernadette Murphy's research and it shows. Incredibly, as recently as ten or so years ago, the ear narrative as fielded by the most influential art historians in the world [like Schama himself] was that Vincent sliced his own ear, albeit just "a piece" of it. According to Schama, who references this snippet of the popular narrative twice, Vincent cut off "only" the lobe, but it was a "large piece" of lobe. In fact it was the opposite. The only piece remaining was a small sliver of the lobe.

The other thing wrong with it, is that Schama's entire narrative in his documentary is framed inside the suicide and within the ear slicing incident. Schama emphasises precisely the fraudulent mainstream narrative that I have been at pains to debunk, but interestingly, as he intuits his subject more deeply, *he* begins to do some of that debunking himself.

Schama inquires rhetorically, from the outset:

"How could a man like that [dramatized as unhinged or mad] make art as stunning as this? [Starry Night Over the Rhône]"

Again and again, Schama invokes a second Vincent van Gogh, one who is in full possession of his craft, and his senses. An "insatiable" bookworm, a thinker, a sensitive conscientious man intent on making his art accessible to the masses, but without scrimping on price.

He also offers this passing remark:

"You didn't get rid of Vincent van Gogh that easily."

No, you didn't, and no you don't.

Schama describes the "real" Vincent as a humble, earthy fellow with a fiery intelligence who was far more than just a man operating on instinct; not just an automaton driven by a fathomless madness. He carefully interprets *Wheat fields with Crows* as far more than a mere symptom of a man painting a suicide note, but the opposite, an artist at the brilliant zenith of his powers.

At 53 minutes into his documentary Schama, standing in front of *Wheat field with Crows* in the museum, states adamantly, and unequivocally:

"I don't think there's the slightest possibility that accomplishing [he turns to the painting] this revelation [on July 10th, 1890], could have been a moment of suicidal despair for Vincent van Gogh. In his art, he'd *never* been more visionary, *never* more brilliant."

In fact, through the course of Schama's deeply intuitive communion with the painter, he unwittingly plucks much of the low-hanging psychological fruit of the counter narrative. Instead of sterility, entropy, hopelessness, mental malaise, disease, depression, dysfunction, darkness or death, Schama offers his audience the opposite. Right there, at the denouement, is a "fertility miracle", "fucking", a Dutch frog kissed by a "high-wattage" French sun, and Theo's optimism, all rolled out in a welcoming, nourishing embrace.

Theo himself is with Vincent before Vincent's supposed-suicide, in spirit, supporting him in Vincent's newfound zeal, supplying him with his ever greater orders for art supplies. Theo is there throughout, and with him afterward.

In terms of the suicide narrative and the ear narrative, Schama gets at least one of these wrong, and as for the other crucial component to Vincent's life story, he doesn't really go into much detail. For an art historian this is inexplicable. What he does do, perhaps without expressly meaning to, is call the suicide narrative into question.

He goes no further, probably because Schama, like most celebrated art historians, must remain beholden to the hand that feeds him, the Van Gogh Museum. He must tip his expert hat to the mainstream narrative and its vested interests, if he wished to be invited back.

No mention is made by Schama whatsoever, of Marguerite Gachet. What Schama achieves is connecting us not with the madness, or the misery of this particular artist, but with his pulsing Life Force. Is that because suicide is a private, deeply personal and thus unknowable quagmire?

Understanding Suicide

"If one is master of one thing and understands one thing well, one has at the same time, insight into and understanding of many things." —Vincent Van Gogh

The dark shadow lingers, his hand outstretched, his silver clipper ready to puncture our ticket. We have come to understand at least some semblance of Vincent's psychology thus far, but we do understand the psychology of suicide? If so, we are ready to punch our ticket. Are we?

We are not yet done at our final psychological marker – the psychology of suicide. We may think we understand what drives someone to destroy themselves, but unless one has lived it, lost to it, or been tormented by it, it's all just hypothetical, isn't it? Getting real about suicide is extremely difficult, because unlike murderers, those who successfully kill themselves never stand trial to explain why. Often, when suicides happen, no one is called to account, not for the life lost or for what could have been done to save them. Why is simply too painful, too loaded and perhaps too uncertain.

Our best hope of skating the polished edge of the sickle track is to slip into a trio of real-life scenarios, an authentic combination of verified suicide and true crime scenarios, in order to test a) whether *any* of them are an approximate fit for this one and b) whether we have developed the *discernment* by now, for telling the difference.

Before we get to our first sample, let's take a cursory look at suicide statistics worldwide, and suicide in France as it is today.

Are you sure you want to hear this?

World Suicide Statistics and Current Norms Around Disclosure

Approximately 1 million people worldwide commit suicide annually. Every 40 seconds, someone, somewhere in the world, takes their own life. For every suicide there are around twenty suicide attempts, which is by inference, 20 million attempted suicides each year, or one attempt every two seconds.

In the last generation, suicide rates have increased by 60%. Suicide is the second-leading cause of death amongst 15-29 year olds globally.

For such a serious affliction plaguing humanity, and a preventable one at that, the murkiness around suicide is vast. This applies to the many suicide victims as well. Instead of telling their families or loved one's their motives, they invariably kill themselves in secret, with no explanation. As one article in *Psychology Today* put it, suicide notes come in all varieties, but most often, silence.

When the authorities or family find someone who has killed themselves, there's often a reluctance to inform the world they committed suicide, instead they do the opposite – they try not to. There's often an attempt to keep it a secret. In the same way when someone changes their mind about committing suicide, they tend to destroy their suicide note [if they've written one], and maintain a pretence that nothing is wrong or amiss. Now, what does this look like in reality? What happens? How does it work?

On April 20th 2018, the world famous Swedish DJ, 28-year-old Tim Bergling [Avicci] was found dead in Muscat, Oman. Most news agencies didn't report anything about the circumstances of Bergling's death, or where it happened. Three days later, his family released a statement thanking fans for their support, while asking for privacy. Five days after his death, it emerged that Bergling had died in his hotel room, at the Muscat Hills Resort. The Resort released a statement, talking up how the celebrity was happy and friendly. Then Bergling's family released a second statement following tabloid rumors of drugs found at the scene.

In the second statement, for the first time, the family hinted at suicide, referring to Bergling as "an over-achieving perfectionist" and "a fragile soul" who "struggled with thoughts about Meaning…" and was "searching for answers to existential questions." The statement added that Bergling was under extreme stress because of the pace of the industry he was in, referring to it as "a machine he found himself in" and Bergling as a "sensitive guy" who "wanted to find peace."

Bergling's spokesman at the time of writing [April 28th, 2018], more than a week after the incident, has still refused to confirm whether the artist took his own life. This is the reality of suicide in the real world. People, particularly family, friends, hotels and business associates, don't like to discuss it, let alone admit it. Even after the death of a person, a lot rides on whether or not it is suicide or not, particularly whether life insurance – often enormous sums of money – can be paid out to dependents. When someone with life insurance commits suicide, life insurance does not pay out.

Exactly the same scenario played out with Cranberries singer Dolores O'Riordan, who was found dead in her hotel room at the London Hilton on January 15th, 2018, three months ago at the time of writing. Initial reports then, and now, reinforce the impression that O'Riordan was happy, and in good spirts immediately prior to her death. Only later, did other information emerge of health problems, and another suicide attempt in 2012. O'Riordan had struggled to cope after her divorce, and admitted to suffering for several years from anorexia, alcoholism, bipolar disorder, depression and a recurring fixation with suicide.

Although an inquest was opened in January to ascertain the 46-year-old Irish singer's cause of death, and was expected to be made public in early April, the inquest was subsequently postponed four months after her death. The status of O'Riordan's death at the time of writing remains unknown.

The reasons for Robin William's suicide [he hung himself at his home] in August 2014, also, are still speculated about today. In all three cases – Bergling, O'Riordan and Williams – no suicide notes were written to their families or anyone else.

The take-out from all this? Even when figures are world famous, there's a concerted attempt to conceal not only the circumstances of their deaths, but the troubling realities they faced in their lives. Vincent van Gogh, like Bergling and O'Riordan, died in a hotel room [the Ravoux Inn]. How did the community find out about his death, and from who? We find additional context to these questions by drilling down into the idiosyncratic history of suicide in the country where Vincent died.

The Taboo Around Suicide in France

In France a person commits suicide every hour. The suicide rate in France is higher than the world average, and also higher than the European average, in fact, it's fairly close to the average suicide rate for Africa. To put this further into perspective, the suicide rate in France is twice that of the Britain and Spain.

More people commit suicide in France than in South Africa, New Zealand or even the war-torn Democratic Republic of Congo. Conversely, Holland has atypically low suicide numbers. Lower than the world average, lower than the European average, and lower than countries like Ireland and Switzerland.

What this says, is that the cultural make-up of a country has a huge bearing on suicide. I lived for several years in South Korea, and was shocked to discover how socialised suicide is in that country. It's the 4th leading cause of death, 40 South Koreans commit suicide each day, roughly twice the rate in France. When someone fails at something in Korea, whether in business, at school or in a marriage, suicide is a typical escape. Unsurprisingly, South Korea has the tenth highest suicide rate in the world, with almost two-thirds of suicides using poisoning as the method of choice.

Why then are the French more suicidal than other Europeans? According to some experts, it's related to a school system that doesn't tolerate failure – but punishes students for it. This culture of winning-at-all costs, and the failure as a tangible social cost to society, means failure is less tolerable to the French than to others. Perhaps this also has to do with French vanity, the economics of France and French history. In France, more than any other European country, suicide is taboo.

Jean-Claude Delgenes, the director of Technologia, a company that collates data on the problem of suicide in France, pointed out to *TheLocal.fr* in February 2018, just how far into history the taboo goes.

"Until the revolution, people who took their own lives had their bodies mutilated, dragged through the streets and buried outside town, because it was considered a shameful act."

Delgenes also cites a rise in anxiety in France:

"A kind of generalized anxiety has afflicted France for 40 years during which time we have been unable to deal with rising mass unemployment. There are two million people who have been out of work for over a year and one million who haven't worked for over two

years. That weighs down on people's moral. People are depressed. They are scared of losing everything."

It's an interesting theory, but not a very convincing one. Spain, Italy and Greece have far worse unemployment figures than France, and as mentioned, France's suicide rate is twice that of Spain. Also, unemployment is very low in South Korea, about a third as high as in France.

Delgenes argues that the culture in France which "doesn't encourage risk taking and punishes failure" only heightens this anxiety, and that originates from the school system... We need to allow our children to grow through failure and not punish them all the time...Failure is a way to build ourselves."

Now we're talking. It's not so much the failure of unemployment *per se*, that creates a sense of personal humiliation, it's the social stigma and stress associated with it that drives deep, existential anxieties. A culture that punishes failure is also clearly one that both drives suicide and refuses to acknowledge it.

But if this was the case, why was Vincent's apparent suicide acknowledged as quickly as it was? Wasn't suicide taboo in 1890, or was it only taboo for French citizens?

In a 2009 study on *Romanticism and the Culture of Suicide in 19th Century France* we see that a large part of the taboo in France for suicide was because of Catholic church. Among the 47 000 religious buildings in France, 94% are Roman Catholic, including the Church at Auvers.

Not only was Vincent's suicide common knowledge after his death, it was so well-known the church he'd painted wouldn't hold a funeral service for the artist, nor would they allow him use of the parish hearse. He was also not allowed to be buried in the church grounds either. One can imagine the disgrace Theo felt, as the son of pastor, being handed this troubling burden of a controversial burial. Initially, Theo had Vincent buried in a wheat field bordering the church property.

According to the study cited above:

Most nineteenth century observers associated self-destructive behavior with mental instability, viewing the individual who sought to put an end to his existence as weak, if not perverse, [but] a certain mystique also surrounded suicide at this time.

In other words, suicide was seen as a product of madness, and thus, there was little incentive to find a scientific explanation. Back to Delgenes on the same topic:

"For the [Catholic] church, committing suicide was a big sin and it was a question that was dealt with from a moral point of view rather than a scientific one...[and] this prevented mental health problems from being treated seriously."

In other words, if you committed suicide in 19th century France, you were doomed, condemned. What's more, people could care less why it happened, they saw it in stark moral tones and weren't interested in cause and effect. One might say the taboo was so severe, by not burying suicides, public and cultural knowledge on the subject was also taboo.

Given Vincent's studies as a lay preacher, his efforts at preaching and his experience as the son of a preacher who'd attended funerals with his own father, it's difficult to imagine he was unaware of the French/Catholic position on suicide, and further, that he'd be insensitive to the burden he was placing on his brother, by committing suicide. Conversely, we can clearly see how quickly and effectively the "mad artist" narrative could have sprung up, in the fertile headspace of the cultural position on suicide as it was at the time.

If we've learned a little about the cultural apparatus surrounding suicide, it's time to integrate that with four practical studies from real life. Are we ready, finally, to fathom the operative psychology?

Sample #1

On Friday April 13th, 2018, at about 01:30, 48-year-old husband and father, David "Dr. Fish" Bellet-Brissaud left his hotel room in Port Elizabeth and promptly disappeared. It was the Frenchman's first trip to South Africa; he'd flown in on Thursday, arriving in the city at 15:00 to participate in the Ironman Championship on Sunday [April 5th]. 10 hours later he was gone.

That was how the story originally played. Sunday came and went and David remained missing. The day after the Ironman event, Monday April 16th, the Frenchman's family [who'd flown in over the weekend] called a press conference. His brother Gael offered a reward of R12 000 [about $1000] while his sister Vanessa, who broke down during the press conference and had to leave the room, described David unhelpfully as "an ordinary guy."

My impression, looking at the coverage, was that Lydia, his wife, seemed quite stoic, given what had happened to her husband. David's brother described her as "very strong", but to me she seemed emotionless, and suspicious so.

I was intrigued by this story for several reasons. Firstly, I've competed in the Ironman in Port Elizabeth myself, and am very familiar with the area in which this incident occurred. Secondly, given my research into Vincent van Gogh, I was interested to know the outcome of this story, especially since Ironman triathletes are extremely motivated people, and my key counter-argument to Vincent not committing suicide was that he'd remained motivated and active until the day he was shot.

In this case, it was difficult to make a call between a high probability of a crime having been committed [knowing the high-crime rate in South Africa], and the possibility of suicide [not knowing anything about the personality and private situation of Bellet-Brissaud].

The fact that Bellet-Brissaud's siblings were offering a reward, suggested suicide was improbable for those who knew him. The reward showed they clearly suspected he was still alive, and had possibly been kidnapped, abducted or robbed. It was difficult to make a call either way, without knowing 1) more about who David Bellet-Brissaud was exactly and 2) the precise circumstances of his disappearance. However, if David's siblings seemed positive and hopeful, his wife Lydia somehow didn't, and she'd been the last to see him alive.

In time, however, more information came to light. In terms of David Bellet-Brissaud it was established that:

1. He lived a clean, healthy, disciplined life. He didn't smoke or drink.
2. He was married to Lydia, and they had two children, Stacey [21] and Anthony [18], both living with their grandmother in Paris.
3. Based on his Instagram page, David had posted a majority of training sessions, the last of them in Paris, but besides this, there was very little else besides the fish and odd selfie. On December 29th, 2017, he posted a rare family snapshot.
4. For the past fifteen years, David worked as a forestry official handling logistics for the SEEF logging company in Gabon.
5. The "Dr Fish" nickname appeared to suggest an unusual interest in fishing and swimming in the sea. He was said to be a good swimmer, often swimming several kilometers in swim training each morning.

In terms of the circumstances of his disappearance:

1. David was staying at the Paxton Hotel, which is close to the seashore and harbour complex.
2. In the evening, David and Lydia joined friends from Gabon for a meal at the Colcacchio restaurant, at the popular Boardwalk Casino Complex.
3. David arrived back at the hotel room, on his own, at about 21:00, while Lydia remained downstairs, socialising and drinking with friends from Gabon at the hotel bar.
4. Lydia returned to their room at around 23:00, and found David already asleep.
5. When Lydia woke up at about 01:20, David was gone.
6. She said: "I thought he had maybe gone outside for fresh air."
7. Lydia would later say it was the first time David had ever gone out on his own like that, a strange claim, giving Ironman athletes are constantly outside training, though not at night.

8. CCTV footage showed David leaving the hotel wearing a black Adidas hoodie, blue jeans and sneakers. The black hoodie indicates he didn't wish to be seen.
9. He'd left his cell phone and wallet in the hotel room, negating the likelihood of being robbed.
10. He was seen walking in the direction of the harbor complex across the road from the hotel.
11. On April 18th, David's family increased the reward for "positive proof of life" more than tenfold, from R12 000 to R150 000.
12. Authorities asked businesses lining the seafront to review their CCTV footage. One recording showed someone jumping between fishing vessels, prompting early speculation that he may have drowned, or may have been kidnapped after witnessing illegal activity on one of the boats in the harbour. This speculation prompted his sister to point out that David was "an excellent sailor" and swimmer. Remarkably, this footage later proved to be a red herring, the man it depicted wasn't David after all; authorities had been searching the wrong area of the harbour.
13. Next, new CCTV harbor footage was handed in. The new footage as more promising; it showed another figure walking along "a different part of the jetty".
14. A bright light shining into the CCTV camera prevented the viewer from seeing what happened next.

On April 19th, six days after his disappearance, cadaver dogs found a trace of David in the harbour area of the second CCTV recording. Shortly afterwards, at about 18:00 his body was retrieved where it had been anchored underwater. He was hauled out and onto a stretcher. His brother Gael positively identified the body. David's ankles had been tied with a green cord to a large tyre, and the tyre weighed down with rocks. An autopsy soon after provided the cause of death: drowning. Gael left the harbour area in tears.

So, did David "Dr. Fish" Bellet-Brissaud drown himself; was this suicide or was he murdered? We can see from this brief personal history that David had no health problems, and apparently no mental illness. He seemed disciplined, but perhaps more regimented and balanced, a perfectionist who wanted, needed, all his ducks in a row. The only useful detail provided by his wife, was her mentioning David becoming quiet after their arrival in South Africa, which she attributed to stress. This would have been his first full distance Ironman, which is a big deal, but he'd run marathons previously, and done a number of half-ironmans. So I'm not sure if I buy into Lydia's explanation. It's not as though David was a total rookie to the sport, and at 48-years-old, he wasn't likely to be quiet because of physical fear. Speaking for myself, in the days prior to an event of this magnitude, one is in the shape of one's life, it's an exhilarating achievement. One's energy levels tend to be – should be – overflowing. So the contention that David had clammed shut on Thursday, two whole days before the event, doesn't resonate with me.

Now, it's incredible how even in such a "small" narrative, a bogus narrative managed to develop, including one involving a phantom figure jumping between boats. Besides that, plenty more speculation was thrown into the vacuum, including intrigues of kidnapping and illegal smuggling. It shows, even with cutting edge technology, it's very easy to become side-tracked when one has an incomplete picture to work with.

So was it suicide or murder?

It was suicide.

In the end, our best information in this case wasn't what we didn't know. What we needed wasn't that CCTV footage burnt out by the harbour spotlight. The key didn't lie in some underworld criminal haystack. Having said that, evidence isn't necessarily in what's there, but in what should be there, but isn't. The absence of Instagram photos from David's arrival in South Africa [he'd posted an image of his airplane ticket on April 9th], visiting the race venue and eating out with his wife and friends, clearly shows that he was out of it from the moment he arrived. I've competed in numerous triathlon events, and it's a big celebration, it's exciting, it's something you want to share and brag about. Why didn't he?

Someone or something was spoiling it for him...

That David's last social media image is from a workout he did in France two days before arriving in South Africa, speaks volumes. One can see from his Instagram timeline, that he was posting at regular intervals, often several times a day, and seldom with more than a day or two passing between posts. Once he's in South Africa, no posts.

My own view is that David was a very disciplined and conscientious guy, very attached to his family, and they [for the most part], were attached to him. While discipline is good, an overly regimented way of living is anal, and joyless, and we can see, with David's obsession with his own training numbers, that very little was going on in his life besides Ironman.

The fact that his wife socialized without him, that he doesn't drink and she was out drinking, and, in her version of events, was asleep when he left the hotel room, raises red flags. It's a very sanitised version of events, which ends with her husband drowning himself.

Lydia doesn't mention her last words to him, or his to her. What's more, in a sense, him being asleep while she is out, and she being asleep when he is out, is psychological code for each spouse drowning out the other. David's death by drowning, is also psychological code. It may seem strange, but suicide is a deeply personal event, and people who wish to kill themselves, wish to do so in a controlled environment, or in a safe place. A hotel room will do, unless it's occupied, and David's was. The next best thing for David was the world he knew best – water.

What's more, her own contention that when she woke up and realized he wasn't in the room, she first thought he'd gone to get some "fresh air" makes no sense. At 01:30 in a strange country? They'd all been out for some fresh air just a few hours earlier. No one would think that, that he'd gone to get some air, at that time of night, unless they'd had a row, and if they had rowed, perhaps it wasn't the first time. Perhaps they'd argued on the plane. Perhaps they'd been rowing for some time in Gabon. Perhaps Lydia wanted to be Paris, not Libreville.

Added to this is the lack of emotion and urgency provided by her throughout. There seems to be a sense that she knows something and isn't telling. If David was upset because of her, and killed himself, Lydia would have every reason not to want to reveal that. It wouldn't make her culpable, certainly not criminally culpable, but she'd have to answer to her children, and bear that burden. And that's the takeout here: *suicide is a real burden for those who are left behind.* Look at what happened here. The entire city was turned upside down, David's family had to fly in, there were press conferences, rewards, an entire boulevard checking their CCTV. And one wonders whether, somewhere in his despair, David *wanted* to expose Lydia, wanted to humiliate her like she'd humiliated him. Wanted to have her explain what had happened, or face the music of the world's attention without an explanation. She chose the latter, volunteering no more than that David was nervous about his race. Had he killed himself because he was too anxious to compete?

If the one take-out from this is to second-guess the credibility of Vincent being a burden to Theo, and that's why he killed himself, the other is to note how secretive a suicidal motive can actually be. David left no note, and no obvious symptoms on his social media. Moreover, suicide by drowning is hardly an instant death; it's got to be pretty unpleasant and wouldn't be everyone's first choice. Finally, David's motivation to train for his race, shouldn't be confused with the will to live. Incentive and intention aren't the same. Inspiration and meaning, or purpose, aren't the same either. For David, there were clearly more important things than sport, like family, and perhaps on that night of all night, he felt eclipsed by how unimportant he was to his spouse.

Is being alone really living?

There are some similarities to the scenario here, and Vincent's in Auvers so long ago. But there is also a *major* difference between what happened here and what happened to Vincent. That difference is in the first, most obvious piece of information we have. David left his hotel room at 01:30, with no phone or wallet, with nothing, and never returned. It's a strange thing for anyone to do, especially someone who is married. It's clear he knew he wasn't coming back, and needed to leave under the cover of dark when no one was around. It was his first day there, and no one knew where he was going, which made his actions even more strange, but also, strangely, *ominously* intentional.

Vincent, on the other hand, left the Inn where he'd been staying for 70 days straight, the same time he always did. He left at a normal hour, and what's more, he took his art gear with him. This suggests that *he thought* it would be a day just like any other. Just as it made little sense for David to take any gear with him on a one-way trip, why would Vincent take his art gear if he didn't intend to return? The answer then, clearly, is that when Vincent left that morning, he *did* intend to return.

Sample #2

Shortly after midnight on Sunday July 24th, 2016, several witnesses at the exclusive Spier Wine Estate, near Cape Town, saw and heard real estate tycoon and multi- millionaire, Jason Rohde arguing with his wife. 47-year-old Jason Rohde's mistress Jolene Alterskye [35] was in the hotel at the same time, attending the same business function as Jason Rohde and his wife. Rohde's wife Susan had known about the affair her husband was having for since June 2015.

At about 07:00 that morning, Jason Rohde called the hotel reception to report the bathroom door had been locked from the inside. When a handyman arrived to unlock it, Rohde's wife was found hanging from a towel hook on the other side, not suspended off the floor, but lying beside the door with an electric hair iron cord twisted loosely around her neck. The other end of the cord looped up to the towel hook.

In late 2017, I attended the court case [still underway at the time of writing] at the Western Cape High Court in Cape Town. Observing him first-hand in court, Rohde appeared to me to be a well-groomed, polished, but high-strung individual. He appeared to have a nervous tick, causing a part of his face to flinch involuntarily.

For the first eleven days following Susan Rohde's death, the cops accepted Jason Rohde's explanation, and treated the incident as a suicide. However, following an autopsy, extensive bruising around his wife's neck implied manual strangulation. The evidence didn't match the ligatures expected from the electric cord, and so it became a homicide case.

In court, Rohde's statement to police on the morning of the incident was read out by one of a phalanx of lawyers. According to *IOL*:

[Rohde] explained that he and his wife had had a disagreement at about 02:30 on July 24, the day of the murder, last year. Rohde added that after deciding to go for a drink at a friend's room, Susan had followed.

"My wife in her gown and no shoes followed me to his room, in which she tripped and cut her foot and left eyebrow."

He said they had both returned to their room to sleep until she awoke at 07:00, still upset, and had gone to the bathroom where she was later found dead. Rohde's lawyer, Pete Mahalik raised the issue of Susan's mental state. He said her father's infidelity, her sister's marital problems and her husband's infidelity might have accumulated and prompted her to commit suicide.

What's interesting in this case, is a scenario where we are asked to believe that someone would commit suicide in a hotel room, with their partner in the adjoining room, and that the partner wouldn't be aware of it. Once again there is no suicide note. Given what we've seen in the Bellet-Brissaud case, it seems unlikely that someone intent on killing themselves would risk botching it, in the sense that someone nearby could interfere with the act before it was completed.

This may seem a silly point, but just as the location and timing of a crime scene in a murder reveals plenty about the psychology of the perpetrator and victim, the choice of location for a suicide, and the timing, reveals a great deal about the motive of the person who wishes to kill themselves. Consider that in the context, once again, of Vincent heading out to a wheat field, killing himself in the open, and his corpse, after being picked on by crows and ants, being discovered an unknown period afterwards by random strangers. Would they know who he was, or what to do with him?

Well, this was precisely what Bellet-Brissaud did, except he was far from home and probably didn't intend for his family to find him, or expect they'd have to identify, just his wife.

I'm reluctant to divulge information about my mother, because it's private, personal and painful, but God knows I have thought about it a great deal. I've also examined my own feelings about suicide more than most normal people should. I feel I can speak with some authority on the burden suicide leaves other family members, especially when they're not explicit about why they chose to do what they did.

My mother killed herself on a Sunday morning, not early, but in a vacant office. Her suicide was on a cold, bright, windy autumn day in October, 99 years and two months after Vincent's tragic end, on the far side of the world in central South Africa. My family endured the same horror his did, with pastors familiar to us who would not consent to a "proper" burial. The one who did, used the service to doom her, using her as a cautionary tale for his fiery sermon. He used the funeral to ask mourning family members who wished to stand up, repent for their sins, and give their hearts to Jesus. Don't end up in hell, like her.

It's not a topic with any satisfying answers. The whole subject is a suffocating burden, even now, almost 30 years later. She obviously didn't want to be found at home by her children. She was found a few hours after leaving home by my father, probably because it had been engineered that way.

In any event, I attended some of the Rohde trial because it was abundantly clear to me that his wife's death wasn't a suicide. When I attended court, images of the deceased, completely naked, spread-eagled on the bathroom floor, with a number of bruises, including to her inner thigh, were displayed in grisly detail. While these images were on display, Rohde showed zero emotion; no grief, and no discomfort – a big giveaway.

The autopsy photos were also shown in horrifying detail, showing how blood had pooled inside Susan's chest cavity, in a horizontal fashion, a clear indication that she'd been strangled while lying on her back. It was very upsetting to see, for me, and I had no connection whatsoever to her. And yet once again, Rohde seemed completely unaffected by it. Murders who meant to kill, are pleased and satisfied with their results, which is why it's difficult and counterintuitive for them to seem upset by something when they consider it a triumph, privately.

Incredibly, WhatsApp messages between Rohde, his dead wife and mistress, were fielded in court, showing all three had been arguing the day before the suicide/murder. Rohde, in one message, referred to his wife following him around at the conference "like a fucking shadow". In another message Susan calls Rohde "a devious fucking bastard".

At 11:35:49, Rohde sent his wife this message:

"...if I call her [Alterskye] it will come up on seri your idiot!!! Now leave, I have had enough. On my work day you are doing this to me. I want you gone now and I don't care about the consequences."

Other messages seemed to involve Susan threatening her husband, and her husband threatening her. At 20:00, Susan sent a message to her psychologist, Jane Newcomb, informing her that she'd met Alterskye directly at the conference.

"I shook her hand and said I hoped we didn't have to meet again."

There was clearly a huge amount of tension within the love triangle, particularly between Rohde and his wife, and never more so on the night Susan died. When Rohde called Susan's brother in Australia, he said: "I killed her, I killed her," but the brother, not knowing the circumstances of the marriage, sympathised, assuming he was just emotional, and simply blaming himself. This mistake may have given Rohde the confidence to believe that others might be misled too.

For several days following his wife's death, Rohde appeared to have gotten himself off the hook. He'd even returned to his home in Johannesburg despite the police asking him to remain in town. At his wife's funeral, he arrived late and left early.

In the case of my own family, my father was also briefly [for a few hours] a suspect in my mother's death. Since she had used his gun, and died at his office, and since he found her, it was automatic [not knowing the circumstances of her life, or what was happening in our family] to make that assumption. I think they did residue tests on his hands. That must have been very painful for him. But it wasn't difficult to prove his alibi, my brother and I were both home the entire morning with him, and my sister had been with my mother, when she'd driven her to church that morning.

Can you see though how ridiculous the idea is that Vincent elected to commit suicide in order to not be a burden to his brother?

Is there *any* doubt about whether the Rohde case was murder or suicide? There are three takes out. The first take-out is *how easily and effectively murder can be explained away as suicide*. All Rohde felt he needed to do was portray his wife as depressed and mentally unstable. Because he was having an affair, and she knew about, she was depressed and unhinged. So what it came down to was a battle between two narratives: her madness [without her there to support her own narrative] versus his anger, and his motive for murder in the context of his infidelity [and having the advantage that he could speak as a witness on his absent wife's behalf].

The second take-out is more subtle, but in a sense, more obvious. *Was Susan really suicidal?* This is an area the court tends to avoid, because it feels like speculation. In fact, the pattern of suicidal behaviour is quite clear. There's no blueprint, but it's easy to show a pattern of self-defeating behaviour, and sometimes, though not always, people who commit suicide tell others close to them repeatedly, they are considering it. My mother did.

If Susan was really miserable in her marriage, would she be at the hotel, with her husband, sharing his bed, confronting him, confronting his mistress? Would she be fighting for her marriage one moment, and despairing, and prepared to give up the next? It may be tempting to imagine a wife and mother might opt out of their own story at the drop of the hat, in the room next door, but the key here is the third take-out. *Susan had known about the affair for over a year.* That shows a tough, resilient, battle-hardened wife, a warrior for herself and her children. In exactly the same way, Vincent was battle hardened to his extended experience as a failure in society, both as an artist, and to some extent as a man. There was no sudden, alarming, unwelcome revelation that they weren't able to acknowledge. Both Vincent and Susan were well aware what was happening.

His persistence was disgusting/Her persistence was disgusting [to Rohde]

He knew very well what he was doing…and he painted in spite of his illness./ She knew very well what she was going…she pursued her husband [Rohde], despite his affair.

He found redemption, in his art, [Susan in her marriage, which she believed she could salvage] and that's where we see his [and her] will to live.

Sample #3

A far tougher, more complex nut to crack, than the Bellet-Brissaud and Rohde cases, is the mysterious death of Rebecaa Zahau. According to Wikipedia:

32-year-old Rebecca Zahau was found dead on July 13th, 2011, at the Spreckels Beach House in Coronado, California, owned by her live-in boyfriend Medicis Pharmaceutical CEO Jonah Shacknai. Zahau's death occurred two days after Shacknai's 6-year-old son, Max, took a fatal fall from a staircase banister in the same beach house. Zahau was the only adult present at the time of his fall. San Diego Sheriff Bill Gore announced on September 2nd, 2011, that Zahau's death was a suicide while the younger Shacknai's was an accident, and that neither was the result of foul play.

There's a similar scenario here to Rohde: an extremely powerful, wealthy man and the woman closest to him dies under strange circumstances. It becomes exceedingly complex when he add the dynamic of the little boy falling down the stairs two days before his stepmother died. Did the one incident have anything to do with the other? It's hard to imagine there wasn't some connection.

It's not the ambit of this narrative to deal with the Zahau case in detail [I've begun preliminary research into a deep-diving narrative investigating the crime]. What matters is to simply compare the skeletal scenario of the Zahau case to Vincent's story, while keeping the Bellet-Brissaud and Rohde cases afloat in our minds.

Ultimately, despite the initial assessment of suicide and no foul play, Zahau's family sued the brother of Zahau's millionaire partner, Adam Shaknai, for $10 million. The Zahau family vehemently disputed that she'd put a rope around her neck, jumped off the balcony and hung herself [completely naked].

In all three of these references case, the method of suicide – like in Vincent's case – is strange, improbable but not impossible. Drownings, hangings and botched shootings are all very common. In the Zahau case, like in the Rohde scenario, it was hard to imagine a woman hanging herself while naked. Why would she wish to be found in such a humiliating state? Conversely, if either of these cases involved a vengeful, angry male murderer, we'd *expect* humiliation to be part of the angry onslaught against the victim.

Back to Wikipedia:

The [civil trial] jury found Adam Shacknai responsible [for Zahau's death] and ruled he must pay the family of Zahau $5 million for the loss of love and companionship as well as an additional $167,000 for loss of financial support Zahau would have provided her mother and siblings.

There are shifting moral implications where there is a murder-or-suicide narrative, but clearly, there are financial implications too. Where a murderer kills someone close to him, clearly, he should not only not benefit in any way from his victim's death, but be punished for his actions. In a suicide scenario, close family don't necessarily benefit either, but no one is punished, and because of the taboo nature of the act, the victim tends to be eviscerated from memory, even in well-meaning, and loving families. As such, the motive behind by far the majority of suicides is never settled. This burden lingers for a lifetime with all those close to the victim, each person that cared for or was touched by the victim.

Since I haven't analysed the Zahau case here, nor provided any proper context regarding the dynamic between Zahau and the Shacknai brothers, the take-out will feel hypothetical. There is a link between the first incident [the fall of the six-year-old, and his death] and the second incident, Zahau's murder. In the Rohde case, there is – I believe – a link between sexual infidelity, and Susan's death. In the Besset-Brissaud case, I believe there is a missing link that has something to do with Lydia, whether this has to do with her infidelity is difficult to say.

How these scenarios play into the allegation of Vincent's suicide is like this:

1. If Vincent was murdered, his murderer felt he had very good reason not to injure him, but to kill him. In the Rohde and Zahau cases, we can see what some of these reasons might be. In Rohde's case, the permanent settling of an ongoing sexual rivalry. In the Zahua case, there's also a sexual dimension, but more pertinently, a sense of opportunistic vengeance, where someone is punished for what someone else thinks or knows they did. It's my view that the little boy was suffocated by his own father, and that Zahau was a potentially costly witness to this.

2. The sexual dimension in Vincent's case was 20-year-old Marguerite Gachet. This was a dalliance that could not be tolerated by her strict, emotionally unhinged father. It's also possible that Marguerite's brother knew about it, and acted against Vincent, whether by informing his father, or confronting Vincent directly, or both. However it's more likely Dr. Gachet himself would have felt personally aghast, and called to action, if he'd found his daughter *en flagrante delicto* with Vincent. One reason the doctor may have felt called to arms, was his knowledge that Theo has syphilis, and Vincent did too, meaning, Vincent posed a clear and present danger to his daughter's health and safety. The warding off of the potential ruin of his beloved daughter, is mirrored in the ruining of Vincent, both in the physical harm he suffered, and in the narrative after his death, impinging on his sanity. Like all good rumors, this one was based to some extent on fragments of truth. We can also see how Gachet, when he was summoned to treat Vincent, would do so with reluctance, and be resistant to repairing damage, if he very much intended to incur it a few hours earlier.

3. It's possible that Vincent acted inappropriately to Marguerite, since he had done so on many occasions previously to other young women that were at arm's reach, including those who'd modelled for him [and Marguerite had]. If true, and if he had tried to force himself onto Marguerite, perhaps while the family were attending church, one can to some extent reason with other family members rallying to her cause. However, the fact that Marguerite took flowers to his grave after Vincent's death, suggests there may well have been a mutual attraction. The latter scenario provides even more reason for a militant father to militate against a persistent pair of lovers, caught up in mutually inappropriate adoration.

Sample #4

There's a final scenario to highlight before we return to more practical matters. It's not only men who murder women and invoke suicide. The case of Kristin Rossum involves an elaborate scenario where her husband, Greg DeVilliers, was found dead in his bed, surrounded by rose petals. Rossum claimed this portrait was symbolic; that the scene was his suicide note. It was his admission about being overly romantic about love in the context of a marriage that was unravelling.

Initially, the suicide was accepted on the terms Rossum provided. But the DeVilliers' family were suspicious; they believed there was more to it. When Rossum was interrogated, she told the cops the right-sounding things, that her husband had been depressed. Her father rallied to her cause, helpfully telling officers about DeVilliers' heavy drinking.

The whole case changed when DeVilliers' autopsy was handed over to a lab outside San Diego. The authorities felt there was a potential conflict of interest in an autopsy conducted at a lab where a relative of the deceased was employed, as well as her boss. A Los Angeles lab found DeVilliers had seven times the lethal dose of fentanyl in his system. It was blind luck that the Los Angeles lab was able to test for it, because most labs didn't. The murderer knew this precisely because she [and her boss] worked in a medical examiner's office.

Rossum, it turned out, was absolutely right. The message was symbolic. The message was about one person getting caught up in a romance and suffering the consequences of drug-fuelled illusions. But that person was her, revealing her own psychology, not DeVilliers. Rossum was arrested seven months after her husband's murder and found guilty in 2002 of first degree murder.

The take-out from this fourth sample demonstrates how easily a person in a strategically powerful position, such as a doctor or someone with access to sensitive medical information about a victim, can commit a crime and control the narrative, ensuring their chances of getting away with murder are virtually assured. Clearly there is a similarity in Rossum murdering DeVilliers, and getting away with it [for a time], based on her medical privileges, and Gachet murdering someone who many thought was mad anyway. If he said it was suicide, if he diagnosed Vincent as mad, who was anyone to argue?

Late 19th Century Shift in Attitudes to Suicide in France

There are about 1 million suicides in the world every year. There are about a third as many murders in the world, over 385 000 murders were recorded in 2016. On a purely statistical basis, for each murder there are likely to be three suicides. Possibly this ratio was broadly true 130 odd years ago as well.

What we know for certain, was that in Vincent's day, the idea of murder was extremely popular in Britain and in France. It was the time of Jack the Ripper and the French Ripper, Joseph Vacher. It was the birth of forensic science and new forensic techniques, such as autopsies, the true crime mirror for Pasteur's work in microbiology, and germ theory, and just as Pasteur was becoming a legend, so were ground-breaking detectives. *Sherlock Holmes*, for example, first appeared in print in 1887.

On July 26th, 1889, a year and a day before Vincent was shot, Toussaint-Augustin Gouffé was reported missing. A fortnight later, half of Gouffé's corpse was discovered in Lyon. The investigation into the Gouffé case preoccupied the French media for the rest of the year, and went on to impact the French for the remainder of the 19th century. Ultimately it was determined Gouffé had been murdered by a couple, Michel Eyraud and Gabrielle Bompard.

In June 1890, at the same time Vincent began his work in Auvers, Eyraud was finally apprehended and arrested, in Cuba of all places. The murderous couple stood trial between in late 1890, and Eyraud was sentenced to death, and guillotined, on February 3rd, 1891.

Interestingly, in late 19th century France, there was a sudden shift in attitude towards suicide. Whereas it had previously been associated with sin, in the blink of an eye, it came to be associated with insanity. In 1882, for the first time, England allowed suicide victims to be buried during the day, rather than at night, which had been the custom.

Much of this had to do with the simultaneous sea-change sweeping Catholic France at the time. France was undergoing massive secularisation, where the powers of the Church were being overhauled, and separated from the state. One of the symptoms of this seismic cultural shift was the sense that suicide had nothing to do with God after all, and everything to do with human madness. If you committed suicide you were insane, end of story. Case closed.

This was the psychological fabric Vincent innocently entered when he arrived in Auvers that summer of 1890. The fact that Gachet knew Vincent had voluntarily signed up for a year at an asylum meant Vincent had condemned himself in the minds of the masses before he even set foot out of the asylum.

If Gachet had had trouble with Vincent [and let's face it, everyone had, from his first landlady, to his parents and extended family, from his neighbors, employers, lecturers and fellow artists like Gauguin, to Theo], and if he felt Vincent's transgressions were severe, well then if Gachet decided he wanted to dispose of him, like Rohde wished to get rid of his wife, and Rossum her husband, and Shacknai's discarding of Zahau, it wouldn't have been difficult.

Émile Durkheim's Study on Suicide Rates between Protestants and Catholics

In 1897, Émile Durkheim, a ground-breaking French sociologist, published his third major work, *Suicide: A Study in Sociology*. Durkheim's third study explored the differences between Protestant and Catholic suicide rates. Durkheim believed social controls [taboos] in Catholics, prevented them from entertaining thoughts of suicide, which accounted for the higher number of Protestant's committing suicide. Vincent, of course, was a Protestant himself. So any allegation in a Catholic community that he was mad, and Protestant, and had committed suicide, was likely to stick, which is why it did.

The shadow in the carriage still hovers. The small, tan ticket seems to float at the edge of cold, white fingertips in a timeless purgatory. The silver clipper glints menacing in the blackness, like the teeth of a salivating wolf. Vincent blinks. No, don't give up the ticket yet.

Last Train to Paris

"Gauguin is very powerful, strongly creative, but just because of that he must have peace. Will he find it anywhere if he does not find it here?" — Vincent van Gogh

1890 – Early Summer – Wheat fields and White House

It's true that Vincent was nervous and fearful at the prospect of leaving the asylum. Though his doctor pronounced him as cured in the asylum record, on May 16th, 1890, the coop that had held him had also become a familiar place, a safe home, a refuge. The bird in the cage pines for freedom, but once the cage door is open, that freedom is fearsome, and crushing.

For this reason Vincent's final artwork in Arles was *At Eternity's Gate*, and indeed, Vincent was. Should he go through? Two weeks before his departure for the north, Vincent wrote a letter to Theo chock-full of psychological insights. There is a message of cautious optimism and simmering creativity. Vincent wants to get back into the saddle. It's almost as if he's asking Theo for permission. Can I leave this place? If I do, will you look after me?

I read your kind letters, then the letters from home as well, and that did me an enormous amount of good in giving me back a little energy, or rather the desire to climb back up again from the dejected state I'm in...Now...you propose [that I come back] to the north, and I accept. I've had too hard a life to kick the bucket as a result, or to lose the power to work...

Could it be any clearer? Even Vincent is aware of the hardship he's left behind him. What hasn't killed him has made him stronger, and as such, he feels new life kicking inside him.

Ah, if I'd been able to work without this bloody illness! How many things I could have done... But yes – this journey is well and truly finished.

Notice Vincent doesn't call his condition "madness" or "insanity", but simply an illness. By saying the journey, his convalescence, is complete, he'd effectively trying to reassure Theo that it's safe for him to return north, for them to see each other in Paris. He won't embarrass his brother with strange behaviour, and he can be relied on to work. His dysfunction is behind him.

Anyway, what consoles me is the great, the very great desire that I have to see you again, you, your wife and your child, and so many friends who have remembered me in my misfortune, as, for that matter, I don't stop thinking of them either.

This seems to be an exaggeration. A symptom of Vincent's lack of friends, and loneliness, was that he would promise his brother a quick exit once he arrived in Paris, and yet when he arrived, he petitioned to be allowed to hang around for a while.

I'm almost sure that I'll soon get better in the north, at least for quite a long time, while still apprehensive of a relapse in a few years' time – but not immediately.

This is Vincent's prognosis for himself. In May he believes he is and will remain mentally fit for "quite a long time", and suggests trouble in "a few years", a clear indication that he may be aware of nature of his true illness [syphilis], and what lies in store.

Then he refers to his entire adventure in the south, the whole two years and two months encapsulating the Arles episode, as a "shipwreck".

I consider this as a shipwreck...[But now] I have more ideas in my head than I could ever put into action...without it dazzling me. The brushstrokes go like a machine. So based on that I dare believe that in the north I would rediscover my confidence once freed from surroundings and circumstances...

Theo was waiting for his brother when he arrived on May 17th at Gare de Lyon in Paris. From the station it was less than an hour north by horse and carriage, to Theo and Jo's apartment at 8 Cité Pigalle, opposite the Musée de la Vie romantique, a favorite haunt for the likes of Charles Dickens, Eugène Delacroix, Franz Liszt and many others.

When they arrived, Vincent's sharp eyes caught Jo waving from a window. It was the first time either of them had laid eyes on one another; in her other arm, was the baby he'd heard about. This was to be Vincent's first contact with Vincent II as well.

Jo herself would later recount her first encounter with Vincent – after all she'd heard, she was surprised to see a man who not only appeared to be the picture of health, but sturdy and strong, much fitter and in far better nick than her own husband:

I had expected a sick person, but here was a sturdy, broad-shouldered man, with a healthy colour, a smile on his face, and a very resolute appearance...He seems perfectly well; he looks much stronger than Theo...He stayed with us three days and was lively and cheerful all the time.

Vincent spent a very short time with the couple and the new-born, given that he'd been absent not only from Theo, but the outside world in general, for 18 long months. In Theo's home he found his pictures everywhere, floor to ceiling, stuffed under beds and couches, hanging on walls, piled against the walls, stacked behind doors. More of Vincent's art was stacked in a storeroom around at the corner, a four minute walk, at 14 Rue Clauzel, Julien Tanguy's gallery. [Tanguy would be one of very few mourners who came from Paris to attend Vincent's funeral less than two months later].

Interestingly, Vincent's pals Bernard and Gauguin were both in Paris while he was there, but didn't bother to look in on him.

Vincent had high hopes of venturing out into the buzzing streets of Paris and capturing "modern" scenes, like the tower. He also offered to paint Jo's portrait, claiming that there was no better tonic for him than simply being in their company. But Theo was nervous there might be an episode, and wanted his brother at a minimum safe distance, and the sooner the better. Just as quickly as Vincent had entered Paris, and the lives of Theo, Jo and Vincent II, he was on a train out of it. Suddenly, on May 20th, Vincent found himself in Auvers, alone again, expected to make a fresh start. It had to feel like déjà vu, it was Arles except the stakes were much higher, the circumstances much harder.

On the day Vincent arrived in Auvers, he made for Gachet's home, following Theo's instructions. Just as Vincent made a far better impression of Jo than we'd been led to believe by others, Gachet didn't leave a particular pleasant first impression on Vincent. Nearly twice his age, Dr. Gachet seemed eccentric, distracted, caught up in his own world. When Gachet – who'd dyed his hair blond – spoke to Vincent, it was to complain. Vincent conveyed his lack of faith in Gachet immediately to Theo, telling his brother in a letter dated Saturday, May 24th, that they should not count on him, and ominously, that Gachet "is sicker than I am."

In fact Vincent used all caps to emphasise his distrust of Gachet:

I think that we must in NO WAY count on Dr Gachet. In the first place he's iller than I am...there you have it. Now when one blind man leads another blind man, do they not both fall into the ditch?

One senses a pathetic, lonely, desperate, pleading tone in this letter, where Vincent advises his brother not to go to Holland to visit their mother, but to visit him instead. He repeatedly suggests the countryside as a better environment for their new baby; quite ironic that the sick man is dispensing medical help, basically amounting to fresh air and sunshine.

Much has been made of this excerpt, from the same letter, suggesting Vincent was hopelessly suicidal:

I feel – a failure – that's it as regards me – I feel that that's the fate I'm accepting. And which won't change any more. But one more reason, setting aside all ambition, we can live together for years without ruining ourselves on either side...

In many of the documentaries, the second half of the quote isn't provided. He felt a failure his whole adult life, and yes, starting again in Auvers, at the end of May, sure, he felt the burden of it all over again. But look at how he frames it. I'm accepting my fate, it won't change, but I'm also setting aside ambition, and let's live together without ruining ourselves in greedy pursuits. We must see this declaration in the context of Vincent just having been to see his brother, a penniless, unemployed, unstable bum in his brother's eyes [even if Theo was too kind to say as much]. Vincent is trying to appeal, here, to Theo's humanity. Let's just spend a little time together, please. Let's suspend thoughts of commerce, and profit, for a whole and just enjoy the simple things. They're not sentiments a new husband with a new-born child is likely to take seriously, are they?

In the same letter of May 24th, Vincent seems to overstep the mark of propriety by suggesting a trip to the countryside will help Jo produce milk. Then Vincent lectures her about raising a child in the toxic and stressful confines of the city. For an unhinged, madman, his emotional blackmail skills aren't bad.

Often, very often, I think of my little nephew – is he well? Jo will you believe me – if you again happen to have more children... don't have them in town, give birth in the country and stay there until the child is 3 or 4 months old. At present – it seems to me that although the child is no more than 3 months old yet, the milk is already becoming sparse, already you're like Theo, too tired.... I'd have you consider not going to Holland this year, the journey is always very, very costly and it has never done any good. Well yes, it does Mother good, if you like, as she'll love to see the little one – but she'll understand and will prefer the little one's well-being to the pleasure of seeing him...

Are you buying what he's selling? I'm not. In the excerpt below he brings up the Holland trip again, exaggerating that there doing so would be the last straw for everyone. Does he mean there wouldn't be any money? As it turned out, Theo's financial woes did worsen precipitously immediately following their trip. But one also senses that costs diverted to holidays, Vincent would prefer diverted to *him*.

Would there be a way of seeing each other again...the journey to Holland [Vincent refers here to their plans to spend three weeks in summer holidaying with their mother], I fear that it would be the last straw for all of us. I still foresee that it makes the child suffer later to be brought up in town. Does Jo consider that an exaggeration? I believe that one must be prudent, though. And I say what I think because you well understand that I take an interest in my little nephew and care about his well-being; since you really wanted to name him after me, I'd wish him to have a less anxious soul than mine.

There's something about Susan Rohde in Vincent's scrapping, isn't there? He's battling, fighting to get these people to Auvers when he's barely arrived himself. He loves them, but he's also completely dependent on them, and he's very meddlesome. And no surprise, he asks in this letter, insists actually, that Theo send him money for rent stipulating that it be "right at the beginning".

To reiterate, Vincent writes about feeling a failure in the context of a very manipulative letter. We can sympathise with his situation, he's desperate to put down roots and to get a sense of safety and security in his life, but his precarious circumstances mean he's also very anxious, and intense, and liable to rub others the wrong way. If he's doing it to family, it's easy to see how casual acquaintances might be repelled by him. And yet, from Jo, we have a sense of a nice guy, cheerful, smiling and resolute. Well, perhaps not after this letter, assuming Theo gave it to his wife to read...

If Vincent's first meeting with Gachet left him "scornful" as Naifeh-Smith see it, Vincent seemed to grow less discouraged as he began to see the doctor increasingly as a means, a way to bridge the gap between brothers. Besides that, Vincent is gradually introduced to Gachet's family; his sixteen-year-old son Paul, and twenty-year-old daughter Marguerite. He becomes familiar with the grounds, and garden. Gachet is rich, which is promising in itself.

I may come to his house as often as I want...

And so, Vincent begins to attach himself to the family, just as he'd attached himself to so many other families previously. And as the days float by, the last precious days of his life, Theo remains absent. Vincent tries to show his brother he has made a friend, and is capable of *being* a friend. Even so, Theo maintains a distance, measuring even his correspondence to his older sibling, but never scrimping on Vincent's voracious appetite for art supplies, lest this prompt his brother to storm back to Paris and demand materials from him in person.

Naifeh-Smith describe Vincent's portrait of Gachet as a man painted in "a thoughtful pose", sitting comfortably "as if listening to a neighbor at a dinner party." I see a morose, moody, miserable, impatient fellow who's prescribing *digitalis*, and who's not a good artist, not a doctor, nor a good man, for that matter. All of it seems too good to be true. In the blink of an eye, Gachet offers Vincent the run of his property. Vincent's allowed to visit whenever he wants, and stay the night if he chooses to. He can dine with the family, paint the garden, and paint their portraits, and so he does. Is this generosity or scheming? What Gachet does for Vincent, he's doing equally for himself. Gachet is desperate to become an artist, and in Vincent's desperation to elevate himself out of failure, he sees an artist that can give him what he wants.

Of all Vincent's portraits, this one shows the most expression and personality, but not in a pleasant way.

...when one blind man leads another blind man, do they not both fall into the ditch...

Is Gachet a blind man leading Vincent into a ditch, or is Vincent, as Gachet's art instructor, leading Gachet? It's an important question, because Vincent did fall into a ditch in Auvers, and it cost him his life. Who lead him to it? Or did Vincent stumble into it himself?

Interestingly, the two books depicted on the table in front of Gachet, both by the same author, appear to be a cryptic reminder to Theo. The one book describes unhappy travails, even death, in the city, while the other is a story about art as a road to salvation.

As the weeks dissolved, one after the other, Vincent's appeals to Theo became more demanding. Instead of a day-trip, Vincent began to advocate for a month-long sojourn. Theo seemed unmoved by these appeals until Gachet visited him in Paris, and invited the family to lunch. Theo immediately accepted and so, on June 8th, a Sunday, the Gachets and the Van Goghs sat down to lunch on a terrace overlooking the River Oise. Vincent insisted on holding Jo's baby, which, if Marguerite was watching, would have endeared him to her greatly. Perhaps Vincent's desire to have his family in Auvers wasn't just to satisfy his own loneliness, perhaps it was to impress this girl.

If Theo thought the outing would satisfy Vincent, and make him less needy, he was wrong. Vincent immediately expected a series of repeat visits every weekend. He reminded his brother about how close to each other they were, and constantly impressed upon his brother how healthy he was feeling.

Eventually Vincent began describing Gachet as "something like another brother". He went event so far as to claim they resembled one another in appearance "and also mentally." Vincent wrote of the doctor spoiling him with four or five course dinners, and becoming friends with Gachets kids. There was no Mrs Gachet, either, which meant no disapproving maternal figure shadowing Vincent when Gachet was away from home.

What's worth noting in Vincent's portrait of Marguerite, which he painted in late June, is that unlike Adeline Ravoux, Marguerite is allowed to play the piano while Vincent painted her. She's not quite got her back to him, she knows he's there, and she knows she's being looked at and evaluated. He's also looking at her, and evaluating her piano playing, isn't he?

It may be that Marguerite was too shy to simply sit and be ogled at. One can imagine, while Vincent painted her, and while she was playing the piano, that a pleasant atmosphere was created, with the artist complimenting her on her piano playing, while the dutiful daughter returned the compliments of her own father, praising Vincent for his creative gift. We can also see how this simple scenario, a decent young lady playing the piano for his pleasure, would have been incredibly charming to a man who'd known the rough, grey, hostile, environment of an asylum for as long as he had.

In any event, the portrait of Adeline Ravoux is on a much smaller, and more modest scale than that of Marguerite Gachet. Naifeh-Smith describe it as "ambitious" and "a careful rendering", which "gave rise to speculation…at the time…on an unrevealed love [affair]…"

Naifeh-Smith then raise an interesting possibility: that Vincent saw Marguerite as a potential companion for Jo. Vincent even wrote to Theo, speculating that "Jo [will] soon be friends with her [Marguerite]." God knows, Marguerite needed some company too. Whether Vincent saw Marguerite as a ploy to get Jo interested in more regular visits, or whether he saw Gachet as someone who might twist Theo's arm, or whether Vincent developed strong romantic feelings for Marguerite, we can clearly see several scenarios in which Vincent hoped to use the Gachets to bring his blood relatives closer to him.

We see this scheme worked, in a sense, where invitations from Gachet *did* lead to visits from Theo and Jo. If anything, the take-out for Vincent from this was that they saw the Gachet's as respectable, and so, if Vincent could get into their good graces – perhaps even marry Marguerite – then they could live happily ever after from then on, as equals. Vincent was prone to overthinking things, and he was a single fellow with a lot of time on his hands. Given his prior history with women he had access to, why wouldn't he try his luck?

Well, because of doctor Gachet. Gachet may have been predisposed to Vincent's art, but that was it. He knew Vincent was a nut, and if Vincent was pleasant to have around for a few weeks, that would wear off as it invariably did with almost everyone. As tension, anxiety and the full extent of his failure [as an artist, as a man, as a nobody and a non-entity] was made manifest again, Gachet's own temper and mental malaise would be triggered. How would the stern 61-year-old with his dyed blonde hair respond to being undermined in his own house?

Vincent wasn't at the Gachet's all the time, however. He took long lonely walks. There were farms, wheat fields, haystacks, and the long sprinkle of human settlement as it peppered the fertile belts of the Oise on both sides. If Vincent was suicidal, this was the natural place – being a Hollander – to put himself out of his misery. All he had to do was jump in. The Dutch know water, the threat of it haunts their consciousness, and so the idea of giving in, is analogous to letting the water have its way over you. Instead of holding it back, fighting against it, plunging in, and letting yourself be washed into oblivion.

Naifeh-Smith very perceptibly note that all Vincent's suicide references – without exception – are about water. And so, if Vincent was suicidal that summer, well, there was the Oise, sparkling, beckoning. What could be easier than stepping into it, just as Bellet-Brissaud did?

Drowning is uncomfortable, but a lot shorter and a lot less painless than a slow death from a small caliber-gunshot wound.

In July, yes, we've come to it – the final month of his life – Vincent's relationship with Gachet began to unravel. It was simply following the same pattern as every other relationship, which was why Theo was wise to keep his distance. His wayward brother had alienated their parents, had alienated everyone, and he didn't want him impinging on their happily ever after either.

What did Vincent do this time? He did what he always did. He was too demanding. It was hard not to be, given how dependent he was on anyone and everyone, but there it is. Gachets frequent absences from his home meant Vincent was an accident waiting to happen. Naifeh-Smith contend that the doctors absence confirm Vincent's fears that he couldn't be counted on. I'm not sure about that. The fact that Marguerite's father was absent, and her mother no longer alive, meant she was vulnerable to Vincent's lechery. The only real question is whether she spurned his advances, or went along with them, or both.

As a result of Vincent's behaviour [whatever it was], Gachet responded by setting strict rules for his patient: *Vincent was no longer permitted to paint in the house*. This implies Marguerite felt uncomfortable with a letch tramping about and ogling at her, but equally, it might have been Gachet who was uncomfortable with what may have been brewing, mutually quite possibly. We know Marguerite put flowers on Vincent's grave – this implies he hadn't acted unforgivably or inappropriately as far as she was concerned.

According to Naifeh-Smith, Gachet's son Paul had a contemptuous view of Vincent, perhaps mirroring that of his father. The teenager described Vincent's painting style as "comical" and "odd to watch". The younger Gachet also provides a description of Vincent tilting his head back and squinting, as he applied his paints. This image strangely invokes Gauguin's slit-eyed impression of the red-nosed, gingerbeard artist.

If things had become fraught on the Gachet front, July was when things went haywire with Theo, Jo and baby Vincent too. It started with the baby becoming sick, crying continuously.

Both parents became desperate. Theo suddenly felt exhausted, like too little butter spread over too much bread. He began to accuse Vincent in his letters of adding to his burden; sketching his brother as part of the load of a heavy cart he was being forced to drag around. Then Theo started complaining about his own failing health. This was no hypochondria; he didn't know it then, but Theo was beginning his own exit from the world.

Vincent felt disturbed, helpless and guilty because of this. He was being assaulted on two fronts, simultaneously. Most terrifying at all, Theo planned to leave his job at Groupil, a scenario that could be catastrophic for Vincent if things went further south. Jo's brother Andries, who disapproved of Vincent's art, was part of the proposed independent dealership. Theo decided to give Groupil an ultimatum. *Pay me more or I walk.* It was with these forces in play, that Vincent arrived in Paris on Sunday, July 6th for a visit. His timing could not have been worse.

Vincent arrived to find Theo and Jo bickering amongst themselves. The outcome of the debacle affected Vincent deepest of all, but if Theo and Jo agreed on one thing, it was that they resented his intrusion, seeing it as interference. Then Jo's brother Andries arrived, and Vincent exploded. He blamed Dries for the whole damned idea. And then things took another turn for the worse: Theo and Jo announced they were moving into the same building as Dries. Poor Vincent saw this as a final rejection of his invitations that they move permanently to the country, to Auvers. Then Vincent railed against Jo's mothering, this time raising his objections to an urban upbringing to her face.

Apparently Jo let Vincent have it then. She'd quietly tolerated the unemployed nobody siphoning the family's income. At another time Jo would ruefully regret her impatience and unkindness to Vincent. We don't know exactly what happened, because the letters around this fateful innocent were destroyed. But if there was ever a time to commit suicide, this was it. Vincent had been shouted at, belittled, insulted, and either chased from his brother's home, or fled from it. Which path it was, it was one shiny with salted tears and breaking hearts.

If there was ever a time to cut off the other ear, or gobble up his paints and hope to die, this was it. But three more weeks would pass, and the season seemed to shift, and life seemed as if it would go on, as it always had.

It was this context that prompted Vincent to write, on July 10th, that his life was "threatened at the very root." This excerpt is also often quoted out of context as unambiguous evidence of Vincent's suicidal mind. Instead, what we see is simply a guy coming to terms with a heated argument, and remaining upbeat towards his sponsors. He's not giving up, or depressed, he's telling them how motivated he is to work. He's fighting to stay in the game.

Jo's letter was really like a gospel for me, a deliverance from anguish...It's no small thing when all together we feel the daily bread in danger, no small thing when for other causes than that we also feel our existence to be fragile. Once back here I too still felt very saddened, and had continued to feel the storm that threatens you also weighing upon me. What can be done – you see I usually try to be quite good-humoured, but my life, too, is attacked at the very root, my step also is faltering. I feared – not completely – but a little nonetheless – that I was a danger to you, living at your expense – but Jo's letter clearly proves to me that you really feel that for my part I am working and suffering like you.

Do you see how selectively quoting from this, out of context, can change the entire perception of Vincent's narrative? There's anguish, danger, threat, sadness, a sense of being weighed down, a storm, attacked at the very root, but at the same time, Vincent's saying I see that you really feel for me, you still care for me. He speaks of deliverance, not despair, proof of solidarity, not abandonment, a shared circumstance, not rejection. Besides all this, Vincent is determined to carry on working.

...once back here I set to work again ...knowing clearly what I wanted I've painted another three large canvases since then. They're immense stretches of wheat fields under turbulent skies, and I made a point of trying to express sadness, extreme loneliness. You'll see this soon, I hope – for I hope to bring them to you in Paris as soon as possible...

On July 15th, Theo visited Holland with his family. He elected not to take his brother along, simply because his mother and sister's probably had no wish to see *him*. Although Theo could have dropped in on his brother in Auvers on his way to, or back from Holland, he didn't. But then, Theo also left Jo and baby Vincent in Holland, where they'd be taken care of, and so he could focus on important business.

While this was happening, Vincent wrote letters about an immense plain of wheat fields, as wide as an ocean. Out there, under the sun, Vincent had to admit, even if Theo was still supporting him, he'd also become withdrawn, perhaps as a sign of future, more serious withdrawals.

In this scenario fraught with danger, Vincent probably drank more alcohol than he usually did. But his sorrows had learned to swim. He worked like a demon now, churning out a canvas a day. He haunted the gardens of the Gachet residence, a troubled soul, not wanting to stir up trouble. Wanting more than anything to make his paintings speak.

In his last letter, Vincent wrote about his painting of a garden, describing it as "one of my most purposeful canvases". A garden is a living thing, something that is watered over time, cared for, tended, nurtured. This was Vincent's final image, a sketch in a letter. Tree roots was his last painting. That too, reflected an excruciating desire to be rooted, secure and safe in the world. A nobody, after all, is easily discarded.

On July 27th, Vincent returned from painting earlier in the day, to have lunch at the Ravoux Inn. This had been his routine for weeks. Then he set off again, lugging his painting equipment under the glare of the midday sun.

Are we ready to hand the train man our ticket now? He hovers in the dark like a ghost, the silver clipper floating like a fish in dark water. His blonde hair glinting gold by the polish of the night. Vincent blinks.

No. Not yet.

Into the Prism of Theo's Disgrace and Death

"You speak of money which you owe me, and which you want to give back to me. I won't hear of it. The condition I want you to arrive at is that you should not have any worries. I must work for the money." — Theo van Gogh to Vincent, October 27, 1888

Mystery mushrooms around Vincent's death, but equally, strange smoke drifts like a veil across the last 30 hours of his life. Art historians and biographers tend to gloss over these aspects, as if death is the most self-evident box of all to check.

Most investigators and journalists tend to regard smoke and mirror scenarios with a shrug, saying effectively: *see, we can't go any further*. Smoke and mirrors are an excellent giveaway in true crime – a symptom that can be seen from a distance, that not only is something not quite right, but someone has gone to the trouble to distort and mislead. The wonderful thing about smoke and mirrors in true crime, is that when one lingers in the smoke, and though watery eyed, and coughing for breath, when one approaches the mirrors to examine their smoky reflections, when you gaze into the reflection long enough, a new reality is revealed.

The new reality isn't the thing the reflection points towards, the vital clue is that whatever clues that are given are intended to draw our attention away from something else.

In a very real sense, Theo van Gogh is a prism into his brother's life. He's not a mirror, in the sense that Theo is not the villain of this story, and so, he has no stake or motive to cover up a crime. How the prism works is we have Vincent's twin, in a sense, occupying Vincent's world, and able to testify about all of it – about Vincent, about the other characters in the story, and about how the stage is set. All of this feels highly theoretical, so let's get down to brass tacks and see how the prism works in practise, and why it's such an excellent tool to penetrate the fog of smoke and mirrors surrounding Vincent in his final hours on the mortal coil.

Ripples in the Pond

Just as Monet painted his pond endlessly, and found revelation in each addition iteration, we must revisit, in these final chapters, the vital final hours of Vincent's life. We begin through the prism – through the lens – of Theo. What did Theo see and experience through his glasses? What did he see, without seeing?

During an emergency situation, the first thing we look at is the first ripple in the pond. Who calls for help, when, how, and who do they reach out to? What we expect to see in a genuine emergency is a single, clear, ripple radiating outward. A clear signal. In some circumstances there may be additional noise, but generally, people in a life-and-death situation act urgently, and effectively. If their actions aren't logical, there tends to be a psychological or emotional cohesion to their behaviour, which boils down to an effort aimed at coming to the aid of their fellow man.

Theo is on the receiving end of the message, on July 28th, that his brother has been wounded. He's not emergency services of course. But he's a vital cog in the chain. So how is it that he's alerted?

We see an immediate problem here. When Vincent's ear had been cut off, Gauguin sent a telegram. One could argue that being shot in the stomach was far more serious than losing one's ear, and in hindsight, we know it was. In any event, no telegram was sent. Instead, Dr. Gachet *wrote a letter to Theo*, and had it hand-delivered. Naifeh-Smith refer to Gachet doing this in order to "avoid the alarm of a telegram". Why would Gachet want to *avoid* alarm? Theo's brother had been shot! Surely timing was everything?

Things get smokier still when Adeline Ravoux offers her version of events:

Since dawn, Father had been preoccupied with how to tell Theo, the brother of Vincent. The casualty then being lethargic could not give precise information. But, knowing that Vincent's brother was a salesman at the Art Gallery of Boussod Valadon…in Paris, Father sent a telegram to this address when the post office opened. Theo arrived by train in the middle of the afternoon. I remember seeing him arrive, running…

Bear in mind, over the course of 30 hours, Vincent survived two nights – the night of the shooting, and part of a second night until he died at about 01:30 on July 29th. Do the math, if he arrived at the Inn at 21:00, then at 01:30 that night, July 27th, the 24 hour clock ticking out the final day of his life began. It's 4.5 hours from 21:00 to 01:30, so adding that to 24 gives us 28.5 hours. If Vincent took an hour to stumble home, then it means he was shot at 19:30 or 20:00, and then survived close to 30 hours after sustaining the bullet wound.

On the first night, Adeline's father Gustave sat with Vincent throughout, while Anton Hirschigg [who stayed in the room next door] hovered nearby. So two civilians held a vigil right through the night, whereas both doctors came and went, and evidently saw no need to stay.

Auvers had no hospital, so it would have made sense to get Vincent onto a train to Paris ASAP. Both the doctors attending Vincent on that first night [I describe their procedures in more detail in the final chapter] were based in Paris, so it would have made sense to both doctors to transport the patient to somewhere with adequate medical care, so that he might have surgery. The fact that Vincent had mobilised himself, meant getting him onto a train wasn't out of the question. Also, the train station was ridiculously close, a four minute walk due west, along the same road as the Ravoux Inn, less than a 1/5th of a mile [230 meters]. So getting Vincent there was no problem at all.

Instead, what everyone decided to do [doctors and civilians], is to allow the night to pass, and then to call Theo for help. Is he being summoned to treat Vincent? Of course not. Is he being summoned to keep Vincent company? That's the more difficult question. Everyone's actions suggest they don't think it's an emergency, although Gustave Ravoux babysitting his lodger through the night, indicates that *he* at least knew it was serious. Hirschigg claimed he heard Vincent screaming through the night, which shows he also knew.

What are we to make of the claim that Ravoux sent a telegram? Records seem to indicate that *no one* sent a telegram, or else Theo wouldn't have arrived relatively late, by mid-afternoon the next day, 16-18 hours after his brother had arrived, critically wounded, at the Inn.

Adeline's description of the younger brother running into the Inn from the station rings true, both because it was a short enough distance to sprint, and because one can imagine Theo wanting to get there as soon as possible.

We also know that Hirschigg did hand deliver a message to Theo, which would not have been necessary if a telegram had been sent.

What doesn't ring true from Adeline is her father knowing anything about *Boussod, Valadon & Cie II*. Since she refers to the new name of the original company, Groupil, one has a sense that Adeline has tailored her story somewhat. Remember she provided it more than 40 years after the events, and by then much had changed, including the names of businesses in Paris.

She may have remembered *something* about a gallery, but I doubt it had anything to do with her father. Rather, I think it was Gachet's letter, perhaps with input from other bystanders, that was eventually dispatched to Paris. And because Vincent wouldn't give anyone his brother's address, they elected, on their own, to hand deliver it to Theo's business-premises.

On Monday morning, when Theo strolled in to work, he'd find Hirschigg there, a Dutchman the art dealer had dispatched to Auvers himself, to keep Vincent company.

Rubbishing the "Burden" Theory

It makes sense that Vincent didn't want his brother summoned. This was a carbon copy of the situation with Gauguin in Arles. Something had happened, and Vincent didn't want to burden his brother unnecessarily with the expense and fuss of coming down. In an excerpt of his letter to Jo [cited immediately below], Theo even suggests returning to Paris that same evening, if Vincent's condition improved. This too is a carbon copy of his rapid return to Paris from his long trip south to Arles over Christmas, in 1888.

One might argue that Vincent was being pig-headed about keeping Theo in the dark about his latest drama, but actually, he was being practical. Every franc Theo spent on unnecessary transport, telegrams or doctor's fees, meant less money for Vincent's living expenses. Yes, things were that frugal, and finances were never more fraught for the Van Goghs than they were then.

What we can see here, though, is how asinine the Burden Theory is. Vincent committed suicide in order to not be a burden. Well, the first thing that was happening was that he was becoming a burden, to everyone. The other aspect, is that ultimately *Theo never quit his job at Groupil*, despite all the drama that surrounded Theo, Jo and Vincent that fateful final July.

"Better than Expected"

When he stepped into the stifling room, sweating, breathing hard, Theo found Vincent looking so unexpectedly well, he took a brief timeout to write a letter to Jo, letting her know precisely that. Theo described his brother as "very ill" but also seemed confident that he'd pull through.

It was just as desperate before and the physicians were surprised by his strong constitution....I promise I'll return to Paris if he's better tonight.

What are we to make of physicians [plural] surprised by Vincent's resilience? We know that Gachet decided early on that Vincent was doomed. Well, how did he know? More particularly, when did Gachet actually treat Vincent? If he treated him on Sunday night, wasn't that when Vincent was still smoking his pipe, talking, and appearing most likely to recover?

If Gachet treated Vincent and was so sure he wouldn't survive, why did he not send a telegram, why did he not get him to Paris [Gachet was wealthy, and had the resources to make this happen], and why was Gustave at Vincent's bedside all night, and not the doctor? Why didn't Gachet return the next night to check in on his patient [because Vincent was *his* patient after all!]

Hirschigg would also comment on the extreme heat of the attic room. The fact that no one – not even the doctors – thought to move Vincent downstairs, to a more bearable location, suggests something sinister. If Hirschigg could go to the effort to travel to Paris, to deliver a letter, and Theo could arrive as quickly as he could, sprinting to his brother's room, was it really too much effort to put Vincent somewhere that was less like a sauna?

It's not as if the nights were pleasantly cool then either. Naifeh-Smith point out that when Vincent arrived, clutching his side, his jacket was buttoned closed, something that seemed odd for the heat of the evening. This incidental fact [which probe more deeply in the final chapter] also suggests Vincent was trying to cover up the wound. He didn't want people to know he'd been shot. Why?

Protecting René Secrétan?

Another ludicrous theory is that Vincent was shot by accident, and decided not to tell anyone, in order to protect whoever shot him by accident. Only those who are completely unfamiliar with true crime would field such a theory.

To illustrate why it's such rubbish, consider the officially unsolved JonBenét Ramsey and Madeleine McCann cases. Both involve unhappy endings of two small children. Some suppose that six-year-old JonBenét was accidentally killed – by her mother, by her father, or by her brother. And so, the family covered it up. Here's why that makes no sense. In every family scenario where a child accidentally drowns, or falls, or is seriously injured, parents will do everything to get the child emergency medical assistance, even when it's obvious the child is beyond rescue.

If a child has slipped on a wet kitchen floor and cracked their head hard during a fall, the priority is saving that child. Innocent people behave with genuine urgency in emergencies, and what's wrong with telling the truth when there is accident? Accidents happen.

Sometimes accidents happen because they are accidents waiting to happen – because there is a pattern of neglect and abuse, some sort of behaviour that's driving things to a particular, unfortunate result. In such as case, an accident is no accident at all, and those involved have every reason to cover-up their ill-disciplined and immoral behaviour that played into a particular end result.

In the Madeleine McCann case, I suspect the three-year-old was sedated, and then fell to her death off the hotel balcony. One might call that an accident, except, because both parents were doctors, and their many friends holidaying with them were also doctors, they ought to have known better. An accident in this sense could have potentially cost not one, but perhaps half a dozen doctors their licenses. If this was the situation they faced, why *not* lie about what had happened?

Killing by accident is such a popular perversion of the truth, murderers use of it in true crime is virtually a cliché. Think about Oscar Pistorius tearfully claiming in court: "It was an accident!"

If Secrétan *had* shot Vincent by mistake, what was the harm in saying so? He shot me, but we were messing about, it wasn't his fault. There's no need to hide the truth. If Vincent was shot on purpose, by someone he didn't know, we'd fully expect him to reveal his assassin, anyone would, right? That's why it's clear that Vincent was shot on purpose by someone he did know, and he couldn't reveal this person's identity precisely because of how much was riding on things working out in Auvers.

Theo's withdrawal and the perilous state of the Van Gogh's financial situation showed that his charity to Vincent was hanging by a thread. For this reason, Vincent didn't want to be more of a burden than he already was. If Gachet had gotten so pissed off with Vincent, that he'd shot him [just as Gauguin had lashed out in anger – Vincent had that effect on people], *he wouldn't want his brother to know about it.*

He wanted to avoid a repeat of Arles, and yet, Auvers was Arles all over again. If it was a botched suicide, why not simply say that? I tried to kill myself but I fumbled with the pistol… I tried to kill myself but I wasn't sure where to point the gun and then it went off…

In a family situation where someone tries to kill themself, I can guarantee you, family *will* pressure family for an explanation. Why? I suspect Theo intuited more than he let on. But given Vincent's worsening condition, Theo had little choice but to humor Vincent in his final hours. Precisely because Theo arrived as late as he did, he only spent about ten of Vincent's last thirty hours, by his side. That may seem like a lot, but Vincent probably spent most of those final hours passed out. Nevertheless, words did pass. The fact that these conversations have never come to light, not even through Jo, suggests Theo knew the truth could be as damaging to them as the scandal of suicide.

Well, what truth could that be? If Vincent had been murdered, which murderer could land a devastating blow to Theo, possibly costing him his job, now that *his* livelihood was hanging by a thread? Vincent's suicide made the thread even more tenuous...

Theo's Burden

When Vincent died, he was breathing heavily and his eyes remained open, staring over life's cruel abyss. There's still no indication that he was spitting or coughing blood. Heavy breathing indicates a strain on the heart. Was his heart fighting off infection?

At this point, the load Theo had to carry got significantly heavier. While Gachet snuck back to sketch a portrait of the dead artist, Theo took a second day off work, and tried to make funeral arrangements for the next day, July 30.

He dispatched telegrams, printed an obituary, and extended invitations to those who were well-disposed to Vincent in Paris. In Brittany, Gauguin received an invite but, still in total asshole mode, pretended he hadn't. He'd later confide in Bernard [who received his invitation, and attended] that it was stupid to be associated with the likes of a lunatic.

While Vincent's body was being disembowelled and embalmed by the local mortician, ironically in the small studio he'd used to splash his yellows, blues and greens onto so many canvasses in the Ravoux Inn, a carpenter got to work preparing Vincent's coffin.

Then the news came that there would be no 14:30 service after all. Theo, with Gustave's permission, set about transforming the shuttered Ravoux Inn into a temporary funeral parlour. Vincent's stockpile of paintings served as decoration [there were enough to turn the interior into a shrine], along with armloads of hastily harvested sunflowers.

Finally Vincent's coffin was hoisted onto the billiard table. Theo ran about in search of a burial plot. This had to be purchased as well. Interestingly, Jo never attended the funeral, nor did any of Vincent's other family members – not his mother, or any of his sisters. It was as if the younger brother knew it was pointless inviting them, whether because of financial limits or the limits of forgiveness, it's difficult to say. Probably both.

On the day of his funeral, July 30th, Tanguy arrived early. Andries Bonger, Jo's disapproving brother, also attended. The mourners were given lunch in the Ravoux Inn's dining room area, while the coffin hovered in the room adjacent. By mid-afternoon, the coffin was hoisted onto several shoulders and loaded onto a hearse that had been seconded from a neighboring town. Theo and Andries led the summer flock through the dusty, sweaty streets.

Gachet spoke at the prepared grave, but did not make much sense. Curiously, he described Vincent as an "honest" man. First and foremost. And incidentally, a great artist. Well of course it mattered to Gachet that people thought Vincent was honest – when he said he'd tried to kill himself. Gachet was saying, implying: "Believe him. He wouldn't lie."

Gachet spoke, but Theo did not. An early obituary reflected the overall mind-set in regards to Vincent. His art was described as the product of "a sick mind."

In the coming weeks, Theo would visit the doctor on numerous occasions, relying on Gachet's version of events for comfort. Theo suddenly felt very empty at his brother's death. Anguish filled the vast, emptied cauldron of Theo's heart. His grief burned through him like acid.

Theo soon implored the doctor to write a book about Vincent, and Gachet agreed. This is another area of great mystery. Gachet worked on his book on Vincent for years, apparently, yet not a page or a paragraph, not a sentence or a single word has survived. It's ironic given how anal the Gachet's were in preserving the artist's work, work they'd arguably stolen and forged.

Theo's Breakdowns

Only one month after Vincent's death, Theo's behaviour turned erratic. He argued with his colleagues at Groupil, then lashed out against his own wife and child. Naifeh-Smith describe Theo mourning his brother by "becoming" his brother. And he was. Now it was Theo's turn to struggle with insomnia, panic attacks and paranoia.

After a month of this madness, Theo did the worst thing he possibly could – he quit Groupil. Two weeks later, Theo was in an asylum in Paris. From mid-October onward, Theo's downward spiral was precipitous. He became violent and enraged. He grew so wild he had to be sedated with chloroform. When he came to, he'd rip his clothes and toss furniture.

Theo spent a single month in the asylum at Passy. The asylum was about an hour on foot south west of the first apartment he'd shared with Jo, at Cité Pigalle, and the Musée de la Vie romantique, and so close to the Eiffel Tower its shadow probably fell over the asylum walls. In mid-November, Jo had Theo transferred to an asylum in Utrecht. Her husband made the trip in a straitjacket.*

Theo spent the winter, the last of his short life, in an asylum much as he's brother had. This knowledge must have felt like a double torment to him – each step down on the spiral, a visceral window into Vincent's world, and the devastating truth that Theo had abandoned his brother emotionally, if not financially, long before his death. The guilt ate at him, just as the syphilis did. There was no escape.

Like Vincent, Theo suffered seizures and appeared mad to those around him. At Christmas, according to Naifeh-Smith, Jo brought her ailing husband flowers. He tore them from her hand and smashed them to the floor. The doctors eventually asked her to stay away, as her visits seemed to agitate him more than soothe, or settle him. Hard as it to believe, smoke and mirrors also surround Theo's death. Even the precise date in January, 1891 is unknown. And just as no family members attended Vincent's funeral besides Theo, none attended Theo's grave, besides Jo. But the Van Gogh wasn't half lifted. By the end of the same year, Elisabeth [Lies] van Gogh, who'd made a living as a domestic worker after her father's death, married her employer. She'd also given birth, in secret, to his child, and given her daughter Hubertina away [to a sweet seller in London] much as Sien had done.

Two years after Cor's suicide in Brandfort, South Africa, it was Willemien's turn to enter an asylum. She wasted away there, for almost forty years. According to Naifeh-Smith she remained mute for almost all of this time, had to be force-fed and attempted suicide on several occasions. Far from sparing anyone anything, the burden of Vincent's death, it turned out, weighed heavily on the rest of his family. Except his mother. Anna simply gave the travails of her brood to God, and turned her eyes to the healing light of the Lord, and all was well again.

The train man shifts. Vincent's eyes stare unblinking through the dark. The ticket remains whole, unclipped, unsung, undelivered.

Not yet.

*Theo would return via the same rail route linking France to the Netherlands, in a coffin, bound for a cemetery in Auvers. It is worth noting that even in death, Theo was "somewhere else", and it was his widow, who had to bring the brothers together again.

Finding Vincent

"Is being alone really living?"— Vincent van Gogh

1890 – Summer – Wheat field under Thunderclouds

A great darkness hangs over everything, drowning all things in it. Everything is oily, indistinct and impenetrable. Has our train ticket really gotten us anywhere? Can a person ever really know another person, even when they're brothers? Having come so far we find it difficult to recognise Theo, after all his letters, and even Vincent has become a stranger.

Who was he?

No one ever really tells you everything about themselves, do they? They reveal the bits they're prepared to let you have, but it's the parts that are held back that really matter. Those secret parts hold the keys to clandestine flaws and failures, weaknesses and torments, faults and fears, the seeds for potential betrayal, the pathetic wretchedness that they'd rather we didn't know about.

I've mentioned this idea of throwing the baby out with the bathwater. When we're not sure about the reliability of something, or someone, we discard all of it in the name of certainty. But nothing is ever certain. No thing is ever absolute. Writing and art are tools that reveal the artist's soul, but never all of it. So where do we find it, here, at the end? Well, we find Vincent's authentic humanity not out there, it's not all in the surface layer of those canvasses, it's deeper. If we are to probe what's underneath those hard, brittle flakes of paint, if we are to bring Vincent to life and press a needle into his freckly forearm, to test his blood, we must do the same to ourselves. We must turn inward, while the night is at its darkest.

Entering the Oil of the Artist

The paint of Vincent's painting is only a surface layer. All the scribbles and sketches, all the rubbing out and scratching over, is edited out by a polished veneer of bright, gleaming oil. And then this oil hardens, cracks and flakes off.

A finished canvas, like a book, or someone who pretends to be an adult, is a trick. What it is, is a charade. Character itself, is a vital lie. The end result seems self-evident, when in fact it is the very end of an endless process of edits, alterations, dabs, touches, alignments, changes, fixes and formats. The final draft is thus an appeal based on a series of modified attempts to be appealing, to be appropriate, to the viewer or reader, but pretends not to be.

In the same way, an adult man forgets that once upon a time he was an incontinent whelp, that had to be wiped, and bathed and fed and soothed, we pretend that our works don't involve similar tears, and trauma. The hinge of history separates us from the pilgrim's progress, but when the door is open, when we accept our own evolution, then we see how the process works across every lifetime. If your mind is bending, like plastic burning in a flame, good, then we have the right substance to enter the molecules of paint, canvas, camelhair brushes, the whorly patterns of a finger and its subcutaneous skin.

It is our job now to step through the darkness of Vincent's paint, because that's where we are, that's this station, and pass through to the other side, far enough for the trees to become a wood, and the wood to bloom from glistening coal to vivid blues, chrome yellows, sparkling emerald greens. We swim now through the desiccated surfaces of time into the vital, liquid oil of the very moment Vincent applied the paint to the brush.

We must follow the electric spark of the creative moment, the eternal, ever-expanding now, along the brush to his hand, and along those quivering, dabbing hands to the conveyors driving Vincent's mind and body. We must penetrate his world like a syphilis bacterium colonising the blood and bone and brain of a man. We must buzz through Auvers of 1890 like a fly, but a fly tethered to, orbiting a single orange sphere – Vincent van Gogh's head.

In that head, through that hand, on Friday, September 14th 1888, Vincent wrote to Theo:

"The uglier, older, meaner, iller, poorer I get, the more I wish to take my revenge by doing brilliant color, well arranged, resplendent."

This letter was written on the other side of time, when Arles was a paradise, rather than a hellhole. These same sentiments were carried into Auvers. In truth, Vincent had been carrying them for years, for all his life. And so do we. Every seven years our bodies complete a total overhaul of our cells and bones, copying each trembling mechanism, replicating each fibre, every brick in each capillary. Our memories do the same. We take the past into the present, hoping to learn from it, improve it, make a better future, even as a sort of decay sets into our hearts.

In those sentiments, Vincent prioritises how he see himself, and how we ought to see him, and coincidentally, ourselves. First of all, his ugliness. Vincent, like Jesus, was not a handsome man. He had ginger hair, like Jesus*, and like all ugly people, their lot in life is harder, and often unhappier. Vincent was the only one of his siblings, including his brothers, not to marry. His ugliness wasn't just skin deep, though, he *was* an unpleasant person to be around. He means to redeem himself – his aging form, his misspent youth, his temper, his social awkwardness, his illness, his poverty, with paintings burning with life and hope. Those paintings aren't the world he sees, they're a world he wishes to be part of. Those farmhouses aren't just farmhouses, they're homes and families he yearns to have himself.

Was Vincent lovable?

Notice in all those factors, ugly, old, mean, ill, poor, there's no mention of madness. What there is is a smelly, rude, but self-effacing man, a selfish, demanding, desperate but sensitive soul, a committed, dutiful, determined but lonely and pathetic individual with an unusual desire to redeem himself. Despite his failures, he remains a dutiful son to an absent father, a loving brother to a sibling that's ashamed of him. All that's left, and he knows this, is the desire for life in his loins, the hunger in his stomach, and his evangelism – through his art.

The emotional connection we make with Vincent is through his suffering, because we are sufferers too. We suffer the same loneliness and humiliation, the same seedy desires frothing with noble virtue. We're comforted in Vincent's journey because we're able to witness the meat of his life offered as a sacrifice, slaughtered by the thing that was supposed to save him –society and culture. What is art, and the artist, if not an offering to culture? And today, what is Vincent's art, if not one of humanity's greatest and most valuable cultural-societal artefacts. The mainstream story offers us solace in the face of mortality and the human suffering he sees, he knows, he lives. But the reality is, even that solace is a lie. Vincent, lying on his bed in that sweaty upstairs chamber, saw life and the lot of the living. There are moments of magic, but a fearsome fire awaits us all. Ugliness, meanness, illness – it waits for everyone. No matter how great our triumphs, not matter how rich or poor, gifted or talentless, quiet or loud, ugly or beautiful, not matter how hard we toil, or whether we are lazy, our efforts will be undone. Tragedy awaits each of us, no matter how vivid we paint the sun, no matter how genuine or fake the friendliness of our smiles, or our letters.

Vincent's sister Anna was right, even early on. The best year of Vincent's life was that first year in London. It was Vincent's most successful year; certainly in the eyes of society, his family and himself. But easy things, like easy people, can seem boring and disposable. Once lost, a lifetime can be spent trying to scratch a small smidgeon of territory lost, but it only recedes further, like a train crossing a far horizon, or a ship, sailing into cotton wool clouds.

We understand Vincent not through his brush, or through his temper, and certainly not through any fanciful notions of madness. We see him best through the prism of a nobody, an outcast. He is *entirely* dependent on the goodwill of his brother, and society. He is pathetic and poor in his social standing, rich in self-possession, powerful in his craft. But poverty in a world of social animals, where one's fate rests on that society's acceptance of you, is poverty indeed.

Whatever anyone may say of Vincent's art, it was unsellable in his time, and unsellable for many years afterward. Without his writing to redeem it, a case could be made that it was unsellable period. The implications of this are much deeper than they appear. Vincent painted dozens of portraits, and yet he couldn't sell those either, not even to the wealthy men – like Dr. Gachet – who sat for him. When he painted children or teenagers, their parents weren't interested in paying for his portraits, not even as a gesture.

That Vincent persisted despite the cynicism of his society, is certainly heroic. But we should be careful not to make him into a martyr, because we harbour our own illusions and delusions of grandeur. Is it more heroic to persist in poverty and waste away one's entire Life Force, living and dying in grinding insignificance, or to adapt and find a way to thrive in the world?

My brother persisted in his art for about thirty years, painting as a teenager, and making a modest living until his mid-forties. A few months ago he returned to university to study artificial intelligence [he already possesses two engineering degrees, in civil and electro-mechanical engineering]. Time will tell if this seismic shift in career will prove fortuitous and fruitful for him. I hope it does. I feel for him, because at times I have been tempted too to abandon the even more modest career of writing books as a fulltime job.

I support my brother in his art, but I've always felt that trading on the family legacy can only take you so far. Every artist must find his own voice, and I daresay my brother floated on the coat tails [or the entrails] of another artist, painting in the same prototypical style as my great grandfather: of Cape Dutch homesteads, vineyards and folded mountains glowing gold in a late afternoon sun. Think about it though – can you name a single famous artist who is the son or grandson of any other famous artist? The point of art that means something to us is that it's unique, that it stands apart and stands on its own as something new and original.

The bane of every artist's lot is insignificance. What does one do with it? Vincent believed that through the force of his brush, he'd break through to the world. Fair enough, he did, but what he meant to do was succeed in his own lifetime. He wasn't painting 70-80 pictures each day in the last months of his life in order to sell out auctions a century later. Many persist, some do to the bitter end, but this should not be seen as indomitable genius, but brute stubbornness. True success is finding a place in the world *while you are alive*; giving the gift of living, but also receiving something; love, redemption, fulfilment, whatever it is that makes us look at our lives and feel a glimmer of peace about it.

Vincent's art is inspiring precisely because of the contradiction between his supreme sacrifice and the way society spurned his work, and his cult status today. We are all born to die, his legacy seems to say, yet we persist, we make hay while the sun shines, even that hay has no value in the eyes of the world. An argument could be made that in a finite world, less is more, but in society, as in nature, it's never about survival of the *lessor*, is it? A bride doesn't chose a mate with the least, does she? For good reason: failure in the world isn't just about bad luck, it's about being maladaptive.

Curiously, bad luck and failure tends to bring out the best in human beings, over time. Failure turns to success, weakness becomes strength, a drowning swimmer finds a way to stay afloat and then to swim strongly. When the swimmer turns against the tide, or as Holland did, turns the tide of the world against itself, the world changes and the whole world benefits as a result. There's a fine line between defying reality maladaptively, and changing reality, in reshaping the world. Vincent *did* become something, especially in the final two years of his life. He could feel it, that mastery, building in him. Theo could sense it, though it didn't bring him any closer to his older sibling in his last months. So what the world saw in Vincent, during his life, in Holland, England, Belgium and France, wasn't heroism, but the thing they wished to escape themselves – filthy insignificance, suffering, poverty.

The Battle for Worth

Swimming through Vincent's blood, and into his salty, charged memories, we feel him sparkling into existence through his letter to Theo from The Hague, on the first Sunday in May, 1882. He's agitated and unpleasant.

Today I met Mauve [Vincent's cousin-in-law, a successful artist who was mentoring him] and had a very regrettable conversation with him [about The Potato Eaters] which made it clear to me that Mauve and I have parted ways for ever. Mauve has gone so far that he can't retract it...I asked him to come and see my work and talk things over afterwards. Mauve refused outright, 'I certainly won't come to see you, it's over and done with'.

In the end he said, 'you have a vicious character'. At that point I turned around – it was in the dunes – and walked home alone.

This was yet another failed relationship, another discarded friendship. It happened for the same reason Vincent argued with anyone – when he thought he was being unfairly singled out for criticism [which was anytime his work was criticised].

...you have a vicious character...

What does Mauve mean? That Vincent is capable of ill will to his fellow man, even violence? Is Vincent a sadist? In my writing, at turns, I've been described as vicious as well. It has to do with criticism of course, especially where criticism seems strategic. But the fact of the matter is an artist with everything invested in his work, when his work is criticised, when he feels it is unfair, it feels like the root of his existence is under threat. An artist sufficiently invested in his work – and Vincent was – feels his life in under threat when his art is attacked. And he may respond, as Vincent did, with snarling, vicious vehemence. And why shouldn't he, his paintings are his children. He protects them as a lion does his cubs. Any artist with little feeling about his own work can't be an artist of any worth, can he?

But there's the rub. If your work isn't selling, and if you're a nobody, then it makes absolute sense that the world can't make sense of you, and so it's your job to endear yourself to the world, through your work, and through your demeanour. Vincent felt by giving up his worldly possessions, he had done enough, but he hadn't. The world of human society wants yielding good heartedness; a gift should be given charitably, not resentfully or worse, contemptuously. And in Vincent's moodiness, the world withdrew in fear and circumspection, seeing his wildness, wild views and wild living as a threat to good society, and civilisation, as indeed it was.

It was only years later, when Vincent's letters revealed his softer side, his sensitivities, *his Dickensian love* for his brother, for the Word, for the peasant flocks, when humanity saw his vast humanness, his handshakes and his hardships laid bare, that his unpleasant side dissolved. In the safety of death, Vincent's sexual sickness was ruled contained and irrelevant, just as his prickly identity and his electric, living works had been judged immaterial in life.

Validation and Significance/Invalidation and Insignificance

We see the reality of Vincent's "unpleasant" character best through Theo. Theo supported his brother, yet he was also conflicted and cringing. Vincent burned *everyone* he knew, and in July, sure enough, he arrived in Paris to burn his brother, Jo and Dries. Theo had seen it all along. But he was so caught up in his own problems, Theo forgot to warn Gachet. And Gachet, in his enthusiasm, had gotten caught up in his own artistic delusions, thus moving beyond the boundaries Theo had set for them both: a doctor patient relationship. Gachet had invited Vincent into the heart of his home, invited him to his table, and into his family. And then, Gachet left…and Vincent was free to turn the tables on Gachet, to occupy the doctor's inner world, and in the giddiness of this, Vincent gave away his true identity.

The doctor, an oddball and a moody misfit himself, wasn't exactly known for his bedside manner either. When the doctor refused to frame a particular artwork, Vincent took this personally. With his identity and his fate so critically dependent on the teetering subjective realties of others, criticisms and insults caused the creaking legs of the chair to buckle, and then snap.

What Vincent needed more than the acceptance of his work, was the redeeming love of a woman. He seemed to know this too. Yet a woman's love seemed forever out of his grasp [as if it was something that could be grasped, and if one did not grasp well enough, it could wriggle out of one's grasp]. Vincent's failure in life to find someone who genuinely loved him, in a word, his *loneliness*, was a source of constant invalidation. It confirmed his insignificance to himself, and exposed it to the world.

In the schema of the Van Gogh brothers, Theo validated his brother, or rather, Vincent's love for Theo validated Vincent as a good and decent person. But it was Jo, who redeemed them both. It was Jo who painstakingly and lovingly collected the letters, and kept the paintings together. It was Jo's love, for Vincent, that eventually shone through, into the world, to validate him in death, as no woman – not even his own mother, or sisters had – in life.

In the same letter to Theo, Vincent intuits in Mauve's scorn, a more general malaise in the mind-set of "the people":

And yet – and yet – and yet…I wish that Mauve regretted it. People suspect me of something... it's in the air... I must be hiding something... Vincent is keeping something back that may not be divulged... Well, gentlemen, I'll tell you – you who set great store by manners and culture…

Vincent goes on to admit, for the first time, his doomed relationship with Sien, the alcoholic prostitute. In his defense of his indulgences, he is argumentative, combative, self-righteous, indignant, hard to get along with yet also humble, self-effacing, conscientious, dutiful. A martyr, with every intention of becoming poorer so that in his sacrifice, he could be found worthy of inheriting the Earth, and entering a "well-arranged, resplendent" paradise.

Farms near Auvers

If we are to find Vincent today, not the dried husks of his bones in a graveyard, but the spirit of him, haunting the hills over Auvers, the glittering Oise, we must visit another candidate for the hallowed title of "last painting."

Intuitively, *Farms near Auvers* looks and feels like it was painted near the Gachet home. That was where Vincent went when he first arrived in Auvers, and was the scene of *Thatched Cottages and Houses*, one of his first paintings in Auvers, in May. So it makes sense that by the end of July, he was a lot more comfortable and familiar, absorbed as he was in the "immense plain" floating like a sea around these homes.

Gachet's home was part of a tumble of cottages just outside of Auvers, to the East, beyond the Chateau, and on the main road. *Farms near Auvers* is less about farms, but farmhouses on the fringe of the countryside. The distant leap and plunge of rolling hills and purple plateaus provides more orientation, it's a view to the crags of the north, away from the river, towards Rouen [once one of the largest and most prosperous capitals of medieval Europe] and Amiens, and beyond that, the North Sea channel. It's easy to imagine Vincent felt at home in these hamlets, because he'd grown up in this sort of small-town, rural setting in Holland. It was the same thing, the same thing, only lifted up and warmed by a bright summer sun.

In Paul Cézanne's muted *House of Dr. Gachet,* the post-impression artist [a contemporary of Vincent who died in 1906] provides a sidelong view of the scene, from the point of view of the main road as one exits Auvers from the East. In front we see a similar tumble of homes, and trees, on the right a hillside rising on the horizon like a grey- green wave.

Vincent looked on this and saw homes, families, green gardens and growing things. He wanted to be one of them, which is why he described his depiction of Daubigny's Garden to Theo in his last letter as "one of my most carefully thought-out canvases…"

In the same letter he sketched tree figures, a clear reference to an earlier panting, *Thatched Cottages in Chaponval.* Chaponval is on the same road East leaving Auvers, passing Gachet's home – it's a little further on. If the scene is a great, shallow C, with Chaponval and the Gachet home at one end, the Ravoux Inn at the center, then Vincent's grave was on the far end, its distance perhaps a symptom of the distance decent folk in leafy suburbs, with lush gardens, wished to maintain with the troubled artist.

What we have in the nomenclature is absolute confirmation that this ribbon of homes depicted in the last letter, and one of the last paintings, *is* around the Gachet residence. That's where Vincent was working, and what he was thinking about, even when he was back at the Inn when writing to Theo.

But that's not all. *Farms near Auvers* is unsigned, so it locates Vincent not only in place, but in *time*, at the Gachet home and surrounds, in his last days. More importantly, it locates Vincent's *psychology*.

He drifted through the wheat fields, yes, and painted the Town Hall, and Church, and the village streets, but *this* is where he wished to belong, in the bright, sun-drenched, lived-in fabric of the world, in the amicable spill and roll of quiet neighborhoods raising their turkeys, chickens, goats and ducks. He wished to be immersed in the Sunday fishing of a nearby river, his ear tickled every hour by the far-off clanging of church bells, his eyes catching on an assortment of stray cats. In the dusty road connecting, knitting a community to itself, he wished, with sexual fervor, to be part of the embroidery.

What lonely, single man, what homeless nobody, which non-entity *wouldn't* look on such a cosy domestic scene with longing, and an upwelling, burning desire for belonging?

Fake Genuines and Genuine Fakes

It's in the subtext of fakery and forgery that Vincent's legacy faces the most serious threat. If true crime is at its core about finding out what's real, then in art, an abundance of phony copies [as there are with Vincent van Gogh] challenges our notions about what's real as regards Vincent.

Many well-known artists have to deal with this blight, my great grandfather was one of a handful of South African masters to see their efforts impinged by forgers. What's staggering with Vincent's work, is that it's the authenticity of some of his most beloved and valuable works, that have been challenged. Vincent's Wikipedia page makes no mention of this aspect, but for the last 30 years or more, forged paintings have brewed across the media landscape.

In May 1998 the *Irish Times* wrote about *Sunflowers*, "the most famous painting associated with Vincent van Gogh" being regarded as "definitely fake" by an Italian art expert, and seven other experts. Since Theo was sending the same materials to Vincent, all of his canvases were typical – in size, the canvas material, the identifying labels. De Robertis, the Italian expert believed it wasn't just the material that pointed to a fake, but the style of work, which was inconsistent, as if painted by two artists.

Ten years before the brouhaha erupted about fake *Sunflowers*, *Sunflowers* sold for a then world record price of $39 921 750 in 1987 [£24.75 million or £53.5 million in 2016 pounds sterling], tripling, almost quadrupling the previous record of $12 million. The buyer, Japan'sYasuo Goto, an insurance magnate, acquired *Sunflowers* from Christie's in London. It wasn't clear whether Goto bought the work for himself, or his company. In any event, a few months later the world record was broken by another Van Gogh, this time purchased by Alan Bond, an Australian corporate criminal. Sotheby's in New York offloaded *Irises* in November 1987to Bond for $53.9 million.

Five years later Bond went bankrupt with debts of about A$8 billion.

In August 1997, *The Art Newspaper* claimed at "at least" 45 Van Goghs were fakes, including *The Portrait of Dr. Gachet*, the *Garden of the Hospital in Arles* and *The Garden at Auvers*. In 2013, a fake, unsigned Van Gogh was deemed genuine, and sold for £30 million by Christie's, who didn't want to tell the media how much they thought it was worth. It's an interesting piece because even the Van Gogh museum decided it was fake, before changing its mind. The museum embarked on a two year study, deciding that Vincent's reference to it in his letters meant it had to be authentic, as well as the fact that the paint was "the same range of paints" Vincent used during that period [an allusion to the palette, nor the age of the paint].

I'm no art expert, but anyone could reverse engineer a description in a letter to recreate a painting, especially if there were millions on the line. To my eye the work is simply too fresh; the sky in particular looks like it was painted very recently. The green dots on the right look like the work of an amateur. And this is why the whole enterprise is so damaging. When a fake could be real, and a real could be fake, what is the real worth of the artist?

The *New York Times*, reporting from the Van Gogh Museum in Amsterdam, wrote authoritatively at the time:

For roughly a century, the painting "Sunset at Montmajour" was considered a fake. It was stored in an attic and then held in a private collection, unknown to the public and dismissed by art historians. But on Monday, the Van Gogh Museum declared the work a genuine product of the master, calling it a major discovery.

At the same time, the *LA Times* threatened to be less sycophantic, but they too threw their weight behind the money and the picture in the end:

The news Monday of a lost but rediscovered painting by Vincent van Gogh has everything art needs to become a big media story: major celebrity, fooled experts, lottery-scale riches and a back-story worthy of "Antiques Roadshow." A canvas by one of the world's most famous artists got dismissed as a fake, tucked away for decades, forgotten in an attic, brought out for re-evaluation and, after two years of scrutiny, declared to be the genuine article. It's a rags-to-riches tale.

Just about the only thing the story doesn't have – only because it doesn't need it – is a very great work of art.

The *New York Times* quotes the museum director glossing over the merits of the artwork, focusing instead on its presumed [and thus assumed] prestige.

"Sunset at Montmajour," painted in Arles in 1888, "is a work from the most important period of his life, when he created his substantial masterpieces, like 'Sunflowers,' 'The Yellow House' and 'The Bedroom,' " said the museum's director, Axel Rüger, in an interview. The painting depicts dusk in the hilly, forested landscape of Montmajour, in Provence, with wheat fields and the ruins of a Benedictine abbey in the distance. The area around Montmajour was a subject that van Gogh revisited often during his time in Arles.

"One or two early van Goghs do sometimes come out of the woodwork now and again, but from the mature period, it's very rare," said James Roundell, an art dealer and the director of modern pictures for the Dickinson galleries in London and New York, which deals in Impressionist and modern art.

Mr. Roundell said it would be hard to predict precisely how much "Sunset at Montmajour" would fetch on the market, but expected it would be "in the tens of millions and quite a few of them."

In 2002, *Sunflowers* was rescued from the abyss, as two experts from the Van Gogh Museum waved their magic wands, and it became the genuine article again. The *Telegraph* mentions a new name here, Schuffenecker, who was a serial forger of Vincent's work. Now the idiosyncrasies of Schuffenecker are used to determine whether Schuffenecker had the opportunity, or the motive, to paint a particular painting. That's how far the narrative has slid from the original artist.

And while [Sunflowers] was known to have been extended [extended is euphemism for forged] by Schuffenecker, the experts [the Van Gogh Museum experts] pointed out that it would have been illogical for him to have forged the main part while adding the rest in a different style. The experts also say that the still life bears similarities to another painting in the Van Gogh Museum which Schuffenecker would not have seen. One of the doubters, French art expert Benoit Landais, whose claims were supported in a Channel 4 documentary, said the investigators [from the Van Gogh Museum] had "failed to come up with incontrovertible evidence".

Counterfeit works pretending to be Vincent's work constantly impinge on the value, and the validity, of the great artist. The line between what was Vincent's art and what wasn't, is like a shifting tide. There have been lawsuits, museums bickering amongst themselves, even Vincent II developed a grudge against Gachet, and Gachet's son, who he accused publically of peddling forgeries.

Perhaps the most tragic aspect of this, is the fact that *Portrait of Dr. Gachet*, Vincent's most valuable painting, which sold for $82.5 million [about $154.5 million today] is also at the leading edge of rabid controversy. Not the work itself, but a copy of it. There is a double act to it that's also considered a forgery, and this distracts from the original work, and the artist. No surprise what the source of this forgery, another one of dozens, turns out to be – it's another pick from the litter from the Gachet Collection.

According to the *Independent* in 1999:

Several of the Auvers paintings...are fakes, painted, most probably, by Dr Paul Gachet, his doctor, sometime friend and the subject of two of the Auvers canvases...The claims and counter-claims about the authenticity of at least four of the works (including one of the Gachet portraits) have already led to two court cases in France and a series of mutually insulting articles by some of the best-known names in Parisian art criticism... Supporters of the "Gachet fake" theory accuse the French museums service of mounting a self-serving exhibition, intended to whitewash...the doubts surrounding several Van Gogh canvases owned by the French state...The experts in the museums service dismiss the critics as amateurs, who refuse to allow scientific proof to disturb their pet theories, which they have erected from false intuitions and circumstantial evidence.

Self-serving museums. No there's a thought. So there's a scenario here of experts hired by museums to come to a particular finding, who are calling out their critics, undermining those who say some of Vincent's work isn't painted by the expert, but by amateurs.

In other words, the show has become Exhibit A in a legal and art-political argument, as well as an exhibition. No matter. It is a fascinating show, as well as a fascinating argument and a fascinating story. The foxgloves grasped in Dr Gachet's hand in the "first", undisputed, portrait have altered colour from mauve to blue. Curiously, exactly the same change has occurred in the second, disputed painting. If Dr Gachet faked this painting, did he use the same cheap paints as Van Gogh?

When art journalists see the authenticity of the world's most famous, and arguably most valuable artist as "a fascinating show", you can see how we've ended up in the quagmire of "post-truth", and "post-reality", whatever that is, but whatever it is, it's a different reality for everyone.

The Forging of Vincent's Reality

It's no theory that Vincent's art was forged. We know who did it, and we have good reason to know how he got hold of Vincent's work, and why.

Wikipedia's description of Émile Schuffenecker says it all, doesn't it?

Émile Schuffenecker [born two years before Van Gogh] was a French Post-Impressionist artist, painter, art teacher and art collector. A friend of Paul Gauguin... Schuffenecker was one of the first collectors of Vincent van Gogh, [and] Schuffenecker was instrumental in establishing The Volpini exhibition [an exhibition of Gauguin's work]. Schuffenecker's own work, however, tends to have been neglected since his death...

So Gauguin and this slippery Schuffenecker were pals. Schuffenecker was a struggling artist, but Gauguin may have found a use for him. Remember those paintings of sunflowers Gauguin swiped from the Yellow House; the one's Vincent wanted back? Well, it's through Gauguin that Schuffenecker would have seen them. But here's the rub.

Some sketches and drawings prove that carefully studied works by Van Gogh in his possession. But there is also evidence that Schuffenecker went a step further and "completed" paintings he considered to be unfinished. In 1927, he himself frankly admitted to have "finished" the Large Tree at Montbriand, painted in Saint-Rémy in October, 1889...Presumably, Schuffenecker also embellished versions of Van Gogh's Sunflowers and Daubigny's Garden slightly, both since 1894 in his possession. This was possibly done simply to adapt a painting to a frame he had at hand, which is the reason he mentioned to Maximilien Gauthier.

Incredibly, the museum experts continue to quibble about whether Schuffenecker was deliberately trying to forge art, or simply interfering here and there with a series of high-profile artists, in order to help the art work fit into a frame. Whether you want to call finishing another artist's painting "completing" them, or forgery seems to be a matter of post-truth semantics. The fact is, in a chapter about Vincent, we've wasted several pages by having to explain what he didn't do, who he wasn't, and why so much certainty exists about what he did.

It's because of this that we can't even be clear on the beginning and end of Vincent's legacy. It's like the bible or a comic book, with bits added to and subtracting constantly, as a greedy laity attempts to exchange its pound of dubious flesh for gold. The fact is, large fractions of Vincent's gilded legacy is fiction, not only his paintings, but also his story.

Forgery isn't some dark art of the past decades either, it's happening in the here and now. On the last day of April, 2018, CNN reported about a French museum finding out half of its paintings are fakes.

Murders Do Happen in the Real World

Our familiarity with Vincent, means at first pass, the contention that he was murdered feels experimental, even exotic. I've endeavoured to explain why this is not only possible, but probable, and that the suicide narrative, is not only improbable, but unlikely, and at its root, outrageous.

Now, as we approach the final chapter in this narrative, it's time to adjust our eyes to the polished railway tracks and the deep darkness that is criminal psychology. In approaching Vincent's murder, I want you to imagine a beautiful black spider, one of the oldest and wisest of its kind. It's not hypothetical, this spider was real, and even had a name: Number 16.

Number 16 was 43 years old when it died, almost twice as old as the nearest contender, a 28-year-old Mexican tarantula. Number 16, an Australian trapdoor matriarch from the Central Wheatbelt area of Western Australia, was monitored throughout its life. Researchers believe Number 16 is the oldest spider ever recorded. Researchers described her life [for it was a she] as "a significant life" that opened the trapdoor for humans to understand the social behaviour of certain spiders. When Number 16 turned 40, one of the researchers wanted to give her a 40th birthday present, a mealworm, but other researchers felt this might bias the study results.

Now the question is, how did the world's oldest spider die? Bear in mind, unlike most spiders, this spider though not in captivity, was in a sense under the protection and care of human beings. The wilderness area, in which Number 16 lived, was thus, sacrosanct. It needed to be for the study to be considered authentic. Nevertheless, Number 16 had a name, and a history. It was being studied when it died, so there was no question what happened to it.

Would you believe Number 16 didn't die of old age, but was murdered? It may seem an exotic contention at first pass, but it's true. Researchers, who marked Number 16's burrow, her home for most of those 40-something years, found she'd been killed by a wasp sting. Number 16 had a very unhappy ending.

According to cbc.ca:

"[Wasps] are quite brutal in the way they prey on spiders," lead author Leanda Mason told As It Happens host Carol Off. "They enter the burrow and then lay an egg either in or

on the spider. And then the egg, once it hatches, the larvae will either eat the spider from the inside out or the outside in. It's a gruesome, gruesome death for Number 16."

Before meeting her violent end, Number 16 lived a long life of solitude inside her burrow, punctuated by regular visits from male suitors, Mason said.

So this wasn't a random killing with no motive either; Number 16 was *targeted* by a parasitic wasp that *typically* preys on spiders. The motive for the wasp was that the legendary spider give up its Life Force to the wasp's offspring; literally exchanging its lifeblood to nourish the larva of its parasite host. It happens in nature, and it happens in human nature every day.

Another Van Gogh Murdered in 2004

On November 2nd, 2004, Theo's great grandson [Vincent II's son's son], also named Theo, was murdered while cycling on the streets of Amsterdam by a 26-year-old Islamic extremist. Theo was a well-known film director and had recently made a film that criticised violence against women in Islamic societies. Theo van Gogh, who many knew as "a controversial figure", was murdered because he was critical of Islam. The Dutch Prime Minister, Jan Peter Balkenende remarked at the time:

"It is unacceptable if expressing your opinion would be the cause of this brutal murder."

*Research into the 6th century Rabbula Gospels, the earliest dated Christian manuscript, has revealed the earliest illustrations of Christ were repainted, changing the original depictions of curly ginger hair, to black.

Who Murdered Vincent van Gogh – and why?

"If you hear a voice within you say 'you cannot paint', then by all means paint, and that voice will be silenced." — Vincent Van Gogh

1888 – Spring – Flowering Orchards

The shadow looms against the polished tracks, the silver thing in his hands playing with a sliver of lunar light. Vincent is nowhere to be seen. Perhaps the darkness has engulfed him. The ticket. Do we give it up, or hold onto it even longer. What are we waiting for? Don't we know what there is to know by now? Haven't we arrived at the station of realisation?

The Murderer

I extend my hand and the train man quickly snatches the ticket. Suddenly, the scene inverts to a sharp, blinding light. The shadow turns into an old, angry man with dishevelled blonde hair, and dancing, anxious, beady little eyes. In his hand is a gun, and the white hot radiance is the spark from it, beating back the darkness.

In the flash, Vincent, who is shouting, scrambles to his feet, and beats a hasty retreat. Someone else is there too, moving through the hay.

And it's for his offspring, to protect Marguerite that the doctor has stung his prey. The egg sown into Vincent's stomach will eat him alive, and then his Life Force will be theirs to do with as they please.

Meanwhile, just as he did in Arles, Vincent is off on his own footrace, bleeding from the stomach, though not badly as his ear had bled that winter's night, shuffling to safety. When Vincent reached the Chateau, equidistant now between the Inn and Gachet's house, he drifted through a hypothetical dilemma.

If medical help was at Dr. Gachet's, and the doctor was his personal physician, why not turn to him for aid? Why go to the Inn and have medical aid sent there, when it was right here? Of course if he was out there, anywhere near the Chateau, going to Gachet was the obvious choice, unless Gachet had shot him on purpose.

In Arles, Vincent had stumbled about with a bloody ear and was soon faced with a mob who had him booted out of his home. He couldn't afford to make the same mistake here. So even though it was summer, and sweltering, he buttoned up his coat. People shouldn't see that he was injured except those he could trust. And they didn't need to know why, otherwise it would be Arles all over again, and worst of all, explaining the nasty circumstance to Theo and Jo. If he wasn't careful, it would be back to the asylum…

So we have a man hiding his injury, and a story that he intended to commit suicide in a public place. We have a man hustling home, away from medical help [and the prime murder suspect], and yet still asking for medical assistance, and a story that he intended to die.

When Vincent arrives, he has to pass a queue of onlookers, before he gets to his room. He hoped to pass them without their noticing him. He certainly didn't engage them. But since he'd missed dinner – unusually – and since the Ravoux's knew him, and suspected something was off, they asked him if anything was wrong.

The Investigation

"Monsieur Vincent, is something wrong?"

Vincent's answer at this moment is telling.

"I have…" He tries to answer, but realizes he can't say what he wishes to say, stops and leaves the sentence unfinished as he stumbles painfully upstairs that seem to have grown immeasurably steeper.

Then, when his wound is revealed, he's interrogated again. Now he says:

"I have…tried to kill myself."

Why not: "I tried to kill myself" or "I shot myself", or, given the loaded dice of suicide in Catholic France, "I accidentally shot myself." If you're going to survive suicide, you might as well avoid the scandal of an honest answer, right? Vincent wouldn't say where he was, or where he got the gun, innocent answers to simple questions, if he had intended to kick the bucket.

But taking the way he meant to frame his answer, where might he have been going with *I have…*

I've argued with Dr. Gachet…

I've gotten myself into trouble again.

I've been caught canoodling with Gachet's daughter.

I've just escaped an angry, controlling father.

I've fallen in love.

Immediately after finding out the skeletal details, the burden fell to the Ravoux's to seek medical assistance for Vincent. It arrived on the scene, via the local doctor, Jean Mazery*. Vincent's breathing wasn't watery or spluttery, which was why he was able to smoke a pipe and speak to his interlocutors. Mazery's assessment was that a small calibre bullet had missed all of Vincent's major organs, and arteries. In other words, Mazery's prognosis was optimistic.

Adeline Ravoux confirmed this assessment, and so did Theo van Gogh, for that matter.

Dr. Gachet Takes the Stand

What's less certain is exactly when Gachet condescended to arrive, to treat his [former?] patient. What is certain, is that once Gachet did arrive he never returned in 24 hours for a follow-up visit. But he did return before Vincent was embalmed, to sketch his patient post mortem. There seems to be something of Gauguin's sadistic pleasure in viewing the guillotine up close, as there is with the doctor scrutinising his patient with more care and consideration in death, than he ever did in life.

One also suspects, if Gachet shot Vincent, this ruse of pretending to treat him was a chore he was reluctant to perform, but how could he explain refusing to respond to a medical emergency?

According to Adeline Ravoux when she was 76-years-old:

I am absolutely certain that [Gachet] did not return: neither that evening, nor the following day. Father told us again: "During the examination and when he was bandaging the wound, Dr. Gachet did not say a word to Vincent."

This stands out clearly, as a mismatch between caring for a patient, and doing his duty, but apparently not caring. If Gachet didn't speak to Vincent, did Vincent not speak to him either? Was someone there while Gachet stalked about on the wooden floor, every creak deafening in the awkward silence?

Gustave Ravoux then escorted Gachet home, as though Gachet had no idea where the Inn was, or how to get home from the Inn. And Gachet apparently had none of his own transport available, either.

Instead of a doctor attending to Vincent, Gustave stays with Vincent all night. What does Gachet do? Hide Vincent's art equipment, gather his brood and conjure an alternate reality. Wash away blood stains? Or does Gachet simply go to bed and get his beauty's sleep?

Adeline Ravoux provides important "before and after" context to Gachet's visit:

Before the arrival of the physician, Vincent had requested his pipe and Father had lit it. He resumed smoking after the departure of the doctor, and smoked thus a part of the night. He appeared to suffer a lot and often moaned. He asked Father to put his ear to his chest to see if he could hear the gurgling of the internal hemorrhage. He remained silent almost all the [first] night, sometimes dozing.

Adeline was a thirteen-year-old girl when she witnessed the incident, some of it first-hand. Her retelling of it 63 years later may be broadly on target, but one can see how confusion can set in between the first doctor and the next, and the first night and the second. Did Vincent suffer on the first night, or the second, or both? Did Vincent's condition worsen after Gachet treated him? If anyone had been in the room with him, it's unlikely the doctor would have poisoned Vincent, but in some versions, Gachet closed the door behind him, and for those outside, all they could hear inside was silence.

Meanwhile in town, just as Vincent feared, the village was buzzing with rumors. Who'd started them, if he hadn't it?

Back to Adeline Ravoux:

[My father] preceded the gendarme into the bedroom, explaining to Vincent that...the gendarmes were here as French law prescribed an inquiry. The gendarme then entered the room, and Rigaumon...questioned Vincent: "Are you the one who wanted to commit suicide?"

"Yes...I believe..."

Vincent answers softly, and uncertainly, another version of the "I have..." response.

When the cops criticise Vincent for his answer, Vincent talks about doing what he wishes *with his body*. Nothing about madness, or his state of mind. Nothing about constrained resources, or lack of money.

My body is mine...

He doesn't breathe a word about why; instead he claims ownership of his body and says he can do as he pleases with it. Of course he can. He can also have it cut open and the bullet removed, which is his next demand. But can he, can anyone, *really* do with their bodies as they please? What happens when certain disapproving fathers and husbands *don't allow* random artists complete freedoms with their bodies, or *won't allow* him to run amok among their daughters?

His persistence is disgusting.

Then Vincent adds: "Do not accuse anybody, it is I that wished to commit suicide."

Vincent refuses to be confronted with the accusation, but then lectures the French police not to accuse anybody else. The reason he is shot is because he wished to commit suicide. But that's not a reason. The cops want to know the reason he tried to commit suicide. Well, Vincent gives them one:

My body is mine...

Isn't that what Marguerite said to her father, or to Vincent?

Vincent provides no explicit motive for his suicide attempt, instead his only reasoning seems to be that no one else is burdened with an accusation. It seems a silly admonition, if he's answered in the affirmative, and the police are calling him on it, saying hey, you know it's against the law, it's pointless asking them not to accuse anybody else, they're accusing him as it is. The whole town is already talking about it as a suicide.

Do not accuse anybody...

Unless he's trying to hint that they consider the possibility of anybody else…

Unfortunately, Gustave then puts a stop to the cops questioning, and the inquiry is over. It's interesting, even facing imminent death, Vincent is arguing, this time with the police.

Back to Adeline Ravoux:

Since dawn [on the morning of July 28th], Father had been preoccupied with how to tell Theo, the brother of Vincent. The casualty then being lethargic could not give precise information. (He had had a burst of energy during the gendarme's visit that had tired him a lot.)

Vincent is alive and awake, and yet his companion is preoccupied with an ongoing dilemma. How does he contact Vincent's brother? Well, didn't Anton Hirschigg know how to solve that problem? Or Dr. Gachet? Or Vincent himself? Why is there this difficulty in contacting Theo, when it's so easy to contact the police and two doctors?

If Gachet hadn't been such a bastard, if he'd spoken to Vincent rather than pretended he didn't know him from a bar of soap, Gustave Ravoux could simply have asked Gachet for Theo's home address. There's also the most obvious issue of all; the letters, half-finished and discarded, littering the small room. Wasn't Theo's address on any of those? Couldn't they wake up the post office dude and get the information from him?

We know that when Theo arrived, he found Vincent's last letter "on his person", literally soaked in Vincent's blood, perhaps because Gustave knew about Vincent's regular correspondence, and wanted the handwritten address if Vincent wouldn't volunteer it. Why didn't Vincent want his brother summoned?

It's clear that initially, Vincent – and everyone else except Gachet – thought Vincent would survive the injury. If that was the case, Theo didn't need to be troubled by the news, or burdened with the expense.

He had had a burst of energy during the gendarme's visit that had tired him a lot.

Why was Vincent to active when the police spoke to him? Since he contributed nothing of substance, wouldn't say where he left the gun, or where he got it from, or why he'd shot himself, there's a contradiction in his activated response and his lack of useful response. Why is he so agitated by the police? Once again, Vincent expect to live, and so a botched suicide was only a hypothetical crime. It basically neutralized any effort to investigate the incident.

I did this, but I'm okay. Don't accuse anyone else. My body is mine…

When Theo arrives, Vincent has about ten hours left to live, and less time than that where he has the strength to remain conscious, to talk to Theo. Adeline Ravoux describes Theo as:

…a man a little smaller than Vincent, thin, an agreeable physiognomy and he appeared very nice. But his face was marked by sorrow. He immediately climbed up to his brother who

he kissed and spoke to him in their native language. Father withdrew and did not help them. He did not go back in during the night. After the emotion that he had felt on seeing his brother, Vincent had fallen into a coma. Theo and my father kept watch on the casualty until his death, which occurred at one o'clock in the morning.

What are we to make of this contradiction?

[Father] did not go back [into Vincent's room] during the night... Theo and my father kept watch on the casualty until his death...at 01:30...

Be fair, we should also inquire why Theo never put Vincent on a train back to Paris, for proper medical treatment. Theo had ten hours to work with, and in those hours, Vincent's condition appeared to deteriorate from him appearing well enough [that Theo thought he'd return to Jo the same night], to comatose, and then dead.

Vincent deteriorated rapidly, but what was does that mean in context? He'd been hurt for 20 hours when Theo arrived, and so the overall assessment had to have been then, that Vincent would live to tell the tale, and continue painting. Since the trip to Paris and proper medical intervention was just an hour by train, and since Vincent wasn't improving, why didn't Theo make use of this option?

It was a Monday night, and Theo had been able to arrive as soon as he'd heard. There was time enough, in Theo's own assessment, that if Vincent's condition *wasn't* serious, he'd be able to return to Paris the same evening. And yet, if Vincent's condition *was* serious, why not return to Paris with Vincent?

The unknown factor here, of course, was Vincent. Did he *want* medical care or not? There are unambiguous reports that he screamed in pain and begged for someone to cut open his belly and remove the bullet.

I may also be that when Theo arrived, Vincent felt contrition and guilt, for being such a financial burden at such a burdensome time. He didn't want to add hospital bills like there's been in Arles, all over again. Perhaps he talked up his chances, or talked them down.

Whatever it was, it didn't make sense not to get Vincent to a surgeon. And so, cue the music:

*I wonder how***

I wonder why

Yesterday you told me 'bout the blue blue sky

And all that I can see is just a yellow lemon-tree

I'm turning my head up and down

I'm turning turning turning turning turning around

And all that I can see is just another lemon-tree

And yet behind the loopy music there is this cold silence when Gachet arrives, and dresses the wound behind a closed door. Somewhere in his delirium, when his companions suggested additional medical care, Vincent may have insisted he didn't want to see doctor Gachet, and his companions may have assumed either that his condition didn't warrant it, or that Vincent didn't want *any* medical care, or that Vincent truly was suicidal.

When Vincent and Theo embraced, and were heard communicating in their native Dutch, it's possible that in the security of this exchange, Vincent may have disclosed to his brother his regret for putting Theo through all this [again], his reason for what happened [true perhaps, but not all true], and his gratitude to see him.

Cue the music:

I'm sitting here

I miss the power

I'd like to go out taking a shower

But there's a heavy cloud inside my head

I feel so tired

Put myself into bed

While nothing ever happens and I wonder…

In his effort to exonerate Theo's friend Gachet, Vincent had to implicate himself, and that meant playing the victim again. He didn't want to live, he said, and if he died, that was fine. If this was a play for sympathy, it's not clear whether it worked. What it did was produce ennui in Theo.

Cue the music:

Isolation is not good for me

Isolation I don't want to sit on the lemon-tree

I'm steppin' around in the desert of joy

Baby anyhow I'll get another toy

And everything will happen…

No matter how moved or unmoved Theo was by all this, he found time to write a letter to Jo, something he would never have done if he really believed his brother was dying. His letter reveals that after encountering Vincent, and finding him in a better condition than he'd been led to believe, by Gachet, he was *still* determined to get the hell out of there, that same evening. It didn't even occur to him to head over to Gachet and ask him if he could sleep over. It would have been the logical thing for him to do.

Theo doesn't call for Gachet either. He's in town, Gachet's a doctor, get the doctor back and see what he can do. If Vincent's suicidal, then the expert in melancholia has failed catastrophically, and he should be called to account. So why wasn't he?

Because Theo was ashamed. That's why there's no emergency telegram from Theo either, even as his brother slipped inexorably along the mortal coil towards death. It's as though Vincent, having being shot, and having slid some of the way towards death by then, decided to allow himself to slide the rest of the way. And Theo accepted this. He could have stopped it, instead, he *allowed* it.

According to Adeline Ravoux:

It was Father who, with Theo, in the morning made the declaration of the death to the town hall.

The Funeral

Bizarrely, though Theo went to plenty of trouble to bury his brother, he didn't invite Jo to the funeral. Everyone else he could think of, but not his wife. Theo didn't speak at his brother's funeral either; too choked up apparently.

At my mother's funeral, my father asked me to speak on her behalf. He didn't, and as far as I recall, neither did my other siblings. Speaking under these circumstances is tough, and yet I wanted to do it. I wanted to honor my mother, I wanted people to know about her hopes and dream in spite of what happened. What was important to her? To make her extinction bearable, I wanted to believe she was in a better place, and I believed it then, just as Theo did. But was she? But how can death ever be a better place for the living, especially when we're less than halfway through our precious apportion of life? Life is fleeting, death is forever, and life *can* go on, even after the end of the world.

I'm turning my head up and down

I'm turning turning turning turning turning around

And all that I can see is just another lemon-tree

Emile Bernard's Version of Events

On August 2nd, Bernard wrote to the art critic Albert Aurier. It was four days after Vincent's death, three after his funeral, and perhaps just a day or two after Bernard returned home. In other words, it was a pretty quick turnaround, and Bernard says as much in his opening gambit.

...I am obliged to tell you without delay. Our dear friend Vincent died four days ago. I think that you will have already guessed the fact that he killed himself.

Strange words for a factual incident. Let's examine then again, more carefully.

I think that you will have already guessed the fact that he killed himself.

Why would Aurier have guessed; why would he need to guess if it was an uncontested and uncontestable fact? I may be reading too much into this, but Bernard had had eighteen months to gossip with Gauguin about Vincent, and Gauguin was all about Vincent being a deranged lunatic. Vincent's suicide seemed absolute confirmation for Gauguin, which is why he had zero sympathy for Vincent, declaring that it was better this was for everyone, including Vincent.

So Bernard saying, on August 2nd *you will have already guessed the fact that he killed himself* is a tad gossipy and presumptuous. It's especially presumptuous because Bernard was there himself, but the arrogance is really in the almost dry reporting of the letter, as if Bernard hoped his account would be published verbatim. There's a distasteful lack of grief for a supposed friend writing in detail about the suicide of a fellow artist. Instead, Bernard seems to be salivating at the prospect of being in possession of salacious gossip.

On Sunday evening [Vincent] went out into the countryside near Auvers, placed his easel against a haystack and went behind the chateau and fired a revolver shot at himself. Under the violence of the impact (the bullet entered his body below the heart) he fell, but he got up again, and fell three times more, before he got back to the inn where he was staying without telling anyone about his injury.

Vincent not telling anyone appears to decisively confirm he meant to die, despite the contradiction of shooting oneself, surviving, then sitting through the 30 hour rigmarole of dying. One thing missing from the post-shooting narrative is Vincent asking that he be put down. If he doesn't want to live, why is he so patient about it?

He finally died on Monday evening, still smoking his pipe which he refused to let go of, explaining that his suicide had been absolutely deliberate and that he had done it in complete lucidity.

The mismatch between Vincent being "completely lucid" and "absolutely deliberate" doesn't hold water, because if he had been lucid, and the suicide both absolute and deliberate, he would have died. He would have aimed at the head, as indeed, the vast majority of suicide gunshot wounds are.

A typical detail that I was told about his wish to die was that when Dr. Gachet told him that he still hoped to save his life, he said, "Then I'll have to do it over again." But, alas, it was no longer possible to save him...

Consider these bland embellishments in context. Gachet told Vincent he still hoped to save his life…really? When? The Ravoux's said Gachet didn't say a word to Vincent, and presumably, if Vincent didn't wish to live, and the doctor was dutiful about performing his duty [as most good doctors ought to be], this *should* have set off a blazing row. But there's no row, there's just silence.

Gachet does treat Vincent, minimally and negligibly, but even so, Vincent doesn't stop him. Perhaps he couldn't, perhaps he was being sedated or poisoned; Gachet could easily claim he was offering Vincent a painkiller, when it was really a slow-working serum. A suicidal man would refuse any and all treatment, however. And yet we have this narrative that after shooting himself, Vincent wanted to die. Where does it come from? Gachet, of course, and Bernard circulates it eagerly, just as he did with Gauguin's story.

Then I'll have to do it over again…

That sounds like something Gachet would say about Vincent behind his back, to justify his lack of involvement throughout most of those 30 hours. The fact that a second doctor had to be called at all, reveals to what extent Gachet was removed from the picture.

Those words are also strangely ironic for a murderer returning to his victim, only to find him detestably still alive and breathing.

Then I'll have to do it over again…

Alas, it was no longer possible to save him…

If it took 30 hours for Vincent to die, and Vincent hiked about town and up a flight of stairs, if he was able to "refuse to give up his pipe" and argue with the police, it really doesn't sound like it wasn't possible to save him. It sounds like there was an abundant lack of trying, especially from those who were most responsible for his care, Gachet and Theo more than anyone.

"I think myself that Gauguin was a little out of sorts with the good town of Arles, the little yellow house where we work, and especially with me." — Vincent van Gogh

Cue the reality shifting music:

I'd like to change my point of view

I feel so lonely

I'm waiting for you

But nothing ever happens and I wonder…

"I think myself that Gachet was a little out of sorts with the good town of Auvers, the little Inn where I lived – and died, and especially with me."

As I've hinted at previously, Bernard's misleading version has some fluffy, seemingly inconsequential information, which is smoke and mirrors, and isn't. Bernard's version locates Vincent at the scene of his crime, and more than likely, receives this information at the funeral from Gachet.*** Gachet, after all, is the artist's go-to-guy and is the closest thing to a witness in Vincent's death, in fact he's arguably the best [or worst] witness of all of them.

While this version cleverly dislocates Vincent from where he probably was at dinnertime, or perhaps the late afternoon [Gachet's home and stables], like all dissembling, this version reveals as much as it hides.

On Sunday evening [Vincent] went out into the countryside near Auvers, placed his easel against a haystack and went behind the chateau and fired a revolver shot at himself. Under the violence of the impact (the bullet entered his body below the heart) he fell, but he got up again, and fell three times more, before he got back to the inn where he was staying...

So what happened to the easel and the revolver? What happened to the last canvas, or didn't he start work on it? The falling three times more sounds dramatic. Who said that? Vincent, or Gachet? If Gachet was standing over Vincent when he shot him, then one can imagine a man scrambling and falling as he flees his attacker.

The shot below the heart implies that Vincent aimed for his heart and missed. In fact, he shot into an area below his ribs, on his left side, and Mazery described a *downward* trajectory. This extremely unusual trajectory suggests:

1) Vincent's murderer shot him from directly above, while Vincent was lying down, on the ground, on his back. His attacker was positioned right behind Vincent's head and shoulders. This also suggests an aim closer to Vincent's genitals than his heart, unless Vincent squirmed at the last moment. This would be hard to do away from the direction of the shooter, if he was lying on his back

2) Vincent's murder shot him while lying on the floor, and Vincent standing over him, somewhat bent over, possibly ducking to avoid another bullet or an overhanging object.

3) Vincent was standing while facing his attacker, who was armed and also standing, and the gun held between them, but pointed slightly downward, went off either accidentally, or during a scuffle, as their torsos or arms tussled and collided.

In sum, whether suicide or murder, the trajectory was not as effective as intended, which suggests active, unexpected movement at the last moment, which is the same explanation for the ear incident not being more serious, and in both cases, why Vincent was able to escape the attack on foot.

Bernard's Version of Gachet and Theo at the Funeral

If some aspects of Bernard's letter appear like heartless reportage, others, like the funeral, seem kinder. It's ironic how, as he lay dying, there didn't seem much point in doing anything to save him, but once dead, there was this feverish activity to prepare his funeral, and cut him open for embalming.

On the walls of the room where [Vincent's] body was laid out all his last canvases were hung making a sort of halo for him and the brilliance of the genius that radiated from them made this death even more painful for us artists who were there. The coffin was covered with a simple white cloth and surrounded with masses of flowers, the sunflowers that he loved so much, yellow dahlias, yellow flowers everywhere. It was, you will remember, his favourite colour, the symbol of the light that he dreamed of as being in people's hearts as well as in works of art. Near him also on the floor in front of his coffin were his easel, his folding stool and his brushes.

Here the easel, folding stool and brushes appear to have done a magic act; moving through time and space from Bernard's haystack behind the chateau, where Vincent left them in the field, and arriving at his funeral.

How do we account for this discrepancy? Either Vincent had a second set of paint equipment, or Gachet had brought the equipment himself from his home, or wherever he may found it lying [or some other anonymous resident], or Vincent never went out that afternoon or evening to paint. Perhaps he went out to write a letter. Perhaps he was fraternising with Marguerite. Perhaps he went down to the river. We simply don't know, but what seems likely, is that Vincent that day, did what he always did – he painted. He had accumulated 70 canvasses in about as many days; so it stands to reason he painted on July 27th as well.

What also seems clear is that if he took his equipment somewhere, it *wasn't* left where he'd left it, it was moved. That's neither here nor there, maybe Vincent painted, maybe he didn't, but as soon as we take the suicide narrative a step further, then we see the gun disappears. A gun disappearing and paint equipment secreted from the scene seem less like suicide and more like murder. But if this is so, why is the easel at Vincent's coffin? Bernard describes the funeral set-up in detail, including the many witnesses; he sees all this first-hand, so it's unlikely it's embellished.

Again, why is the easel there?

Isn't it obvious? In the same way that Gachet would have raised more suspicion by not treating Vincent, than by doing so unhelpfully, Gachet also wants to minimise suspicion around Vincent's things. His easel, his chair, his tools of the trade, are pretty obvious. Theo would have wanted to know where they were if they weren't there. Gachet had plenty of opportunity to put it in place while Theo rushed about town, making various arrangements, including printing invitations and purchasing a burial plot.

There's also the possibility that, if Vincent's equipment was absent, Anton Hirschigg may have provided his rig as a sort of stand-in. But wouldn't Theo have noticed? It makes more sense, if there was a murder, that things would be moved about to cover tracks. A gun hidden, blood rinsed, the dead fellows stuff secretly returned to the artist's shed while everyone else gathered in the upstairs room.

Bernard describes Theo "sobbing pitifully" at the funeral, the whole time, and the sun "terribly hot" as they climbed the hill outside Auvers to the new cemetery. The atmosphere is redolent with summer, or as Bernard puts it, fields under wide blue skies that were ripe for harvest. Well, Vincent had just been harvested, and was perhaps floating with the crows above the yellow fields while his corpse was lowered into the grave.

But here, at last, Bernard provides a first-hand account of Gachet. Theo was too choked up to say anything, but Gachet, can-do trooper that he is, suddenly rises to the occasion and speaks for the man who hours earlier he saw no hope.

Bernard's account is that Gachet could only stammer a very confused farewell. Part of it involved Gachet crediting Vincent for being honest. Gachet said he didn't know Vincent very well, or for very long, but thought of him as a great artist. Gachet reckoned Vincent prized art above everything. I'm not sure if that was true – Gachet prized art above everything, for Vincent the thing he yearned for was love, family, belonging, an end to his excruciating solitude. Art was a means to that end, a means to giving solace and perhaps one day receiving it.

Gachet – A Final Retrospective

Dr. Gachet's job was to cure Vincent of his melancholia. He failed spectacularly. After just ten weeks of treatment under Dr. Gachet's care, his patient committed suicide. Whatever Gachet was doing, he failed to come to the aid of his patient. He was forewarned about Vincent's condition, and as an expert in the field, he ought to have had at least some of the tools to recognise Vincent's condition, and also treat it.

Not only did he fail to come to Vincent's aid before June 27th, when he knew his patient was injured, he was disassociated and dismissive, not wishing to involve himself either in treating Vincent himself, or in providing any kind of ongoing support or comfort.

In hindsight, Vincent was actually better off, safer, alone in the asylum in the south of France, than he was in Auvers. He lasted just two months in Gachet's so-called care, and what's more, once Vincent was shot, the good doctor Gachet was again unable to do anything of value to save the patient with the bullet in his stomach.

All of the above is absolutely true even when we accept the mainstream view. It takes on a completely different hue, however, when we regard Vincent's demise while in the hands of Gachet, not as neglect or accidental, but as intentional murder.

We can see from the record going on into the future that Gachet was, just as Vincent said right in the beginning, a man we cannot count on. But Gachet could count on himself, and his art dealer son, to maintain strict control over their portion of Vincent's legacy. And so they did, and how well they did for themselves!

You may recall, Dr. Gachet removed about a dozen of Vincent's paintings from his lodgings immediately after his death, including The Portrait of Dr. Gachet [an image Gachet himself was above purchasing from the artist while he lived], claiming these as payment for his medical services to Vincent.

55 years later, in 1945, museums in France owned just seven Van Gogh paintings. In 1949, Paul II [Gachet's son] and Marguerite each donated a Van Gogh picture to the Louvre. In 1952, after Marguerite's death, Paul II gave the French state *The Church at Auvers*. To be technical about it, Paul II didn't just hand it over, what he did was sell it to an anonymous Canadian, along with priceless and very personal Van Gogh artefacts: his palette board, tubes of paint, and the original plate for Vincent's one and only etching. So the Canadian sold it to the French museums, and presumably, the middleman and the fencer got their first pot of gold. So far so good, there was still plenty of the black spider's remains left to dismember and distribute.

In 1954, a year after Irving Stone's *Lust for Life* appeared in print for the first time, Gachet unloaded five more paintings, and a drawing, bring the total donations at that date to nine art works.

Fourteen years after the end of World War II, and significantly, just three years after *Lust for Life* hit cinemas in America, the Gachet Collection – sixteen paintings in all – was given "as a gift" to the French state. Marguerite had died in the meantime, so it was up to her art dealer brother to set up the "donation". Well, like the artefacts, this wasn't a gift, or as some in the mainstream have reported, it wasn't "left" to the French state. The French state bought the collection from Paul II Gachet for an estimated 100 million francs [$28.2 million in adjusted currency].

According to Henk Tromp's *A Real Van Gogh: How the Art World Struggles with Truth,* the flurry of donations in 1954 and 1959 coincided with the release of a damaging book accusing the doctor of causing Vincent's death [a euphemism in itself]. The offending work was cryptically titled *Van Gogh le suicidé de la* société [*Van Gogh: The Man Suicided by Society*]. I disagree with Tromp that the Gachet Collection was dumped on the market to avoid a potential drop in value. The opposite was happening; publicity around a book and blockbuster film meant in the late 1950's, Vincent's legacy was at its zenith, or seemed to be.

Ironically, the claims made by the author of *Le suicide,* Antonin Artaud were debunked as the work of madman. Like Vincent, Antonin spent an extended stay [three years] in an asylum at Rodez, where he was treated with electro-shock therapy.

Gachet II vs Vincent II

In June 1953, celebrating the centenary of Vincent's birth, Gachet II sent Vincent II [aka the Engineer] a seemingly seminal work, *Garden of the Asylum, Saint-Rémy.* **** In exchange, Gachet became an honorary member of the Vincent van Gogh Foundation, effectively boosting Gachet's standing amongst the art crowd as an authentic dealer, and a credible spokesman – for himself.

Despite the exchange, Gachet's membership for the painting, Vincent II didn't take to Gachet's gesture as the art dealer may have hoped, even though Dutch newspapers at the time went gaga over the "new acquisition". A year later, Vincent II handed the painting over to be assessed by the Stedelijk Museum. The verdict: fake. Nice one Gachet II.

Vincent II offered it to other experts. Some said it was "definitely" a Van Gogh, others, such as the director of a museum in Arles [whom Vincent II sent photos of the work], said it was definitely not genuine. Vincent II didn't put the painting on a wall, but relegated it to a vault, which in itself speaks volumes.

Tromp raises an interesting question: if Vincent II was so convinced the painting was a forgery, why didn't he publish his findings? Why *not* publish them? Unless I'm misunderstanding him, Tromp sees this as evidence that Vincent II couldn't have been very convinced either way. Perhaps. On the other hand, why impinge on his great, great uncle's legacy unnecessarily. If a painting was a fake, it could call into the question of the entire collection, and at a time when Vincent's legend was just starting to take off.

In 2001 the Van Gogh Museum conducted extensive analysis on the painting and found that it was genuine after all. Well, I supposed if you have enough experts examine a work, you'll eventually get the green light you're looking for, and in just the right tone of green, too. And consider the stakes: this painting is fake [$0.00]. Hold on, no, it's genuine, KA-CHING. [$__ million]

The Murder of Vincent van Gogh

The reality is Vincent wasn't murdered once, but over and over and over again. There may have been an attempted murder in Arles, and since Vincent gave up booze after that, perhaps alcohol had something to do his disastrous home share with Gauguin. Whatever it was, when Vincent was dead, Gauguin couldn't bring himself to let sleeping dogs lie.

The real mystery in this story is Marguerite. What were her true feelings towards Vincent? I have only ever seen my father come to blows with a stranger once, and it was when he punched a teenager who'd been secretly *kafoofling****** with my young sister [about fifteen-years-old at the time]. I remember the incident quite clearly, even where it happened. Unusual for the suburbs, there's an overgrown alley next to our home where the mice, the youngster and my younger sister, would meet and steal the cheese while the cat was away. But my father eventually caught him, shouted at him and threw a few punches. Not skipping a beat, the young buck charmed my father, telling him that he had great respect for him for being such a protective custodian towards his daughter. They [father and daughter] he flattered, were a credit to each other.

There was also no question of the punk fighting back when confronted; instead he slunk back again when the coast was clear. My father's intervention had evidently transformed a so-so fling into a high stakes live-by-the-seat-of-your-pants red-hot romance. Dangerous, but exciting.

Without Marguerite's say-so, it's almost impossible to confirm her intentions, although it seems likely Vincent would have had intentions to *her*, or any available woman for that matter. What we can say with certainty is what Vincent said about her, in his letter to Theo on June 28th, 1890, a day less than a month before his death.

"He has promised to make her pose for me another time at the small organ. I will do one for you."

Gachet had promised Vincent to MAKE his daughter pose for the artist AGAIN. France in 1890, as now, was a patriarchal society, where women performed a role, were treated as domestic or sex objects, possessions more than equal partners. This may have made the lot of the artist sexier, especially when it came to paying [and possessing, for a few exquisite moments] a retinue of young models. When an artist has slept with one model, isn't there a temptation [even just in the mind of the artist], to sleep with all of them?

One can imagine the naïve and distracted Dr. Gachet waving his arm and ordering his young daughter to pose for Vincent, and so, if she was following orders, she was that much more available to Vincent's spell [or to be put off by it].

What's clear, though, is my father acted against the letch that pursued my sister not so much because she objected to his affections, but because – more likely – that she permitted them. His defense, as I recall, was based on their mutual youth and naiveté, as he saw it. I'm not sure if there was much more to it than that, besides the fact that it was also becoming obvious over time, that they were both defying him.

Now, consider how undesirable a first love may be in the eyes of a conceited, well-to-do, patriarchal doctor, who as a widower is in a sense even more "married" to his daughter than a father would otherwise be. When the Romeo is a loser infected with the French disease,****** a terminal sentence in those days, his potential advances *were* a matter of life and death. Since Gachet had spent some time in the Prussian front with French soldiers, he would have known better than most how the French disease could tear through a platoon, or a community.

Had Marguerite *not* had feelings for the young pretender, I daresay it would have negated a strong reaction from her father. But it was nevertheless a fraught and confusing situation. Come into my home, paint me, paint my garden, paint my daughter's portrait, look but don't touch. And equally for Marguerite: let him paint you, let him eat at our table, but don't be too nice to him. If Marguerite was a solitary creature [and we know that she was], doesn't this suggest that she probably did have feelings for the dirty bad-boy, artist? If Gachet held him in high regard, and disapproved of him in other ways, Marguerite would certainly have felt stimulated by this, and even curious.

Curiosity killed the cat...

A gun could only have been warranted if Gachet had been alerted to trouble in an escalating pattern of complaints, disputes and concerns. He may have become activated through inference, and then directly, through interference, leading to a confrontation with Vincent and his daughter. Rules were erected to keep Vincent at bay, but Vincent being Vincent, he persisted.

My body is mine...

His persistence is disgusting.

The gun was the last resort of a desperate father, desperate to protect his daughter's life from the deadly affliction that was also part of Vincent van Gogh; it was in his blood, in his brain, in his loins, in his every fibre.

As it happens, in the hillside above Auvers, in and around the Gachet residence, there are many nests, nooks and crannies for furtive grabbings and sweaty snogging amongst the buzz of animals. There are caves semi-converted into barns, and a labyrinth of farm-style enclosures poking between cottages. So, the uninhabited alley that was available to my sister conveniently close to home, was also available to Vincent, and Marguerite.

What's more, witnesses heard a shot, and arguing, in this area, above the main street, outside Auvers. It's virtually the only ear witness testimony, and one imagines, on a Sunday afternoon or evening, the sound of a bullet had to have been audible somewhere, and due to the lie of the land, inaudible in other places.

Once Vincent had been stung by the wasp, he attempted to escape, but the wasp pursued him, pretending not to, and pretending a kind of fatalistic, studied indifference. The funeral, the post mortem sketch and extended pilfering, anal copying and strategic peddling, prove this indifference to be a charade.

Marguerite took flowers to Vincent's grave, every day, after his death, some undertaking since his cemetery was so far out of town, and on the opposite side of Auvers to where the Gachet's lived. Did she feel guilty for her part in precipitating Vincent's downfall? Did she not marry because she never did escape the suffocating weight of her father's thumb, or his hair-trigger temper? Is that why she kept Vincent's portrait of her, hanging on her bedroom wall, for 44 years?

Postscript

In a midday break from writing this last chapter, I met a successful South African artist for coffee. I wanted an artist's take on certain aspects of my research. I knew she'd spent months as a resident artist in France, and I'd heard she'd been to Auvers, and to Vincent's grave. I wanted to ask her about the lie of the land, the feel of the place, and to show her *Farms near Auvers*, to get her reading of where that be.

I got more than I bargained for. The artist told me about the hills that rise up, to the north of Auvers, lifting as they fly out from the river. She said there are still big flocks of black crows haunting the wheat fields, the houses today look like they did then ["the French are like that, they like to keep things a certain way"].

When I asked her about the grave, she blinked her blue eyes, and seemed to see them there in front of our coffees. Two small graves,******* side-by-side, both covered in green heather. The heather is a cutting from Gachet's garden.

The graves lie right beside a low wall, and just beyond it, wheat fields stretch like the backs of large, lazy cats warming themselves under the sun. And even now, there are very much the same wheat fields with crows that Vincent saw in his day. Crows cackle and joust noisily with each other.

"Vincent was buried, facing East, facing the sun…" she tells me, hinting that she too, doesn't believe he killed himself. Apparently, neither did those burying him.

I explain my theory about a picture a day suggesting that each picture locates the artist.

"Yes, because he was painting *en plein air* – what was in front of him."

I ask about Gachet. Remember him sobbing and not making much sense at Vincent's funeral, calling him a great artist? Or as Bernard put it:

…he spoke about how sublime [Vincent's] goal was and how great an admiration he felt for him…

Not so great an admiration, it turned out, that The Great Gachet would wish to be buried in the same cemetery at his hero, Vincent, however. When Paul Ferdinand Gachet died in 1909, he was 80-years-old. He lived more than twice as long as Vincent did, and enjoyed almost twenty years of life after Vincent's miserable end.

He chose to be buried at the Pere Lachaise Cemetery in Paris, the most visited cemetery in the world [it receives more visitors than the Van Gogh Museum]. In its hallowed grounds lie the likes of Oscar Wilde, Molière, Eugène Delacroix, Jim Morrison, Marcel Proust, Maria Callas, Collette – in other words, a certain class of high calibre individual that Gachet, frankly, saw himself equal to, or better than. Well, was he?

On a distant field just north of Paris, a flock of black birds rise out of the yellow, flashing the sun off their oily backs. They drift towards, then over Gachet's house, a small white block with red chimneys, staircases, and a gleaming garden. They laugh as they ride the warm, brisk thermals. It's a derisive laughter.

Then, as yet another Van Gogh tourist scrunches along a well-worn gravel path, approaching the modest graves, someone coos in sympathy. What a *wonderful gesture* from the doctor, to have the brothers connected by this tangle of green foliage from Gachet's garden.

KARR KARR KARR

The birds know better, and now, one of them swoops lower and farts a splodge of shit onto the tourist's shiny, blue shoulder. The dripping swirl resembles, for an instant, *Starry Night,* or perhaps a giant lemon smashed through the middle, floating in the night sky.

In the enormous, all-seeing eye of the crow, Auvers and the whole world, swims, swirls into the brown of a coffee. The coffee pours down my throat like a river of poisonous sludge, and the artist beside me, gulps down hers.

In the ether of wings and weather, in the metal of earth and water, whatever remains of Vincent stirs in the silent soil. A single soil particle tumbles over another, a microscopic avalanche, unseen, and therefore, unreal.

If he could, he would rise from the grave on the black wings of crows and the electricity of the wheat fields. He'd rise through the ants and soils, he'd lift through the invisible magnetic forces that hold the Earth to itself. And with those ghost hands, those fingers that once set canvasses alight, he'd grasp and tear Gachet's garden at the very root.

He would brush every last twig from the soil, turning the soil into a kind of bare, brown canvas. A substrate for planting genuine things, not parasitic things. And from his brother's grave, his ghost fingers would do the same weeding, casting the clinging detritus over the wall, ridding himself of it, as if it were an oppressive green snake, pressing down on his still bleeding stomach.

*Some sources suggest Mazery was from Paris, and was vacationing in Auvers at the time of the incident.

**Lemon Tree lyrics by Fool's Garden

***Bernard, in his letter to Albert Aurier, claims Gustave Ravoux as his source.

****More information at the paragraph: "Still lifes too pleasing to be by Van Gogh" at this link.

*****Let's just say that *kafoofling* is the clumsy, teenage virgin version of the more adult, and more elegant canoodling, itself a forerunner to the hanky-panky.

******Syphilis is Latin for "The French Disease". It was spread through Europe in its initial phase by French soldiers during their campaigns in Italy, in the late 15th century.

*******In 1914, shortly after publishing her memoir and Theo and Vincent's letters, Jo had Theo's body exhumed in Utrecht, and laid carefully alongside Vincent's grave in Auvers.

About the Author

Nick van der Leek *[@HiRezLife on Twitter and @Nickvdk on Instagram] is the author of over 70 books, including several trilogies dedicated to unravelling the world famous, and still officially unsolved JonBenét Ramsey and Madeleine McCann cases. In 2016, Van der Leek profiled eight of South Africa's preeminent landscape artists.*

Instead of journalism, Van der Leek studied law, economics and marketing. After cutting his teeth in Rosebank, Johannesburg in the Times Media newsroom, he became a full-time investigative writer and photographer. Today he is one of South Africa's most diverse and successful freelancers.

The next Shakedown title, TREACHERY, *available in May 2018, focuses on the unsolved Casey Anthony case.*

For more information on new releases, reviews, blogs and discussions, visit www.shakedowntitle.com

Printed in Poland
by Amazon Fulfillment
Poland Sp. z o.o., Wrocław

60595891R00143